E. M. FORSTER:
Our Permanent Contemporary

E. M. FORSTER:
Our Permanent
Contemporary

by
P. J. M. Scott

VISION
and
BARNES & NOBLE

Vision Press Limited
Fulham Wharf
Townmead Road
London SW6 2SB

and

Barnes & Noble Books
81 Adams Drive
Totowa, NJ 07512

ISBN (UK) 0 85478 255 9
ISBN (US) 0 389 20368 8

Printed and bound in Great Britain by
Unwin Brothers Ltd.,
Old Woking, Surrey.
Phototypeset by Galleon Photosetting,
Ipswich, Suffolk.
MCMLXXXIV

Contents

Acknowledgements

I should like to thank the Provost and Scholars of King's College, Cambridge, for kindly allowing me to consult some of the unpublished material by Forster in their Library, and their Archivist, Dr. M. A. Halls, from whose actively helpful assistance, which always distinguishes him, I have felt conscious of appreciable benefit.

A testimony of indebtedness is also due to Mr. P. N. Furbank for his biography of this author. It is not a book I have 'enjoyed', and I do think that possibly it is based on a misconception—namely, that Forster's life history should be told as much as possible from his own point of view and (rather like Florence Hardy's life of her husband) in his own words. But this faithfulness of self-effacing discipleship is not only an object-lesson in humility and charitable intention, it constitutes of course a real critical value, which will be still more appreciated in future time, when pretty well all of Forster will be published and people will be able to see for themselves how judiciously, through what acres of literary legacy, Mr. Furbank has sifted and selected.

The painstaking and illuminating toil of the Editors of the Abinger series cannot be often enough mentioned with gratitude by any writer on Forster in these days.

References: these are miscellaneously derived. In the case of several works I have used the Abinger Edition versions where these have been hitherto provided, well aware, as its first and principal editor to date, the late Oliver Stallybrass has remarked, 'there is conclusive evidence that [Forster] was exceptionally careless in checking typescripts and correcting proofs.' But there is a problem (in my view). Mr. Stallybrass was so estimably dedicated a servant of his author's intents, he was capable of being too officious. As the prologomenon to the *Source and Textual Notes* section makes clear in *Two Cheers for Democracy* (No. 11 in its ultimate sequence but one of the two launching volumes of this edition) he is willing to correct 'when Forster misquotes from other writers' (Ibid., p. 360). A glaring instance crops up, e.g., in *Aspects of the Novel*. Forster there (Ch. 8) summarizes the plot and pattern of *The Ambassadors* and himself concludes 'So Strether loses them too. As he says: "I have lost everything—it is my only logic." ' Yet this almost drastic misquotation the Abinger editor silently corrects to the actual phrases of the James novel: ' "That, you see, is my only logic. Not, out of the whole affair, to have got anything for myself." ' But the original *Aspects of the Novel* version is surely very revealing—at least as much about Forster's awareness of James's achievement as of that achievement in itself; and therefore we want his (Forster's) text to stand. Accordingly I have quoted from the Abinger Edition for (1) *Where Angels Fear to Tread*, (3) *A Room with a View*, (3a) *The Lucy Novels: Early Sketches for 'A Room with a View'*, (4) *Howards End*, (6) *A Passage to India*, (8) *The Life to Come and Other Stories*, (9) *Arctic Summer and Other Fiction*, (13) *Goldsworthy Lowes Dickinson and Related Writings*, (14) *The Hill of Devi, etc.*; but not for *Two Cheers for Democracy* nor *Aspects of the Novel*. There and for volumes not yet appearing in the Abinger series I have used Forster's latest texts, faulty as they are.

Introduction

E. M. Forster's life makes dreary reading; certainly from Mr.
P. N. Furbank's, and perhaps inevitably from any, hands.
There we have the all too classic wretched tale of a child
brought up to be a thoroughgoing pathetic muff by a household
of dominant female relatives who early instilled into him
exaggerated worries about east winds, overcoats, wrapping up
and shawls; who grew up bullied at school and timid in adulthood; who was walled by his sexual inversion into an existence
of much loneliness and misery; whose artistic inspiration and
fulfilment lasted little more than a quarter of his days; and who
spent most of his slow long 91½ years basically marking time.
('The irony of fate' seems operative. Forster's conviction during
his first three decades that he could die a youngish death[1]
perhaps betokened a wish and legitimate need. Jane Austen,
denied a whole half-century of the time he was allotted—unlike
her own nonagenarian brothers—was cut off in creative mid-
stride?) Though his was signally a late-Victorian and Edwardian
predicament, such individuals are still to be met with, potter-
ing in shabby old raincoats about the reading-rooms of public
libraries or looking lost on the promenades of coastal resorts
out of season in overcast weather.

For oh! that he had had the gift of happiness, had lived with
the *brio*—and the religious faith—of, say, Francis Poulenc: the
French composer whose own work's stylistic self-containment
has some affinity to Forster's, who was also a single man and
for the same reason. A recent biographical note informs us that
this latter 'expansive character . . . (1899–1963) enclosed'

> two quite different personalities. One was the clown, the jovial
> buffoon who entertained his friends with sly mimicry at the
> piano and doted on gossip. When, at his country home, he
> needed to go on an errand into the village, he would don his
> peaked cap back to front—'Like Blériot!' he joked—and roar

9

off in a cloud of dust, his awkward bulk swaying dangerously on a scooter. This was the man who wrote the farcical *Rapsodie nègre*, the uproarious *Mamelles de Tirésias* and the jaunty *Embarquement pour Cythère*. The other Poulenc, by contrast, was a humble and very devout Catholic. 'Mine is the faith of a simple country priest', he would declare. Unlike his friend Darius Milhaud, whose religion was as much a part of him as the sunshine of his native Provence, Poulenc lived his Catholicism with the intensity of a Goya painting.[2]

If Forster had had any of these characteristics (well, minus the gossip bit), how much less merely depressing—unfocused, contingent and sad—his life-story would seem.

Taupe he was called (i.e. French for 'mole') in the Bloomsbury circles, from his habit of sitting silently through tracts of their talk only to come up conversationally in another place. (In my view he was often more acutely discriminative than the whole of the rest of them put together—this is not to disparage *their* intellectual equipment—and Virginia Woolf did well to be nervously more respectful of his opinion than of any other in her acquaintance.) But as Noel Annan remarked in a radio-review of Mr. Furbank's biography, 'this mole grew quills.'

What sets Forster's career apart from all other sad muffs is that his astonishing intelligence found astonishing embodiment in the novels which, for a limited period, against all likelihood and athwart all the currents of disablement which possessed him, his genius somehow managed to produce. That Shakespeare and Emily Brontë created as they did makes their work unique: in English—in world—letters. But Forster's achievement, and he is one of our great writers, is still more implausible-though-actual than theirs. His is the *unlikeliest* art in the tradition of British fiction.

This is so, not only on account of the given biographic facts, but of that art in itself. What almost disconcerts one, beyond mere gasping, is the way an artist with *this* tone of voice could spring like Pallas Athene so fully formed, clad, armed from the head of Jove. *Ab initio*.

It is his narrative attitude which makes Forster one of our great human resources, and upon that that the following study intends to concentrate.

Introduction

1. P. N. Furbank, *E. M. Forster: A Life* (London, 1977–78), Vol. I, p. 19.
2. From the record-sleeve which accompanies the disc ASD 3299 of Poulenc's *Gloria* and *Piano Concerto*, issued 1976. This extract comes from its first paragraph in the commentary provided by James Harding.

1

The *Manques*

First, however, we must take the measure of the Forsterian inadequacies, so that they may leave his positive achievement to a clearer view.

Perhaps his most evident failing is as a fictionist of homosexual relations. Here he falls between all conceivable stools. He does not make of homosexuality an insight into other human issues, as do Plato or Proust—or as Wagner and Dante make of heterosexual affinity in *Tristan und Isolde* and *The Divine Comedy*. Nor does he treat it fairly on any other terms.

In Plato's argument homosexuality is not only itself, it is also symbolic/symptomatic of the nature of Love: a creature which roams through the world seeking its completion and fulfilment in restored unity. Man suffers the condition of being divided, spiritual amputation even, until he finds his other half. (As a metaphor and explanation of Love at all levels this surely is potent and illuminating.) Hence Socrates, in *The Symposium*, though in love with Alcibiades who is for him what W. H. Auden has finely called 'the vision of Eros',[1] is unwilling to have physical relations with the young man, though the latter offers to seduce him, because they would be essentially a misdirection of the divine impulse. Sexuality here involves, in its profoundest implications, not a physical itch which wants scratching but a religious revelation which should be honoured as godly and—in Plato's thought at least (I am not expressing an opinion in the matter)—buggery is not a relevant expression of, or response to, that vision.[2]

Proust makes something else of the issue: a brilliant metaphor, because archetypal instance, of a fundamental human

13

embarrassment. People keep—like the Baron de Charlus—constructing elaborate *personae* of high dignity for themselves, only to have these remorselessly sabotaged from within by contrary impulses which make a mockery of their scheme of decorum. The Baron de Charlus conscious of a lineage and manner beside which the rest of Europe's inhabitants are so many vulgar *parvenus*, is also the rouged posturing cat's-paw of a working-class violinist and the besotted client of flagellating male prostitutes.

Also the phenomenon is used to incorporate another of the *Recherche*'s main themes—the protean character of human nature, though here it is used much less convincingly. Men and women have an idea of themselves as fixed identities with permanent leading interests, when in fact they change, radically, from one decade to another. Proust assails the illusion in many ways over the course of his novel. One of them is that Saint-Loup, the virile orthodox young soldier, starting off as the pursuer of beautiful actresses, gets obsessed in middle age with boys instead. (It is a weakness of course, that we don't find this credible. It may happen in ordinary life—I don't know—but Proust does not make it happen in his pages.)

The whole gap between the public image of an individual—indeed his or her self-awareness—and the realities which make up that person, the great French artist finds most comically, poignantly expressible with this central impulse in many of his characters' lives, an impulse they cannot abolish but—such is its social stigma—they will not acknowledge.

No analogous claim of profound insights can be made for Forster's handling of the element. The story he completed in his eightieth year, 'The Other Boat', has attracted high praise, but this seems to me misplaced. It begins with an encounter between the March family, sailing back from India to England in the very beginning of this century, after the father of the five youngsters, a major in the sub-continental army 'went native'.

> 'With a girl or with a boy?'
> 'A boy? Good God! Well, I mean to say, with a girl, naturally—I mean, it was somewhere right away in the depths of Burma.' (Section 4)

14

The children have played with 'Cocoanut', a half-caste child, at one end of the ship on that first occasion, till rescued from him and sunstroke by their stern, racialist, mother. Ten years on, Lionel March sails out to *his* new career in the military service of the Raj, meets 'Cocoa' again and the two young men have an affair which ends in murder and suicide.

> The sweet act of vengeance followed, sweeter than ever for both of them, and as ecstasy hardened into agony his hands twisted the throat. Neither of them knew when the end came, and he when he realized it felt no sadness, no remorse. It was part of a curve that had long been declining, and had nothing to do with death. (5)

The author himself explicated this idea in conversation with his biographer not long after its writing:

> *21.10.58.* M., at the Reform last night, . . . Said he thought the tragic theme of 'The Other Boat'—two people made to destroy each other—was more interesting than the theme of salvation, the rescuer from 'otherwhere', the generic Alec. That was a fake. People could help one another, yes; but they were not decisive for each other like that.

Yet however true or not that remark may be as a philosophical observation generally, we are entitled to question whether it is justified by the *procédé* which is this particular story. *Why* are the murder and the suicide inevitable? Lionel March is not *presented* as having a tragic kind of self-consciousness, of being a man aware of some desperate contradiction in his soul which nothing but death—or murder—can resolve, even if his creator has chosen so to view him.

The whole work itself only very fugitively supplies reasons for these events in counterpoise to the immense improbability (thank Heaven) of such an upshot, so that it seems much more the expression of a gruesome sado-masochistic fantasy on the author's part than a treatment of some inalienable logic in human affairs. When Antigone and Creon clash in Sophocles' play and bring about each other's ruin, they are both 'in the right' and the inevitable victims of the way things are in a tragically ordered universe. Sororal piety and the exigencies of a high political morality become an irresistible force meeting an immoveable object. But nothing in 'The Other Boat' argues very convincingly why March could neither have extricated himself from his entanglement nor have 'gone native' like his father years before him.

Indeed, when we consider how the two other pieces of Forster's homosexual fiction which he wrote with the greatest sense of being serious and inspired, 'The Life to Come' and 'Dr. Woolacott', are set in fantasy-regions—a foreign exotic never-never land, a dream-world respectively—and also treat of man-with-man sexual encounters that are accomplished, concluded, consummated in violent death, one is moved to enlist practically the sarcasm which distinguishes this passage from the 'Terminal Note' that in 1960 he supplied to his *Maurice*:

> Unless the Wolfenden Report becomes law, it will probably have to remain in manuscript. If it ended unhappily, with a lad dangling from a noose or with a suicide pact, all would be well. . . .

If homosexual relations are, of their own inner logic, murderous, suicidal, sadistic—or anyway essentially destructive and unhappy—there seems little point in campaigning for anything other than their total suppression: in oneself, in other people, in society and law at large. But is it not a real 'perversion' so to render them—at least, without arguing your case?

For when we turn to the same opus—*Maurice*—in which

> A happy ending was imperative. I shouldn't have bothered to write otherwise. I was determined that in fiction anyway two men should fall in love and remain in it for the ever and ever that fiction allows,

the performance which greets us is no less inchoate. On the full-length canvas of a novel what becomes finally clear is that Forster cannot conceive of men *being in love* with each other. Indeed the phrase cannot be used meaningfully about any of the characters in his homosexual fiction, unless it attaches to Maurice and Clive's relationship early in their friendship, and significantly 'the physical' is there never to be admitted.

That phase of that particular fiction excepted—and it offers us only half a glimpse of a falling-in-love process—Forster's homosexual protagonists are represented simply as having copulative encounters (in essence); the process of a developing acquaintance and interest in a whole personality on both sides he seems incapable of rendering; likewise the after-history of a commitment.

I put thus the complaint against this whole boggy tract of his literary endeavour—wading through which my own spirit certainly wilts—because it seems to me that if a writer with such a subject cannot imaginatively *either* project a courtship or 'marriage' in the kind, *or* use the subject as (at once) illustration, instance and metaphor of some issue in which the human race participates as a species, he is left with no standing ground, there is nothing to treat of in this dimension, at all.

Romance, passion, philosophy in the form of human relationships fiction can feed upon and illuminate, yes. But *relationships* in Forster's accounts of 'Uranian' temperaments are principally what one misses. Any treatment of heterosexual natures and activities is subject to exactly the same strictures. As Auden has usefully remarked, 'All of us know the few things Man as a mammal can do.'[3]

To say the above is not to lose sight of the signal disadvantages under which Forster lived and worked. Perhaps his was the generation in which it was hardest to be homosexual of any of the past few centuries' in Britain. Even to conceive such a book as *Maurice* in 1913 signifies a freedom, range and courage of thought which was out of the ordinary. And that novel has strengths as well as fatal weaknesses. One of its good features are Alec Scudder's letters, another is the brilliant scene of his meeting with the central character at the British Museum (Ch. 43). They and other felicities I look forward to drawing upon in later pages of this monograph. But in the main the segment of Forster's *oeuvre* here under consideration has, as emotional, intellectual, moral nutrient, a negative charge. In the concluding portion of his 'Terminal Note' already mentioned he deals with the issue's historical development:

> *Homosexuality.* . . . Since *Maurice* was written there has been a change in the public attitude here: the change from ignorance and terror to familiarity and contempt. It is not the change towards which Edward Carpenter had worked. He had hoped for the generous recognition of an emotion and for the reintegration of something primitive into the common stock. And I,

17

though less optimistic, had supposed that knowledge would
bring understanding. . . .

But what his own fictional practice brings, with its ability for
the most part only to articulate loneliness and lust, not *love*
between two persons of the same gender, is a cramped sense of
mere human defeat.

In his Diary for 16 June 1911 he decides to 'analyse causes
of [his] sterility' as a writer at that time and under the second
heading names what his editors have advanced as the principal reason for the frustration of his creative gift in most of the
years which followed: 'Weariness of the only subject that I
both can and may treat—the love of men for women & vice
versa.'

I think the most significant auxiliary verb in that sentence is
not 'may', but rather 'can'.

A more divided view may be evoked by the essays Forster
has left behind. The collections *Abinger Harvest* and *Two Cheers
for Democracy* are, taken in single draughts, depressing in their
scrappiness, but not on that account alone. As political thought
they constitute *in toto* so inadequate a response for the human
predicament to which they address themselves. Individual
notes are fine: for example the marvellous baiting of Anti-
Semitism in 'Jew-Consciousness'—so aptly ruthless in its
mockery (or likewise in 'Racial Exercise', *Two Cheers for Democracy*,
Part I). Yet just as Forster fails to ask 'how this disgusting thing
has grown up in the human bosom, this horror in our mortal
midst?' and, by penetrating to the weed's origins, help prepare
the ground for its eradication: so with the freedom of the arts.

It is noble and right of him, especially under the conditions of
a war-time censorship, to insist on Society's need to keep its
artists freely self-expressive—'Three Anti-Nazi Broadcasts',
'The Duty of Society to the Artist', 'The Tercentenary of the
Areopagitica', etc.—but he does fail, quite explicitly in the last-
named paper, to engage with the no less serious problem 'How
total should publishing licence be?' The nation where porn-
ography and child-rape has become a way of life; where violent
scenes, whether from newsreel or fiction, flood almost every

18

juvenile mind daily and blunt its sensibility to the terror and misery of such things; where we are now offered a huge extension of such benefits by cable television and an ever-deteriorating standard of reaction to human affairs in the public prints and broadcasting media: such an outcome ought insistently to pose the question 'How much permissiveness equals liberty?' It is an issue which lifelong liberals of Forster's kind have all too deliberately ignored during the current century. When the dotty, pointless and largely self-indulgent, prima-donna-ish Students' Revolutionary *annus mirabilis* of 1968 was upon us at Cambridge, a sit-in going forward at the Senate House and the Vice-Chancellor's burning effigy or hard fact being discussed, our author remarked to me 'But I cannot understand why they want to write smut upon the walls.' Yet that student radicals should find relief in that activity rather than something more rational follows inevitably enough in a society where freedom of utterance has become so sacred a cow that it has opened itself to absolute commercial and emotional exploitation. His part in speaking for the Defence in the *Lady Chatterley's Lover* court-case is one of the least exemplary episodes of Forster's public career.

Some of these essays make marvellously witty reading, reading with sharp-edged point. 'My Wood' is a lovely un-answerable treatment of the private ownership wedge; how 'In the first place, it makes me feel heavy'; in the second begets ever and anon more greed upon itself; in the third it offers as a pretentious substitute for real creativity; and in the fourth it increases one's egotism. Yet Forster has the good sense, whether here or in his 1935 'Liberty in England' address (*Abinger Harvest* supplies both these papers), to reject asceticism, Sovietism and other extremes. Indeed there is generally the feeling that during the Slump and then the no less nerve-wracking crisis of the '30s, that 'low, dishonest decade', he kept his nerve when other intellectuals (by definition lesser thinkers, smaller fry) embraced Communism or Fascism (or Theocracy) or other deadly nostrums. This is largely just. Forster in the latter speech declares

> I am actually what my age and my upbringing have made me—a bourgeois who adheres to the British constitution, adheres to it rather than supports it, and the fact that this isn't

19

dignified doesn't worry me. I do care about the past. I do care
about the preservation and the extension of freedom . . .

and it is all to the good, also, that he has noted that literary
freedom is important even though it does not *immediately*
answer to the needs of those exploited peoples in an empire or
unfed classes in a society to whom the very term suggests only
the twitterings of a fat-paunched intelligentsia in a salon.

But his defence of the *via media Britannica*, which eschews
Revolution on the one side and conservative changelessness on
the other, is far from emphatic enough to ring like a clarion
call through what were terribly dark hours. 'A Note on the
Way' as late as 1934 admits

> We are all harder and more disillusioned now than we were
> then, the League of Nations lies behind us instead of before, and
> no political creed except communism offers an intelligent man
> any hope. And those who are, like myself, too old for communism
> or too conscious of the blood to be shed before its problematic
> victory, turn to literature, because it is disinterested.

Yet anyone who bothers to read the classics of the Soviet
Revolution, as Forster (see *Commonplace Book*, p. 118) had been
doing, can deduce for himself, as Forster had done, that the
net result of all Hegel's, Marx's, Engels's and Lenin's thought
has of its own intrinsic logic to be an absolute human hell.

The Forsterian trumpet, so much more creditable than
many others at that date, gives an uncertain sound. He is not
bold enough to emphasize the virtues of the English Ideology
which swallows crises and gets results—though after a very
unexhilarating and lumbering fashion—*in the middle term*. It
will never appeal to the Romantic in all of us and the heroic in
human nature: on the political scene that will just go on
busying itself with a various course of bloodshed, tyranny and
torture. But in an age of appalling despotisms (now as then)
Forster could have infused a little more vigour into his
'adherence' to the British constitution.

It may now be remonstrated 'Nay but that is exactly what
he did and in the most critical hour of all, with his 1938 credo
"What I Believe".'

> In search of a refuge, we may perhaps turn to hero-worship.
> But here we shall get no help, in my opinion. Hero-worship is a

dangerous vice, and one of the minor merits of a democracy is that it does not encourage it, or produce that unmanageable type of citizen known as the Great Man. It produces instead different kinds of small men—a much finer achievement. But people who cannot get interested in the variety of life, and cannot make up their own minds, get discontented over this, and they long for a hero to bow down before and to follow blindly. It is significant that a hero is an integral part of the authoritarian stock-in-trade today. An efficiency-régime cannot be run without a few heroes stuck about it to carry off the dullness—much as plums have to be put into a bad pudding to make it palatable. One hero at the top and a smaller one each side of him is a favourite arrangement and the timid and the bored are comforted by the trinity, and, bowing down, feel exalted and strengthened.

Superb the psychology and morality of that analysis and classic its statement. Likewise its concluding, and comforting, words about totalitarianism's ultimate weakness, even in its tremendously empowered twentieth-century forms:

And as for individualism—there seems no way of getting off this, even if one wanted to. The dictator-hero can grind down his citizens till they are all alike but he cannot melt them into a single man. That is beyond his power. He can order them to merge, he can incite them to mass-antics, but they are obliged to be born separately, and to die separately, and, owing to these unavoidable termini, will always be running off the totalitarian rails.

There are, throughout, in short some splendid characteristic remarks in this essay. But most of it is based on very shallow assumptions.

For one thing it demonstrates a wholly inadequate sense of human motivations. Forster pleads here for 'Tolerance, good temper, and sympathy' as the essential desiderata for a human renewal in our fraught precarious modern world, but these virtues have to be grounded in something more substantial than a vague affectionateness to become decisively operative on critical occasions. He instances the conduct of people inside Parliament towards each other and towards other nations in comparison with that of folk purchasing a newspaper from the vendor outside the Westminster building and comments the experiment of earthly life cannot be dismissed as a failure. But it may well be hailed as a tragedy, the tragedy being that no device has been found by which these private decencies can be transmitted to public affairs. As soon as people have power they go crooked and sometimes dotty as well, because the possession of power lifts them into a region where normal honesty never pays.

The reason however why—if they do—'anyone who takes a paper is sure to drop a copper into the cap' of the newsvendor outside the Parliamentary railings is that the stakes are so much lower. Within the Mother of Parliaments—and Forster's essay rightly, decisively supports that institution with ' "private" moderate enthusiasm for democracy . . . [which] served good purposes by not being cheapened propaganda'[4]—whole reputations, careers, power-games of (to their participants' view) a 'major' order are to be won or lost; sometimes by bending the truth, squaring the circle, or being less than wholly generous and honest all the time. Losing a penny for your newspaper to the man who sells it represents a much smaller sacrifice. The 'private decencies' Forster leans upon turn out to be thinly rooted where the bribes come high—though not in every case of course. As always the devil Screwtape has an appropriate word on this:

> This, indeed, is probably one of the Enemy [God]'s motives for creating a dangerous world—a world in which moral issues really come to the point. He sees as well as you do that courage is not simply *one* of the virtues, but the form of every virtue at the testing point, which means, at the point of highest reality. A chastity or honesty, or mercy, which yields to danger will be chaste or honest or merciful only on conditions. Pilate was merciful till it became risky.[5]

In secular language his argument is easily paraphrased. Call no man decent until he has been decent under heavy fire. When the great love of his life, the young ex-policeman Bob Buckingham, grew ever keener to enlist during the anti-Hitler conflict, Forster tried to dissuade him.[6] Yet both believed it was a just and necessary war, one in which the able-bodied, the physically serviceable ought to fight. Where was the transmission of private decencies to public affairs in *that* Forster attitude?

Further, a tradition of even such minimal morality as 'the

22

penny in the cap' represents is no *donnée* of human nature. Unfortunately. Forster assumes when writing this credo that people will always at least be thus much equitable. But in 1983 it would be a foolhardy newsvendor who decided he could 'safely leave his papers to go for a drink and his cap beside them'. We have arrived in the interval at the much more secularized and faith-less society Forster wanted all his life-time; our spiritual capital from the earnest religious Victorian days is practically all used up (in regard to the citizen as an individual moral agent); and most Britons, though much better off on average than pre-Second-World-War, are now magpie-thievish in all public areopagoi, generally holding themselves far less accountable to one another than in 1938 they did. (In that year my mother knew an all-but-destitute young man who, walking home fruitlessly from the Labour Exchange one day, found £100 in a notes-bundle on the pavement in front of him. Automatically he took it to the nearest police station for reclaiming by its rightful possessor: a rich man who had dropped it and who did claim it and gave its discoverer a pitiful reward. Would such honesty—on the part of the young man—be almost inevitably witnessed today?) Public morality has vastly improved meanwhile—the corporate way we treat each other, so that we don't now tolerate the living and work conditions and salaries of yesteryears. Private personal integrity has nose-dived.

A society's ethical tradition depends upon many things and is a complex product of, *inter alia*, a discipline of enforced norms and uncontemplated options. Some of these constituents in Edwardian England Forster and several of his contemporaries dedicated their efforts to sapping without perhaps considering carefully enough where, how far along the route of hobbled values, they would bring us out.

He begins well on personal relationships in the testament presently under consideration:

> Here is something comparatively solid in a world full of violence and cruelty. Not absolutely solid, for Psychology has split and shattered the idea of a 'Person', and has shown that there is something incalculable in each of us, which may at any moment rise to the surface and destroy our normal balance. We don't know what we are like. We can't know what other people

are like. How, then, can we put any trust in personal relationships, or cling to them in the gathering political storm? In
theory we cannot. But in practice we can and do. Though A is
not unchangeably A or B unchangeably B, there can still be
love and loyalty between the two. For the purpose of living one
has to assume that the personality is solid, and the 'self' is an
entity, and to ignore all contrary evidence.

Likewise with the need to make a similar pretence about the
personality's environment and the terms of its existence themselves, if healthy living is to ensue:

> The people I respect most behave as if they were immortal and
> as if society was eternal. Both assumptions are false: both of
> them must be accepted as true if we are to go on eating and
> working and loving, and are to keep open a few breathing holes
> for the human spirit.

A lot of agony would have been spared, and not only to the
likeable Horatio, if he could have got his unlikeable friend
Prince Hamlet to digest and appropriate that nutritive attitude.

However when we get to 'the heart, which signs no documents', a snake has emerged in the grass. How can reliability in
human dealings exist without undertakings of the kind—if not
literally signed as such, certainly commitments expressly
made? Forster's dictum there rules out marriage, real friendship and any sort of relation which depends upon slogging
through rough and smooth feelings, fair and foul weather, both.
Likewise it is easy enough to praise personal relations above
Causes (same paragraph 4 of this essay)—not least because
they look less dangerous. But firstly that ignores the fact that if
you betray your country, you betray a lot of other people's
friends as well (some of *them* good people whom others rightly
care for); and secondly that the problem cannot propose itself in
those simple terms. What the individual may have to decide is
between the political reality of his nation-state and some other
value. E.g., should one betray one's friend to the police if they
are the secret police of a wicked régime?

For anyone after 1930 in Britain to attempt subversion of the
state or give aid to an inimical other country is simply
mischievous because the one-person one-vote parliamentary
system obtaining since that date has meant that, while no

earthly paradise has been erected, the community as a whole has been sufficiently free to veto the actions of government and the conspiracies of factions. The present voting system is inadequately representative (our current rating method for that matter has its inequities), but if enormities too gross be imposed upon the people, they have an effective means in their own hands of repulsing and reversing these. If we suffer or care and think sufficiently hard, we have ourselves the recipe for reform; to elect a wholly new Parliament of entirely fresh members recruited to extirpate the abuses which oppress us. In other kinds of political reality the matter can be morally more complicated, but of course a good man by definition is well aware that revolution or subversion are terrible last resorts; only would-be tyrants turn to them except under insupportable duress and in the evident lapse of a real impartial rule of law, for 'it is easy to break eggs without making omelettes.' The villainy of a few Varsity men of the 1930s (Burgess, Philby, Maclean, etc.) who took it upon themselves to work for an alien power (of which the principal accomplishment and sole support was its secret police) has few parallels in history for arrogance and causelessness, in justification. What terribly stupid, egomaniac *little* men they must have been—and what a pity that Forster, with his trusted voice, should in this document have placed so self-endorsing a text into their hands: 'if I had to choose between betraying my country and betraying my friend, I hope I should have the guts to betray my country.'

'Ah!' their shades may protest and in the very words of King Edward VIII immediately before his abdication, but 'Something had to be done' about the Slump of that time, the poverty, the worklessness, the huge general condition of misery among such as the Jarrow Marchers—for whom Parliament provided no remedy. Yet the fault lay with the individual members of the *demokratia* and *their* collective decision-making. In 1927 the Liberal leader (Lloyd George) and his Party had told J. M. Keynes to go away and work out an economic blueprint for Britain's future. This he did. It was adopted by the rank and file of that movement; introduced four years later by Franklin Roosevelt with enormous success in the U.S.A.; ignored by the Conservative and Labour Parties who continued to practise ancient economics and out-of-date attitudes to labour and production; and the terrible Depression which followed in 1929 just deepened and lengthened here for a decade more. (On 1 January 1940 one million men were still in Britain's dole queue.) The working classes of this country were entirely to blame for not having bothered to read, or learn about, the election manifesto of the Liberal Party, and not having voted for it instead of their apparent new friend the Labour Party which was bankrupt of real creative thinking in the period 1924–44. If the tormented proletariat of Great Britain during the '20s and '30s had cared to vote Liberal, not 'Socialist', they would have had the post-war boom seventeen whole years earlier.

They had a real opportunity too. The Liberals fielded candidates in 512 constituencies during the 1929 contest; nor did they enter the fray looking merely a fringe 'crank' party with little support. As their historian/obituarist has proved:

> All of the features which a political party needs for victory seemed to be present: unity; a sense of purpose; enthusiasm; personalities; money; organisation.[7]

Yet they were only awarded 59 seats at the declaration of results. When one considers how

> It was Keynes who saw the way out of the slump while Snowden [Labour Chancellor] was screwing down the meagre reliefs for the unemployed. It was Sinclair [Liberal leader from 26/11/35] who saw that standing up to the dictators required military preparedness, while the Socialists were still drifting in the dreams of disarmament.
>
> It was Beveridge who provided the ideas for the great extension of welfare while the Labour leadership was still obsessed with nationalization.[8]

one can only endorse Dr. Douglas's drastic epitaph:

> . . . the Parliamentary weakness of the Liberals in 1929 was not merely the loss sustained by a political party; for the dynamic which the leading Liberals possessed was not to be found anywhere else. Britain and the whole world were to be losers when nonentities without vision came to control our country at one of the great turning-points of the human race.[9]

26

In the face of their terrible exigencies at that epoch the British working class, now at last fully enfranchized man and woman together, had a full creative option; and they chose not to exercise it.

This is, precisely, *not* to say that the 'right answers' should have been imposed by a clique of dangerous ruthless men operating an élitist politics of their own. Democracy is not simply the rule of the stupid. As Forster affirms it deserves 'Two cheers' because 'it admits variety and . . . permits criticism'; thereby snuffing the hopes of the Blackshirt types in our midst (or the Stalins). You can take a horse to water but you must not make him drink. Prolonged parched thirsts are sometimes the price electorates have to pay, in British-style democratic systems, for not thinking hard enough in a given crisis. But as long as they have held on to their constitutional ritual, liberty at least sufficiently continues for debate to be rejoined and corrections made to the national mistakes. In much of the globe today no alteration is imaginable prior to the Second Coming: hell on earth seems fixed.

One respects also, very much, the testimony of any one in the younger generations who for the second time in the first half of this twentieth century had to go off and fight or to live under fire. Adverting to this very essay, Mr. G. D. Klingopulos (then of the University College of South Wales, Cardiff) in 1960 quoted

> . . . I believe in aristocracy though—if that is the right word and if a democrat may use it. Not an aristocracy of power based upon rank and influence, but an aristocracy of the sensitive, the considerate, and the plucky. . . . They represent the true human tradition, the one permanent victory of our queer race over cruelty and chaos.

and recalled

> This is the voice that spoke just when many of Mr. Forster's readers were embarking in troopships and learning to 'travel light'. They seemed frail words, even, at such a time, slightly absurd, but they represented much of one's ration of moral generalization for the next six years. It was surprising how the timely words travelled and what a good influence they had. Those out of range of the nine o'clock news missed the rhetoric

27

of the Great Men, and when they read about it years later it seemed only rhetorical. The essay 'What I Believe' was the meeting-point for many different sorts of people between 1939 and 1946, and it seemed, with all its frailty and absurdity, exactly right. . . . A later generation may not easily guess that the thought of this writer's mere being, somewhere in England, has seemed at times, to many people, distinctly reassuring.[10]

Such witness makes any carping otiose and before it one ought humbly to bow the head. When Mr. Klingopulos goes on immediately to say

In a half-century which has produced a surfeit of Great Men, bullying, brutality, dogmatism, and noise, Forster has represented an attractive, though not easily imitable, intellectual shrewdness, delicacy, and responsibility.[11]

he packs into one sentence the whole theme of my own study. The difference is, I see those things at work all over the novelist's best fictions, not his other writings in a manner anything so sustained. The integrity here elicited means testifying to one's own perceptions and I find 'intellectual shrewdness' and 'responsibility' in Forster's famous Credo very patchily at work. It does not at all seem to me a coherent basis for living or a piece of careful thought.

This last comes to show for the chief problem with the same author's literary essays. (His musical ones are more impressive, especially 'The C Minor of that Life' (*Two Cheers for Democracy*).)

Aspects of the Novel can be made to stand for Forster's work as a critic of the writer's art, though I have here a disabling sense of dealing a little too summarily with a corpus considerable in all senses: quantity, variety and quality. It is like so much of the rest of his *oeuvre*, an extraordinary admixture of the brilliant insight and the superficial comment which has been simply not examined or thought through sufficiently. Indeed much of Forster's writing outside his good fictions merits that description—and perhaps the man himself. Was there ever through Europe's literary history such a combination of the profound and the shallow in one human being? Well perhaps. James VI of Scotland and I of England looks curiously like;

and is it a coincidence that both men—our present subject and that 'wisest fool in Christendom'—were self-indulgent homosexuals given much to flexing their intellectual powers upon life seen as a fierce exercise in social morality? Note Ben Jonson's fine sly treatment of this 'dichotomy', if such it be, in his sovereign-and-patron's personality/career with the portrait of Justice Adam Overdo in *Bartholmew Fayre*, written for acting on St. Bartholomew's Eve 1614 in the king's own face![12]

For 200 years for instance students of the Novel had needed to hear the following eulogium:

> . . . this power to expand and contract perception (of which the shifting view-point is a symptom), this right to intermittent knowledge—I find it one of the great advantages of the novel-form, and it has a parallel in our perception of life. We are stupider at some times than others; we can enter into people's minds occasionally but not always, because our own minds get tired; and this intermittence lends in the long run variety and colour to the experiences we receive. A quantity of novelists, English novelists especially, have behaved like this to the people in their books: played fast and loose with them, and I cannot see why they should be censured. (Ch. 4)

He has just confessed that this shift of view-point 'came off with Dickens and Tolstoy'; he insists that Dickens 'is actually one of our big writers'; yet in the same breath offers the most fatuous analysis of Dickens's method as a fictionist ever to be coined by a first-class mind:

> Dickens's people are nearly all flat (Pip and David Copperfield attempt roundness, but so diffidently that they seem more like bubbles than solids). Nearly every one can be summed up in a sentence, and yet there is this wonderful feeling of human depth. Probably the immense vitality of Dickens causes his characters to vibrate a little, so that they borrow his life and appear to lead one of their own. It is a conjuring trick; at any moment we may look at Mr. Pickwick edgeways and find him no thicker than a gramophone record. But we never get the sideway view. Mr. Pickwick is far too adroit and well trained. He always has the air of weighing something, and when he is put into the cupboard of the young ladies' school he seems as heavy as Falstaff in the buck-basket at Windsor. Part of the genius of Dickens is that he does use types and caricatures, people whom we recognize the instant they re-enter, and yet

achieves effects that are not mechanical and a vision of humanity that is not shallow. (*Aspects of the Novel*, ibid. cap.)

Without exasperating ourselves by working round to Mr. Pickwick, we must demand 'How on earth can anyone who has ever in fact read *Great Expectations* and *David Copperfield* characterize their narrator-heroes in that way—given their manifold shifting moods which these novels represent, their accreted experience of life, their (far from painlessly bought) gaining and gained maturity of human consciousness deepening and spreading all the while?'

Forster has swallowed whole the Bloomsberry that Dickens was a stagey prestidigitator who dealt in cardboard puppets with a glittering manner and has not bothered to attend to the texts with his own intelligence operating at the level of wakefulness whereof it was well capable.

There is, maybe, a case against Dickens (admit I, for whom personally Dickens is the biggest thing yet discovered in the world's prose fiction), but it cannot begin to be formulated after such a fashion as that.

In fact we are not seeing there the formulation of a case. We are just presented with a few gaudy fiats of arrived-at judgements re-minted as epithets and foisted on us in an after-dinner-speech sort of blandness. The chatty manner of Forster's remarks on the question of novelistic viewpoint above reflects honourably the way in which a good novel is actually a most tightly disciplined form (will it, nill it), which yet operates by giving the impression of looseness and a free-ranging human voice. The chattiness has however altogether got out of hand, is built far too much into the conception of these Clark Lectures and is really a dishonest device, stigmatized, when under another guise, by Forster himself on the very next page: 'It is like standing a man a drink so that he may not criticize your opinions.' The voice is so urbane and amusing and witty, with its little digs hither and yon, and its nudges there and here, that we are (at least invited to be) beguiled into not considering what it actually says.

> Time, all the way through, is to be our enemy. We are to visualize the English novelists not as floating down that stream which bears all its sons away unless they are careful. . . . (Ch. 1)

We appropriately roar, with a somewhat uncertain cackle, but where does the laugh really come out? What does that mean? Which impropriety of mortal thought does the bathetic added conditional clause there suitably nail? When Jane Austen enjoys—in apparently completely a-rational discourse—a dig at a successful 'rival' (who is not such really), we can sit down and parse both her statement and our shouting mirth in reaction to it with cold bald 'practical criticism' if we wish. It will stand up to pages of the same: ·

> I would wish Miss Lewis to be of a silent turn and rather ignorant, but naturally intelligent and wishing to learn;—fond of cold veal pies, green tea in the afternoon, and a green window blind at night. (*Letters*, No. 81, p. 317 of the 1959 Collected Edition)

(Already three-quarters of a human personality and half a way of life have been embodied before us for one thing.) But the sort of rhetoric which features in much of *Aspects of the Novel* yields less the more it is leaned upon for its signification.

The whole lecture-series alternates between offering individual *aperçus* which are finely hit out and 'wit degenerating into clenches' where, if we are diverted it is somewhat against our will. More disconcerting still, this process is unitary. Forster's strictures on Meredith are deadly and very funny, both. Yet if we assent it is because we know Meredith's work ourselves and agree with them, not because Forster has argued and proved his case anything like fully enough:

> The tailors are not tailors, the cricket matches are not cricket, the railway trains do not even seem to be trains, the county families give the air of having been only just that moment unpacked, scarcely in position before the action starts, the straw still clinging to their beards. It is surely very odd, the social scene in which his characters are set: it is partly due to his fantasy, which is legitimate, but partly a chilly fake, and wrong. What with the faking, what with the preaching, which was never agreeable and is now said to be hollow, and what with the home counties posing as the universe, it is no wonder Meredith now lies in the trough. (Ch. 5)

And when he throws in a tangential tilt at the Victorian Laureate our amused agreement (in a measure) feels still more

31

compromised with regard to the rules of fair play: 'I feel indeed that he was like Tennyson in one respect: through not taking himself quietly enough he strained his inside' (ibid. loc.). Does a great poet deserve a one-sentence despatch like that? Legitimate occasionally enough, maybe, these parenthetical digs, but not surely as frequently as they occur in this book.

The wit, the humour, the perception are not extricable from the injustice of Forster's proceedings here and through much of his writing. Nor would we, ultimately, have it otherwise for the ingredients will recurrently produce prose far more formidable:

> *D. H. Lawrence's Frieda* seen last week after an interval of 15 years, still uttered the old war cries [that people didnt *live*, that England was done for, that she and her husband had their fights out, that they were trumpets calling to the elect] but her manner was nervous, almost propitiatory, and I realise that she, and perhaps he, were as afraid of me as I could have been of them. There was something both pretentious and rotten about her, as in his pictures. She would rebuke me for disobeying the Message and then stop and watch me with a shy smile. Very proud of having no friends, equally so of her apparatus for collecting and compelling them.—And the tripe without the poetry was not attractive, and I retired unashamed into my academic tower. He and she haven't had a bad life, but it seems vulgar when they proclaim it as an Ensample and a Mystery. (*Commonplace Book*, p. 68)

Verily one of Forster's leading values in the legacy of English letters is his ability to cut people, situations and controversies down to size in the most apt and exemplarily discriminative manner. Time and again we turn a page and find that, effortlessly as it seems, some grand appallment or impressive rhetoric which has clouded the judgement of a generation has been (as above) shrunken in most appropriate fashion. The one-line heading of one of the *Commonplace Book*'s entries illustrates this power in its ability to be brief: 'Notes on the Coleridge-Wordsworth Bother' (p. 88).

What we don't suffer in that vade-mecum or the novels is the fundamental *accidie* which seems to lie just behind or beneath the lectures on the Novel and other parts of Forster's arts-criticism. As often as not an insinuation is playing below the surface that considering the Arts in action is rather small beer; for instance, at the beginning of the Meredithian 'analysis':

> Meredith is not the great name he was twenty or thirty years ago, when much of the universe and all Cambridge trembled. I remember how depressed I used to be by a line in one of his poems: 'We live but to be sword or block.' I did not want to be either and I knew that I was not a sword. It seems though that there was no real cause for depression, for Meredith is himself now rather in the trough of a wave, and though fashion will turn and raise him a bit, he will never be the spiritual power he was about the year 1900. (Ch. 5)

Yet that particular artist is not the sole casualty there. He takes with him not only *Aspects of the Novel* and all literary criticism but more besides. We appreciate that almost all the universe has never trembled at the name of George Meredith; the sardonic quip moves us, however, at high speed to a focus where all mortal activity looks like a mathematical point in relation to its environment, the cosmos, and the depreciation of one Victorian novelist is as nothing beside the invalidating of the speaker's own *locus standi*. If, viewed from a distant constellation, the rise and fall of literary statuses are as trivial as Forster's opening metaphor concedes, then how much point has imaginative literature itself, let alone public discussion of it? Over and again some imp of an essential impatience sticks out its tongue. Norman Douglas and D. H. Lawrence controverting are given the left-handed accolade 'the hardness of whose hitting makes the rest of us feel like a lot of ladies up in a pavilion' (Ch. 4)—which is mockery, depreciation that really 'drinks the cup and all'. For it is significant that Forster's image is of himself and his auditors being merely decorative onlookers at an event which may be a joust (a life-and-death battle about essential issues) or 'just a game'.

Either literary appreciation is a fit exercise for adult minds or it is not. In both cases, literary values are human concerns translated into retrievable and analysable form. If criticism deserves this cavalier tone, then so does human life. The whole business of our existence (on that understanding) isn't worth taking all that seriously.

A later entry in the *Commonplace Book*, made circa 1930, ponders Coleridge's Dejection Ode:

Is not this the watershed I seek? Here he describes the death
of creative power, not knowing that his description means the
birth of critical: an inferior infant, yet it lived and made
remarks beyond the powers of its inspired predecessor. Turning
over of the genius in sleep, so that criticism comes uppermost.
(p. 91)

And already Forster has become well aware of what potent
keys may be turned by the application of a fine critical intelligence. On page 61 he has noted

> *Thought and Logic.* I possess the latter faculty. The former,
> classed by G. Heard as an emotion, has only been serviceable
> twice, once in a paper on Dante, written over 20 years ago, and
> once, more recently, in 'Anonymity'. Here there was a process,
> as of a living thing developing, it was a pleasure to create, and a
> satisfaction afterwards, and the detection of flaws in my argu-
> ment left the general cleanliness and beauty unaffected. Why
> has this noble quality come so seldom to me? After 'pure
> creation', from which it is separated by a boundary I can't yet
> define, it is the most desirable quality for a writer, and, unlike
> pure creation, it ought to strengthen as he grows older. It is
> impressive without being pompous: that separates it from
> rhetoric. It isnt the same as thinking things out, which only
> demands acuteness and pertinacity. It is a single organic
> advance, not a series of isolated little attacks. It may survive
> when there is nothing left in the universe either to be fanciful
> over or to criticise. (*Commonplace Book*, circa 1929)

A better definition of great philosophical excogitation or
critical writing could scarcely be wished: 'It is a single organic
advance. . . .' Yet not only *Aspects of the Novel* but whole
swathes of *Abinger Harvest* and *Two Cheers for Democracy* are
built upon the shaky foundation of Forster's failure to cling
tenaciously to that guiding light or at least to think through
the equation delineated above. In the main his essays suffer
from their own chatty tone, inherent in which particular style
of chattiness lurks the concession 'oh well all this doesn't
anyway matter all that much.'

There are several important exceptions to this depressing
rule, however, and to them and (first of all) to the works of
'pure creation' I now turn.

NOTES

1. In his Introduction to Shakespeare's *Sonnets* ([Signet Classics series] New York, 1964), pp. xxix–xxxiii.

2. If this seems too curt a synopsis, then let me offer the following supplementation. Auden gives an accurate paraphrase of the thought in question here: 'Both Plato and Dante attempt to give a religious explanation of the Vision. Both, that is to say, regard the love inspired by a created human being as intended to lead the lover towards the love of the uncreated source of all beauty. The difference between them is that Plato is without any notion of what we mean by a person, whether human or Divine; he can only think in terms of the individual and the universal, and beauty, for him, is always beauty in the impersonal sense . . .' (pp. xxxii–iii of essay cited immediately above). Now the two ultimate problems with erotic love at its most intense are (1) that it is very insecure. One of the parties, both, will die one day. (And for the Christian the consolation of an after-life is little less severe than disbelief in the same for the most convinced materialist. Though St. Paul assures us that whenever a man and woman couple they set up a transcendental relation which must eternally be enjoyed or endured—itself a promise not without grim fringes—still higher authority has informed the world that 'in Heaven there is no marrying or giving in marriage.' The blessed among the dead have 'saintly shout and solemn jubilee' in a 'perfect diapason' which makes earthly loves, at their idealest, like the mere tuning-up of an orchestra before its symphony begins. But is that consoling to 'the young In one another's arms', given that (a) that 'celestial consort'—I am quoting the while, of course, from Milton and Yeats—is unimaginable and (b) the this-worldly experience is valued in itself, not just as a footstep on a ladder? Speaking myself as a believer, I believe that inevitably God will harmonize all this; that the acceptable among the dead really do hit the jackpot and *get everything*. ('Seek ye first the kingdom of heaven, and all these things shall be added unto you.') But I cannot in this state of existence imagine how.) Problem no. (2): even the act of sexual intercourse itself does not accomplish two perfect lovers' greatest desire—that of achieving absolute integration of spirits and bodies, the dissolution of the fleshly bond-and-barrier between them. Here, I think, the special validity of Plato's instances come in. Where the love is between persons of the same sex this inability to conjoin and make a new total blended unity is in the corporeal dimension still more explicit than between heterosexual partners. Thus it was artistic tact of the deepest insight no less than convention's exigence which led Wagner to represent his hero and heroine, when Tristan and Isolde at last in Act 2 do have free time alone, spending it by sitting on a bank singing immortal melody together and not in what *Sense and Sensibility*'s Colonel Brandon calls 'intimacies'.

3. W. H. Auden, *Collected Poems* (London, 1976), p. 643.

4. From the *Daily Telegraph* review of *Two Cheers for Democracy* upon its appearance in the Abinger Edition (1972).

E. M. Forster: Our Permanent Contemporary

5. C. S. Lewis, *The Screwtape Letters* (London, 1942), pp. 148–49.
6. *E. M. Forster: A Life*, Vol. II, p. 248.
7. Roy Douglas, *History of the Liberal Party 1895–1970* (London, 1971), p. 206.
8. Foreword to above, by the then [1971] Leader of the Liberal Party, ibid., pp. xi–xii.
9. Ibid., p. 207.
10. Boris Ford (ed.) *The Pelican Guide to English Literature, Vol. 7* (['The Modern Age'] Harmondsworth, revised edition 1964), pp. 246–47.
11. Id. loc. (p. 247).
12. There are other similarities too. Both were sired by fathers they never knew who died before they were really consciant and supposedly, on the side of some relatives and onlookers, of 'neglect'. Elizabeth of England had a good case for being short with the Scotch Ambassador about Henry Darnley's demise and 'The blow [of Edward Forster's death] was a shattering one for Lily. It left her grieving and bewildered, and conscious that Edward's family secretly half-blamed her for the tragedy' (*Life*, Vol. I, p. 11). Both men were brought up as royal babies, the unique central foci of their environments' consideration and felt themselves to be magically endowed and possessed of a great destiny (which was true enough for the matter of that). As for the parodying of James VI & I, well I call Ben Jonson's treatment fine and sly because *Bartholmew Fayre* as a whole seems that to me. We are left by that play with an image of London (and by extension contemporary England)'s habitual sins and characteristic vices, both—and we would earnestly desire, in any announced plebiscite or campaign as it were, to endorse the view of its exasperated J.P. We are ourselves exasperated, more manageably, through the course of the whole and wish him all speed when he steps forward near the conclusion (the drama does not, cannot have an ending) 'to take enormity by the forehead, and brand it' (Act V, sc. iii). Yet we are diverted also throughout, 'against our conscience', by not only some of the other characters' inventivenesses or rascality but also Overdo's own absurdities.

As I see it, this play is a very major achievement in remonstrance-and-charity on the part of such a temperament as its author's. Thus the world wags, it informs us; it stinketh, Vanity Fair, and somehow nevertheless life keeps going—including the possibility of virtue. In the keeping going itself and the equal fact of attentive critical intellect able, *as* a human feature, to hold complex feelings about it in a single mode of cognition, lies the justification. Also we have all got skeletons in the closet: and the chief embodiment of law and morality present (Adam Overdo/King James) *tout le premier*! We agree with Overdo; he is sympathetic as well as in the right. But we have to laugh at him too.

'O rare Ben Jonson.' Jacobeans like him must have wondered how to bring into one focus a sovereign who wrote powerful tomes in support of traditional morality (even James's arguments on regicide/political assassination are still, I suppose, very respected *points de départs*, at least, in moral science debates, and no one has yet refuted his scourge against smoking); who deserves much of the eulogium with which commences the greatest translation of the Bible for his commissioning and political support of that—then very controversial—enterprise; who grappled with the much thornier problem still of Church Government and got it right; yet who slobbered over his male courtiers and had them posing for him with rings and jewels in their ears.

Mr. Furbank tells us E. M. Forster did not enjoy being laughed at by his friends (*Life*, Vol. II, p. 296). If *he* 'winced and bristled so visibly under teasing', how on earth did the Stuart monarch cope with being so broadly satirized in full open court? *Exempli gratia inter tanta alia* amidst this text is the lengthy (and very funny) take-off (latter part of Act II) of certain of James's known fulminatings:

> *Justice Overdo.* Neither do thou lust after that tawny weed, tobacco. . . . Whose complexion is like the Indian's that vents it! . . . And who can tell, if, before the gathering, and making up thereof, the Alligarta hath not piss'd thereon? [etc., etc., etc., punctuated by bemused interjections from his wondering auditory till one of them can stand no more.] I will conclude briefly—
> *Waspe.* Hold your peace, you roaring rascal, I'll run my head i' your chaps, else.

One most gratefully marvels all over again, wondering what they are, at those elements in the British tradition (unlike, say, the Russian or Chinese) which have inhibited even our few absolute rulers from punishing whole provinces with mega-deaths when they fancied someone so much as coughed at them. Indeed in the remaining eleven years of his life what did James do but keep *this* poet laureate in income and commissions for his pains?

Now in that historical instance, and both sides of the footlights, just that 'Tolerance, good temper and sympathy' were decisively operative which Forster pleaded for. But they have to have big deep roots, as Asia's long histories agonizingly show, and can't just be arranged by hanging up a few flags suitably marked with the fine words.

2

The Pre-War Fiction, Part 1

I agree with other critics (e.g. Leavis[1]) that *Where Angels Fear to Tread* is Forster's most accomplished pre-First-World-War work. Indeed in a specialized sense it seems perhaps too accomplished, and I have recurrently wondered over the years if the 'block' this author suffered from, creatively speaking, after 1910, was due not so much to the usual alleged reasons—his own sexual psychology, the drastic change in the civilization whose *mores* he had been accustomed to record—as to some more fundamental, inexorable law in the nature of artistic development itself. Is there something suspect, is there a price to be paid (fearful in its way) when a writer has perfect command of brilliant equipment at the age of 25? In poetry's case, that hierophantic art which can breathe tranced inspiration into the mouths of babes and sucklings, such early competence is not unique and bewildering—though we shall hold our breath for the development of a Keats or a Wilfred Owen. But the novel, the short story set in an actual social world or not too distorted mirror of it, requires a matured experience of life and the technical control to reproduce that verbally (the fruit of yet more maturation)—something which usually lags behind in the mere logic of human processes. Jane Austen had her sister and supreme confidante Cassandra shouting with laughter behind their locked bedroom door at the early drafts of *Pride and Prejudice* circa 1796–97; and well (no doubt) she might. But we are not to assume that it read as finished and brilliantly then as the

38

version she eventually gave (in her thirty-eighth year) to the world in 1813.

Yet the following description of Harriet and Philip Herriton's journey into Italy (Ch. 6 of *Where Angels*) is as rich and comprehensive, effectual and multi-faceted in its operation, as anything else one can produce from the annals of imaginative novelistic writing:

> They travelled for thirteen hours downhill, whilst the streams broadened and the mountains shrank, and the vegetation changed, and the people ceased being ugly and drinking beer, and began instead to drink wine and to be beautiful. And the train which had picked them at sunrise out of a waste of glaciers and hotels was waltzing at sunset round the walls of Verona.
>
> 'Absurd nonsense they talk about the heat,' said Philip, as they drove from the station. 'Supposing we were here for pleasure, what could be more pleasurable than this?'
>
> 'Did you hear, though, they are remarking on the cold?' said Harriet nervously. 'I should never have thought it cold.'
>
> And on the second day the heat struck them, like a hand laid over the mouth, just as they were walking to see the tomb of Juliet. From that moment everything went wrong. They fled from Verona. Harriet's sketch-book was stolen and the bottle of ammonia in her trunk burst over her prayerbook, so that purple patches appeared on all her clothes. Then, as she was going through Mantua at four in the morning, Philip made her look out of the window because it was Virgil's birthplace, and a smut flew in her eye, and Harriet with a smut in her eye was notorious. At Bologna they stopped twenty-four hours to rest. It was a *festa*, and children blew bladder whistles night and day. 'What a religion!' said Harriet. The hotel smelt, two puppies were asleep on her bed and her bedroom window looked into a belfry, which saluted her slumbering form every quarter of an hour. Philip left his walking-stick, his socks and the Baedeker at Bologna; she only left her sponge-bag. Next day they crossed the Apennines with a train-sick child and a hot lady who told them that never, never before had she sweated so profusely. 'Foreigners are a filthy nation,' said Harriet. 'I don't care if there are tunnels; open the window.' He obeyed, and she got another smut in her eye. Nor did Florence improve matters. Eating, walking, even a cross word would bathe them in boiling water. Philip, who was slighter of build, and less conscientious, suffered less. But Harriet had never been to Florence, and

between the hours of eight and eleven she crawled like a wounded creature through the streets, and swooned before various masterpieces of art. It was an irritable couple who took tickets to Monteriano.

'Singles or returns?' said he.

'A single for me,' said Harriet peevishly; 'I shall never get back alive.'

'Sweet creature!' said her brother, suddenly breaking down. 'How helpful you will be when we come to Signor Carella!'

Anyone who can pen those two pages has nothing more to learn about the management of narrative—in the sense that they perfectly set down the very much he has to say. They crowd into brief space, and with the apparently effortless relaxation of supreme art, a wealth of comedy and information. Apart from being so funny, even thus cut out of their context, look how much of Italy they give us to see and how much further, in slight compass (as to word-total, not covered canvas) is developed the contrast of Italy's culture with England's.

Indeed it is the tonal control, the variety of notes and their perfect management which, in the *biographico*-critical look at Forster's art, is amazing to the point of giving cause for alarm. Perhaps Emily Brontë wrote *Wuthering Heights* (to give another instance of what I mean) at nearly the same age—*aet. suae* 26; perhaps she did not. But though *Wuthering Heights* strikes most of us as one of the really greatest novels, it also appears a kind of sport—which, if one regards the matter properly, lessens neither its distinction nor its value. All sorts of control are operative there, and of a deliberate craftswoman's kind, over material wide-ranging and even—otherwise than by Emily Brontë's genius—intractable. But a note she does not have is Forster's easy urbanity, a tone in his case quite distinct from world-weariness and cynicism and the foreshortened views of human conduct which they portend; and Emily Brontë's collocation of latinate discourse for the style of civilized society's language, in her book, and Anglo-Saxon-derived terms of speech for the semi-barbarous rurality around, seem equally a donnée of her reading and environment and the uttermost of her range. We don't have the sense of her as capably handling other social notes than those which are

uttered in the homestead at the Heights or round the Lintons'
hearth; so much as that we may confess while insisting that no
other artist could manage her elements and compositional
masses as she, perfectly, does.

That is why it is impossible to imagine her writing another
novel in contradistinction to her sisters. It is not just
a question of reading inevitability back into what simply
happened.

Yet already at an equally young date, or earlier, E. M.
Forster seems capable of registering any social situation and
nuance. So much has been perceived and digested, as it were,
before he starts.

Verily the substance of his shown world gains much from
something central to this author's method. After he had first
read Proust and was writing *A Passage to India* he attributed it,
with typical self-misprision, to the example of the author of *In
Search of Lost Time*, though in fact Forster always worked it in
much fuller measure: the echoic ploy of a little phrase, a scenic
detail, which, as he says, commenting on the *Recherche*, 'gives
memory a shock' (*Two Cheers for Democracy*, 'Our Second
Greatest Novel?').

In his own *oeuvre* these things are present from the beginning
and have in fact a more major role than in Proust. They
substantiate the world he is building. For instance, in *Where
Angels Fear* we have the fact that the book starts and ends with
a train-journey—the same journey at the conclusion, only this
time in reverse. Still more pointedly perhaps there is explicit
mention of a famous tower in the opening when Philip
Herriton is speaking of it: 'the Campanile of Airolo, which
would burst on her when she emerged from the St. Gotthard
tunnel, presaging the future' (Ch. 1); and at the end where it is
the last thing of Italy he beholds, and the gained development
of his thought, his attitudes is signalized thus, as he and Miss
Abbott travel northwards: 'Philip's eyes were fixed on the
Campanile of Airolo. But he saw instead the fair myth of
Endymion. . . .'

When he gets to Monteriano on his first abortive rescue
mission (to stop Lilia's marriage) he is met by two men with
cabs, one of whom is ready waiting at the station for the
train—as it were efficiently (the reader may decide to reflect)—

the other 'driving two horses furiously' to meet it. In its own minute way that looks forward to the crisis of the tale where two drivers—the same ones?—going at very different paces, because one is cautious and one is not, in view of the weather, precipitate the catastrophe on the way (again) to the station.

More famously there is mention of the said weather as early as Chapter 6—' "there will be rain, he says, by tomorrow evening" '—which plays its own part in the fatal outcome: the coach overturned in the muddy path, the baby killed, Philip's arm broken, Harriet raving in the dark (Ch. 8).

The ironies are multiple throughout, are the very loom upon which the book's wonderfully sensitive prose shuttles. But indeed 'ironies' is a wholly inadequate word for them. Because a multitude of earlier evidences chime with and qualify so many later ones, in this fashion, they constate life itself. We have the sense of more things than we can number perceived in their characteristic nature, and a whole world apprehended and mediated in its substantiality. For these things are very gently present, they have no contrived air—they are there as things are in life itself. We may not even be conscious of them till they are pointed out; yet they impinge on us so that we feel the created world in its aspect of coherence looming upon us as a whole out of the book.

The story is a chapter of disasters owing to the interference of some English tourists in the life of a local lad (and an old city) in a different culture. Firstly, the Herritons—who are mother, son and daughter—pack off Lilia, a blowsy, flirtatious woman who has married into their family and been widowed there, to Italy. They send her with a chaperon, Caroline Abbott, in the hope that foreign travel will ease off the embarrassments she causes them in Sawston, the stuffy Home Counties town they inhabit.

Established in the small hill-city of Monteriano, the boisterous 33-year-old accepts a marriage proposal from the son of an Italian dentist; is aided and abetted in this initiative by the hitherto staid and conventional Miss Abbott, who is also fully a decade her junior, and the pair are wed before Philip Herriton has arrived to stop them.

Lilia's new marriage is a mistake. She has 'no resources. She didn't like music, or reading, or work', and her husband, who is handsome, caddish, unfaithful, and uncertain of her position in Italian society, effectually imprisons her in an existence far duller than ever she led at home.

Her one attempt at escape fails and she dies giving birth to a son.

The Herritons would here close the matter but that Gino sends a couple of postcards 'from your lital brother' to Irma, Lilia's English child who is being brought up in the Sawston establishment, and the secret is out. Caroline Abbott, guilt-stricken ever since the unfortunate expedition of the previous year, announces her intention of rescuing the child herself from what she now conceives Monteriano to be: 'a magic city of vice, beneath whose towers no person could grow up happy or pure' (Ch. 5).

This obliges Mrs. Herriton to mount a rescue-party of her own, since she has no desire to be disgraced in her home town by a baby-in-law being brought up in another of the neighbouring households. But when all three English people get there—Philip and Harriet Herriton and Miss Abbott—they find something unexpected: that Signor Carella wants his child for its own sake and will not part with it at any price.

Caroline Abbott, having once seen the father and infant son together, is eager for the two rescue-parties to leave at once; and she urges Philip to take a stand on one side or the other and fight. 'You ought never to see him again. You ought to bundle Harriet into a carriage, not this evening, but now, and drive her straight away.'

Habituated to being an 'honourable failure' he does not; and that evening, parting for the station in a cab, he encounters his sister who has the baby with her 'waiting for them in the wet, at the first turn of the zigzag.'

It is a perilous road in such conditions, the driver is fast and careless and the carriage overturns. When Philip, who breaks his arm here, comes round from a brief swoon he hears Harriet still screaming that the baby has slipped from her arms and that she stole it.

The child has been killed and Philip decides he must bear the news back to Gino. In the Italian's home he explicitly holds himself accountable for the tragedy. Carella responds, in a mania of grief, by torturing him—it would be to death, but that Miss Abbot intervenes, having anxiously followed after, and stops the hideous scene (Ch. 9).

All is patched up. Harriet gets over her hysterical illness which has followed the disaster, and its guilt. Philip and his sister are protected by Gino who lies for them at the inquest. He and the Italian are now fraternal friends and it is not only in a spirit of goodwill that Philip Herriton leaves the country at last, determined to have little more to do with Sawston. He is in love with Caroline by this time—and learns with a shock that her affinity is to Carella; that she has been subjected to the full process of falling in love with him because she had to come back and see him one more time, that night of the fatality.

> This woman was a goddess to the end. For her no love could be degrading: she stood outside all degradation. This episode, which she thought so sordid, and which was so tragic for him, remained supremely beautiful. To such a height was he lifted that without regret he could now have told her that he was her worshipper too. But what was the use of telling her? For all the wonderful things had happened.
>
> 'Thank you,' was all that he permitted himself. 'Thank you for everything.'
>
> She looked at him with great friendliness, for he had made her life endurable. At that moment the train entered the St Gotthard tunnel. They hurried back to the carriage to close the windows lest the smuts should get into Harriet's eyes.

In a letter to R. C. Trevelyan (28 October 1905, reproduced in Appendix to the Abinger Edition of *Where Angels Fear*) Forster was explicit about the novel's theme: 'The object of the book is the improvement of Philip'; yet while that may have proved a happy guiding scheme from his, the author's point of view, it by no means answers to all that the work achieves. For this novel articulates the insufficiency of both the English and the Italian worlds. On the one side we have the middle-class-oriented stuffiness, its 'petty unselfishness' and muddle-headed values, Sawston life as a pointless power game in status and repute. On the other the southern immediacy and barbarism predominate, warmth which is puppyish as well as (intermittently) considerate.

We can see these things in the passage I have already quoted from Chapter 6. The first paragraph—'They travelled for thirteen hours downhill. . . .'—presents the opposite norms: Harriet and Philip Herriton move from an environment of Protestant glacial stolidity to Italian grace, which is picked up in the change of verbs ('travelled' turns into 'waltzed') and the liquescence of the grammar.

But such are the superficies of two cultures. Immediately hereafter we have the menace implicit in the Italian climate. It can be killingly hot, though for the present this is tempered for us by the fact that its effects on Harriet are mainly comic. It is not just a question of the English duo having come with the wrong attitudes ('But he had a strange feeling that he was to blame for it all; that a little influx into him of virtue would make the whole land not beastly but amusing'). 'Eating, walking,' as well as 'even a cross word would bathe them in boiling water.'

We are confronted now with the fierce unromantic 'romance' of the Latin demesne, the 'true self' which is revealed 'in the height of the summer, when the tourists have left her, and her soul awakes under the beams of a vertical sun' (beginning of the chapter). Going 'to see the tomb of Juliet' is a costly mistake, delineates a wholesale misprision of what in such a season they are able here to apprehend—presumably an appreciation of the people, not the antiquities ('Love and understand the Italians, for the people are more marvellous than the land', Philip counsels his sister-in-law at the start of the story). Altogether, traditional reactions prove useless.

Harriet's sketchbook is, symbolically, stolen. Everything conspires against the prudential-'profitable' touristic approach. Indeed Italy makes thoroughly short shrift of northern devices and proprieties. 'The bottle of ammonia in her trunk burst over her prayerbook, so that purple patches appeared on all her clothes.' It is worth noting the joke here. We see the transferring, under Italy's cruel competence, of religion used as a device for self-endorsement ('purple patches') to outward living, all disconcertingly publicized. Every device for making life safe is snapped, and we can refer for a gloss to the passage in *Maurice* where Forster diagnoses the existences of the suburban middle classes; their highest desire, we are told

> seemed shelter—continuous shelter—not a lair in the darkness to be reached against fear, but shelter everywhere and always, until the existence of earth and sky is forgotten, shelter from poverty and disease and violence and impoliteness; and consequently from joy; God slipped this retribution in. (Ch. 42)

Here harassment is unmitigated:

> At Bologna they stopped twenty-four hours to rest. It was a *festa*, and children blew bladder whistles night and day. 'What a religion!' said Harriet. The hotel smelt, two puppies were asleep on her bed, and her bedroom window looked into a belfry, which saluted her slumbering form every quarter of an hour. Philip left his walking-stick, his socks and the Baedeker at Bologna; she only left her sponge-bag. Next day they crossed the Apennines with a train-sick child and a hot lady who told them that never, never before had she sweated so profusely. 'Foreigners are a filthy nation,' said Harriet. 'I don't care if there are tunnels; open the window.' He obeyed, and she got another smut in her eye.

It is also worth remarking once again, the utter mastery of such writing; how the narrative is all character-delineating, the scenic here all narrative, the comedy includes serious information, the episode looks backwards and forwards through the tale (not least with the 'petite phrase' *Harriet with a smut in her eye*). Look how much movement these two pages have: the packed rapidity of the telling—we cannot but respond to the way here condensed is a whole, full experience of Italy, in brief space—but without us feeling rushed or trampled. This is partly due to the double-sided character itself of what is happening. Several events here convey the harassing *and* colourful character of the Herritons' *rites de passage*, but also Forster shows himself able to vary the pace and the mood with Life's own fluency.

There is likewise his absolute possession, as one may say, of the micro-life of dialogue, so that the ways in which his characters talk render them entirely convincing and further substantiate the thematic life of the work. Here for instance the personages speak in character and what they declare also embodies the scene's double-natured import. 'They are remarking on the cold' is Harriet's phrase. The word 'remarking' is a concessionary one from her, an irritable woman who easily condemns and dismisses other people. She is nervous. Yet it is also a gracious word in its tiny way, relatively elaborate for its purpose, and reflects the kind of social interchange going on (among the locals) around all this Herriton bother. We realize from this that Miss Herriton really is scared by the weather which now environs her; and therefore admire the more her conscientious visiting of 'various masterpieces of art' under a meteorological dispensation that is nearly fatal, even while (in a degree) thinking her self-discipline misplaced, laughing at her and being appalled by the Italian mid-summer climate.

His skill in dialogue, let alone the other parts of a novelistic narration, disposes of Forster's own claim (again, right off the beat) that he is 'not a great novelist' on the plea that he only handled a limited number of human types: 'the sort of person he thought he was, the sort of person he wanted to be, and the sort of person he disliked'[2]. All types *are* present in *Where Angels Fear To Tread*, however much *in potentiâ* and fugitively. We feel that he knows two whole worlds, the English and the Italian, inside out and can insert at will a cameo of anybody from either of them. As he does; there are the curates at Sawston—'Both are chinless, but hers had the dampest hands. I came on them in the Park. They [the curate and Lilia] were speaking of the Pentateuch' (Ch. 1), or the personnel associated with the Monteriano railway station:

> His feet sank into the hot asphalt of the platform, and in a dream he watched the train depart, while the porter who ought to have been carrying his bag ran up the line playing touch-you-last with the guard. Alas! he was in no humour for Italy. Bargaining for a *legno* bored him unutterably. The man asked six lire; and, though Philip knew that for eight miles it should scarcely be more than four, yet he was about to give what he was asked, and so make the man discontented and unhappy for the rest of the day. He was saved from this social blunder. . . . She made room for Philip and his luggage amidst the loud indignation of the unsuccessful driver, whom it required the combined eloquence of the station-master and the station beggar to confute. (Ch. 2)

47

'Eloquence' and 'confute' there utterly bring to life the minor personages of that scene. Or there are the *dogana* men, later on, and their young relative (Ch. 6).

Such finely realized vignettes of folk with wholly different antecedents and psychologies from the Sawstonians' suggest that Forster can represent a limitless variety of the human beings under his purview from within.

All the while we are conscious, on the other side of the balance, of Italy's malefic character. Just as the heat rises to dangerous levels, so there is more than enough irrationality here. It is all very well parroting ritual hymns in praise of instinctive corporate life and so on from the cool collectedness of a northern environment, but does it really make sense to have a *festa* in such a season? Experience of hot climates has taught me that a key element for survival amidst their rank baking and humidity is plenty of good sound sleep. That way the body can be ready for the total assault course which is its next white boiling day. The human frame is perhaps the most adaptable among animal organisms and, agreed, the children of Bologna will be acclimatized to their August weather as Anglo-Saxons from Kent are not. But this adaptability operates within essential needs and constraints. Eskimo die in the Arctic almost as quickly as Italians, if condemned to exposure. Chinese in Canton find their own summer all but insupportable unless mitigated by fans and cooling drinks; and that the infants in Forster's account choose Italy's hottest weather to banish somnolence with 'bladder whistles night and day' not only offers us a comic image of the stiff Harriet's tormenting, but suggests also that on occasion there is something of the mad dog about Philip's vaunted Italian people no less than the malignity of the 'terrible and mysterious' landscape (Ch. 4) which helps unsettle Lilia's nerves. A rabid canine is not to blame, if you will, for his condition; but this makes him no less frightening and destructive.

The duality that finds expression even here, where the main object of the narrative is a tilt at certain English preconceptions and rectitudes is more fully worked out elsewhere in the tale, principally in the agony which Lilia's marriage becomes for her. But generally Italy is weighed in the balance and found no less wanting than, culturally speaking, the English alternative.

We are every bit as shocked by the attitudes of Gino Carella and his friend Spiridione Tesi (Ch. 3) towards women—or we ought to be—as by Mrs. Herriton's species of brutality; and the more depressed in that both cases represent attitudes predominant in their respective societies. Carella and Tosi really deserve the epithet, often now too freely flung about, 'male chauvinist pigs' except that it seems unfair on the thoroughly decent porcine creation. For them women are a convenience to be pulled in and out of the domestic cupboards as their emotions require and they positively rejoice in their odious double standard. The fact that Italian women acquiesce in this revolting ethos does not mend the matter. Females are required to be faithful, men are not. Women are to go to church to keep up the religious side of family life; men can skip it. Women are to stay at home living narrow restricted lives among the relatives of their own sex; for men the world is to be their oyster (Spiridione spends his holiday 'travelling over Italy at the public expense'). Any defence of this morality on the grounds that it functioned and was/is the custom of the country, is very two-edged. Cannot we apply such words to the rule of the worst Pharaohs? 'Yes, but slaves in Pithom and Rameses and cities of that kind *expected* to work till they dropped and then be bricked into the rising walls. It was the world they were born into and the only reality they knew.'

Lilia in fact gets the worst of Italian life for reasons Forster makes clear. She has been so punished by family life in Sawston she stamps on the chance of it in Monteriano and, not really belonging to any class, her husband is nervously uncertain how to integrate her into the rest of his society, so ends by practically just locking her up.

Sickening is Perfetta the servant's unconsciously deadly invocation of the whole morality when Lilia rounds on Gino and tells him 'all she knew and all she thought' of his infidelity: 'What courage you have! and what good fortune! He is angry no longer! He has forgiven you!'

The cruel 'democracy of the *caffè* or the street' which is solely a democracy for males throws, in its working-out upon the tragic fate of the younger Herriton widow, the Sawston modes of human relation into an attractive light. We see afresh what

English culture has, over the centuries, spared and built of mortal amenities and through the eyes of this supreme victim of Italy herself:

> If she were to disobey her husband and walk in the country, that would be stranger still—vast slopes of olives and vineyards, with chalk-white farms, and in the distance other slopes, with more olives and more farms, and more little towns outlined against the cloudless sky. 'I don't call this country,' she would say. 'Why, it's not as wild as Sawston Park!'
>
> One evening, when he had gone out thus, Lilia could stand it no longer. It was September. Sawston would be just filling up after the summer holidays. People would be running in and out of each other's houses all along the road. There were Bicycle gymkhanas, and on the 30th Mrs. Herriton would be holding the annual bazaar in her garden for the C.M.S. It seemed impossible that such a free, happy life could exist. (Ch. 4)

Our sympathies will fluctuate throughout a reading of the whole. In the presence of Mrs. Herriton's sterile domestic and social scheming the wonderfully vital, hilarious-happy scene at the opera (Ch. 6) embodies a livingness which seems to have been all but cancelled within the English shore. The sincerity-amid-hypocrisy and hypocrisy-amid-sincerity of Italian manners is typified by the letter Gino sends to Mrs. Herriton when the latter has offered to buy his child.

> For a moment Philip forgot the matter in the manner; this grotesque memorial of the land he had loved moved him almost to tears. He knew the originals of these lumbering phrases; he also had sent 'sincere auguries'; he also had addressed letters—who writes at home?—from the Caffè Garibaldi. (Ch. 5)

The delicate superlatives which characterize the epistle '—superlatives are delicate in Italian—' have a delightful grace that is missing from the life of the northern household, but then one remembers that it is in externals, so much of the time, that Carella's most gracious living is done, not in essentials. Yet such recollection is also qualified by the fact that the matriarch to whom he writes so politely has offered a bribe, a disgusting insult indeed, from what on her side is a heartless cause.

In brief—over the course of several hundred such episodes, incidents and touches—we shall compare and evaluate one system of behaviour, one world of values, with another until eventually we perceive that, like Henry James's 'transatlantic' histories, this novel, passing through its portrayed environments, attains to a vision of human possibilities which transcends the two; for both are shown to be inadequate, both are revealed as bristling with virtues.

Gino's modes of gaiety and grace, we realize, Lilia's directness, Harriet's courage—these as elements individually and culturally derived are to be cherished. Their species of caddishness, vulgarity and bigoted dishonesty respectively, are worth eschewing. What the novelist is after is the integrity of which all these people and scenes exhibit the fracturedness; and he reaches it by the very act of his narration. In that the whole book operates at one level after another of irony which is not unsympathetic or sentimental, Forster presents himself and us with a vision which is much more inclusive than the outlook obtaining in any one of his exhibited personages, and he registers the glimpseable lineaments of a society which does not exist, yet is deeply needed.

The theme of transcendent vision or knowledge is itself taken up in the fate of Caroline Abbott, and Philip Herriton in relation to her. (The suggestion now offered by some critics that this hero's blushing conversational fumble towards her during their train-journey together at the end conveys the agonized difficulty of a homosexual declaration, seems to me very unhelpful; in fact a magnificent instance of reading the extraneous and irrelevant into a text by the light of later biographical information; in proof of which no convincing answer comes back to the question 'So what? What does that idea illuminate—in the book?' Suppose at this time of day we learned that Shakespeare had been a bothered and hectic transvestite, what a field-day commentary would have with *Twelfth Night*, *The Merchant of Venice*, etc.; and how little of import in his *oeuvre* it would intrinsically clarify.)

Across the larger revelation of human values in different societies that the book deals in as a whole there moves also Forster's interest in the problem of integrating the life of the body and the life of the mind. This is his first larger-scale assay upon the issue and not his least successful. What, in the shorter tales of the previous years—e.g. 'The Story of a Panic', 'The Road from Colonus'—figured as metaphysical *données*, so that a given human identity was invaded, *ab extra*, by red-integrating spiritual power, is here worked out, unsuper-naturally, by a social process.

Caroline Abbott starts off from Sawston as a frigid piece of single blessedness dedicated to a dull life of good works and conscious that her existence seriously lacks important vibra-tions. In an attempt to repair these *manques* she sets off for Italy with Lilia Herriton; and there swinging from one extreme to the other, loses her head:

> 'We were mad—drunk with rebellion. We had no common sense. As soon as you came, you saw and foresaw everything.'
>
> 'Oh, I don't think that.' He was vaguely displeased at being credited with common sense. For a moment Miss Abbott had seemed to him more unconventional than himself. . . .
>
> 'Lilia is dead and her husband gone to the bad—all through me. You see, Mr. Herriton, it makes me specially unhappy; it's the only time I've ever gone into what my father calls "real life"—and look what I've made of it! All that winter I seemed to be waking up to beauty and splendour and I don't know what; and when the spring came I wanted to fight against the things I hated—mediocrity and dullness and spitefulness and society. I actually hated society for a day or two at Monteriano. I didn't see that all these things are invincible, and that if we go against them they will break us to pieces.' (Ch. 5)

In returning there however, on her own rescue mission, she is subjected to the process herself of falling in love. It is not a passion which can hope for reciprocity. She is but little interested in repeating Lilia's mistake and Gino is anyway already bespoke in another marriage even if he could respond to her feeling. But the emotional upheavals of the year which now is ending have taught her to accept physical attraction as a part of life which neither vitiates nor justifies the whole:

> 'Don't talk of "faults". You're my friend for ever, Mr. Herriton, I think. Only don't be charitable and shift or take the blame. Get over supposing I'm refined. That's what puzzles you. Get over that.'

> As she spoke she seemed to be transfigured, and to have indeed no part with refinement or unrefinement any longer. (Ch. 10)

We can see this as looking forward to the fine moment in *A Room with a View* where, under Mrs. Honeychurch's cross-questioning, Lucy finds that

> the case for Cecil, which she had mastered so perfectly in London, would not come forth in an effective form. The two civilizations had clashed—Cecil had hinted that they might—and she was dazzled and bewildered, as though the radiance that lies behind all civilization had blinded her eyes. (Ch. 13)

It is the hint of a vision of Charity, or indeed New Jerusalem, and vindicates a little the words of Auden which otherwise are sloppy-sentimental merely; 'As I see him, Morgan is a person who is so accustomed to the Presence of God that he is unaware of it: he has never known what it feels like when the Presence is withdrawn.'[3]

Still, this part of the novel is somewhat insecurely achieved, *voulu*. For wholesale conviction we could do with having more, in one mode or another, of Caroline's inner life.

But meanwhile, fully effective already, is the play of Forsterian nuance. Like Jane Austen, but entirely *sui generis*, this author has a habit of subjecting motive and response upon the human scene to peculiarly close scrutiny and with a rhetoric which is perfect because it is sly for prinking out the gaps in their various incarnations.

> Charles died, and the struggle recommenced. Lilia tried to assert herself, and said that she should go to take care of Mrs. Theobald. It required all Mrs. Herriton's kindness to prevent her.

More subtly still:

> Just then Irma came in from school and she read her mother's letter to her, carefully correcting any grammatical errors, for she was a loyal supporter of parental authority. Irma listened politely, but soon changed the subject to hockey, in which her whole being was absorbed. They were to vote for colours that afternoon—yellow and white or yellow and green. What did her grandmother think?
> *Of course Mrs. Herriton had an opinion.* . . . (Ch. 1, emphasis added)

Again and again we run into psychological moments, characterizations of moral loyalties, which are as complex as possible but unparalysing; which feed back an invigorated sense of life *because* they are so faithful to the complexity of human experience.

> As they drew near, Philip saw the heads of people gathering black upon the walls, and he knew well what was happening—how the news was spreading that a stranger was in sight, and the beggars were aroused from their content and bid to adjust their deformities; how the alabaster man was running for his wares, and the Authorized Guide running for his peaked cap and his two cards of recommendation—one from Miss M'Gee, Maida Vale, the other, less valuable, from an Equerry to the Queen of Peru. . . . (Ch. 2)

It is a sorrow, it is a joy, that Italian society should be like that.

Enough has been said to intimate the view that *Where Angels Fear to Tread* is a perfect major work. *Is* that my opinion? Well I certainly think it is one of the great prose fictions in our literature, yes, but am not bold enough to claim perfection for it.

Two faults seem to inhere. It is not long enough to hold comparison with the very richest novels, and in one aspect it suffers from a young man's heartlessness.

It is not long enough. When one thinks of an Austen novel one calls to mind a more extended narrative (even *Northanger Abbey* and *Persuasion* are considerably more protracted than this text) and the slower pace with which the earlier writer unfolds her scroll of life. That mediates to us a solider sense of a whole world *in its daily routines*. This is the case in spite of the fact that Forster and Austen have in nearly equal degree the ability to imply the life history of a character in a few phrases, gestures and remarks. We know that Austen could immediately describe for herself the nature of Mrs. Norris's underclothes (in *Mansfield Park*) or that her successor can say from memory which are Harriet's favourite psalms; and both would do so in a degree sympathetically. One recalls the poignant moment where her creator points out how Mrs. Norris would have made a better manager of nine children on a small income than her sister Mrs. Price; and of Harriet, Forster can honestly tell us

> She kept her promise, and never opened her lips all the rest of the way. But her eyes glowed with anger and resolution. For she was a straight brave woman, as well as a peevish one. (Ch. 6)

Yet *Where Angels* does inevitably suffer from its novella-type scale in any attempt to convey the slow-accumulating density of time and experience upon mortal sensoria.

Secondly Philip and Forster both take the death of the baby too lightly. Up till its demise the child is superbly handled. It is wonderfully fleshed; a moving epiphany, a tiny egoist, banal and revelatory together, it is all that a healthy infant portends and can be. The fact however that it dies by accident, not deliberate murder, hardly much mitigates the horror of its loss. Yet the narrative, no less than the hero whose *Bildungs-roman* Forster saw the whole tale as constituting, gets over the baby's abduction and killing with an ease that is a false note. Something too dreadful has happened for the *dramatis personae* to quit the scene with heads as full as they are (and even cheerfully in Philip's case) of other topics.

But those are weaknesses, not fatal flaws, and this book goes on being the most extraordinarily mature effusion of a 25-year-old in England's imaginative prose literature.

It is noteworthy that the most achieved of the same writer's short stories at that season are partially or wholly set in a foreign ambit. It is as if, during the Edwardian epoch, by going to Italy and Greece in person and then in his creative role, he was able to focus his interests to the cutting out of all self-indulgence and emotional loose ends. 'The Story of a Panic', 'The Road from Colonus', 'The Eternal Moment' and 'The Story of the Siren' are much the most impressive of Forster's briefer tales.

'The Story of a Panic' addresses itself to the preoccupations which distinguish *Where Angels Fear to Tread*. To what extent can the individual break out of a cramping social environ and an insufficient cultural inheritance so as fully to realize himself and achieve happiness? How much can the society of our day be revitalized and turned aside from, on the one hand, the 'metalled ways' of technologico-materialist development and, on the other, the moral inhibitions it has gained?

The virtue of this tale—like 'Colonus' and the 'Siren'—is that, with its supernaturalist paganism, it crystallizes and clarifies Forster's positive commitments, embodying concretely the liberations to which he looks as a goal and the values by which he wants society to be reoriented.

Following a visitation from the god Pan amongst his party of fairly dense British tourists, the 14-year-old Eustace Robinson loses his feebleness of body and attenuation of mind to become invested with a livingness for which the only problem is the opacity of spirit in *mankind*.

> He spoke first of night and the stars and planets above his head, of the swarms of fireflies below him, of the invisible sea below the fireflies, of the great rocks covered with anemones and shells that were slumbering in the invisible sea. He spoke of the rivers and waterfalls, of the ripening bunches of grapes, and of the smoking cone of Vesuvius and the hidden fire-channels that made the smoke, of the myriads of lizards who were lying curled up in the crannies of the sultry earth, of the showers of white rose-leaves that were tangled in his hair. And then he spoke of the rain and wind by which all things are changed, of the air through which all things live, and of the woods in which all things can be hidden.
>
> Of course, it was all absurdly high faluting: yet I could have kicked Leyland for audibly observing that it was 'a diabolical caricature of all that was most holy and beautiful in life.'
>
> 'And then'—Eustace was going on in the pitiable conversational doggerel which was his only mode of expression—'and then there are men, but I can't make them out so well.' (Ch. III)

The specimens of mankind around him try to deny him that liberty in and through Nature which he needs as a kind of pagan baptism, but fail owing to the good offices of Gennaro, a waiter at their hotel, who helps the boy to escape into the completion of his epiphany at the cost of his own life. This price and the fact of the story's telling by a second-rate narrator who, a sufficiently pompous impercipient legislator among the tourist party, does not see the whole meaning of what has happened and speaks for a kind of humanity which is all but effectually dead, heightens the value of the young hero's experience into a moral absolute.

The other Italian *contes* above-mentioned form a descant or commentary upon the theme of this value. While 'The Eternal Moment' is a more personal drama, as it were Forster's own attempt to guard the emotionally liberating experiences he has had in the South from any implication of fatuity which the passage of time of itself may make adhere, 'The Story of the Siren' is a fiercer plea than any other in his pages for a return to the pagan values of the Mediterranean world B.C., values he much more clinically summarized in his 1956 Introduction to Goldsworthy Lowes Dickinson's *The Greek View of Life*:

> Religion is a puzzler: all-pervading yet having little connection with what the Christian regards as faith or as conscience; mainly concerned with making Man feel at home in this world, and offering him only the vaguest intimations of immortality. The State is a puzzler of another sort: unthinkably small, so small that the people in it know each other personally, and the same citizen could be farmer, judge, legislator, soldier, etc. The Individual is easier to grasp, but remains definitely B.C.: if fortunate, he is well-to-do and healthy and so can enjoy the operations of his body and his mind and can contact other fortunate individuals; his life is not a preparation for a better one, and the end of it is regrettable unless he has become unfortunate. And Art: art is aesthetic, but it is also ethical; it is individual but it is also social, for the reason that the individual is closely integrated in his city-state.

I think we should not underestimate the degree in which the attitudes to life developed in Ancient Greece (especially Athens) appealed to Forster and constituted his court of appeal against the historical world he experienced. 'Simply the Human Form' (editorial title), an unpublished writing which belongs to this period, though in Elizabeth Heine's words

> at a superficial glance only an essay, . . . is on closer inspection a story, the first person report of a visitor from outer space, of non-human form, who is intrigued by human reactions to nudity in art and life.[4]

It combines key-aspects of Forster's longing for a renewal of the human experiment made in the golden Athenian epoch:

the elevation of athletic beauty as a moral principle and the integration of the physical and intellectual capacities of human nature which he saw the Christian era as having fractured and divided.

> You will say, 'They have the same natural distaste to their own appearance, that they have to yours.' No. Otherwise they would not admire the Ilissos. They know themselves to be beautiful, but they only acknowledge it in their art, and nudity at the present day signifies the highest standard in art and the lowest standard of civilization.
>
> Since the race prides itself on an intimate connection between the two, the situation is strange. But once the connection did exist. In that peninsula, of which I have already spoken, the aspirations of art and the dictates of civilization were for a brief period the same, and the memory of that period will never pass from the human mind. Men would recall it if they could, but things have passed between which not even men can understand. By their inconsistency they now render it pathetic homage, for though they have not the courage to unclothe their bodies, they have not had the heart to clothe their statues. . . .[5]

'The Story of the Siren' is a much more desperate, heart-broken cry against Europe's later priestcraft and its achievements, the character of the civilization Forster found himself actually born into. That the ultimate key-note of his complaint against the Christianized organum is that it has meant 'Silence and _loneliness_'—in the closing words of the Sicilian boatman (emphasis added)—interprets for us, if you will, the central location of his hurt: the non-acceptance and non-integration of his kind of emotional life in the post-Attic societies; but it does not devalue the attempt to see things from a pre- and indeed anti-Christian pagan viewpoint.

Such an attempt at an _otherness_ of vision, a paganly apprehended world, is much more successfully accomplished here, it seems to me, than in the more lurid savagery of 'The Tomb of Pletone'[6] (a narrative of events touched upon in the last paragraph of Forster's 1905-published essay on the same theme 'Gemistus Pletho'). That is more merely savage than anything else; a sort of undigested sadism informs but does not meaningfully shape the murderous incidents.

With its plot basis in reincarnation or transference (at any rate the transmigration of a soul) 'Albergo Empedocle'[7] raises a problem inherent in most of these stories: the status of the supernatural in them. As an element, does it clarify or obscure? Do we perceive a human issue more focused by this means than otherwise it would appear to us or does the supernaturalism leave questions begged and the mortal choices (here under examination) blurred?

It is best handled in the most important of them, 'The Road from Colonus'. Here we have an elderly traveller, Mr. Lucas, who is at last making the trip to Greece and who begins it thoroughly jaded. The famous places he has always dreamed of seeing have struck him most unremarkably and he realises that he is up against old age and an *ennui* as large as life itself. Ahead of his small tourist party however, and in proximity to a group of plane trees which shelter 'at Plataniste, in the province of Messenia', 'a tiny Khan or country inn, a frail mud building with a broad wooden balcony', he discovers a hollow tree with a living trunk, from the roots of which gushes springwater which in a continuous stream covers the road, while inside the bark the country people have created a shrine. Determining in his new resolute mood of discontent to take possession, Mr. Lucas enters, leans back and undergoes a sort of epiphany.

> He was aroused at last by a shock—the shock of an arrival perhaps, for when he opened his eyes, something unimagined, indefinable, had passed over all things, and made them intelligible and good.
>
> There was meaning in the stoop of the old woman over her work, and in the quick motions of the little pig, and in her diminishing globe of wool. A young man came singing over the streams on a mule, and there was beauty in his pose and sincerity in his greeting. The sun made no accidental patterns upon the spreading roots of the trees, and there was intention in the nodding clumps of asphodel, and in the music of the water. To Mr. Lucas, who, in a brief space of time, had discovered not only Greece, but England and all the world and life, there seemed nothing ludicrous in the desire to hang within the tree another votive offering—a little model of an entire man. (Ch. 1)

The others in the travelling-group arrive now, however, and determine to make of themselves a rescue-party when he announces his intention of staying at the Khan. This scene is extremely well managed by its author. Though the old man is put astride his mule by force, in its upshot, and dragged from 'the place which brought him happiness and peace' even in spite of the physical defence offered his scheme by the Khan's younger inhabitants, we are conscious that he could still have stopped there if he had made enough efforts of his own.

> By one of those curious tricks of mountain scenery, the place they had left an hour before suddenly reappeared far below them. The Khan was hidden under the green dome, but in the open there still stood three figures, and through the pure air rose up a faint cry of defiance or farewell.
> Mr. Lucas stopped irresolutely, and let the reins fall from his hand.
> 'Come, father dear,' said Ethel gently.
> He obeyed, and in another moment a spur of the hill hid the dangerous scene for ever.

The next episode, indeed the dénouement of the little drama (Ch. II) reveals to us his life back in London: permanently querulous, dissatisfied, meaningless and not even conscious of its essential loss when his daughter, translating from an old Greek newspaper which has wrapped some bulbs just sent to them from Athens, discovers that on that very day in which they left Plataniste ' "A large tree . . . blew down in the night and . . . crushed to death the five occupants of the little Khan there, who had apparently been sitting in the balcony" '—just Mr. Lucas's choice of seat for the evening he intended to spend with those people.

> She put her hand to her heart, scarcely able to speak.
> 'Father, dear father, I must say it: you wanted to stop there. All those people, those poor half savage people, tried to keep you, and they're dead. The whole place, it says, is in ruins, and even the stream has changed its course. Father dear, if it had not been for me, and if Arthur had not helped me, you must have been killed.
> Mr. Lucas waved his hand irritably. 'It is not a bit of good speaking to the governess, I shall write to the landlord and say, "The reason I am giving up the house is this: the dog barks, the children next door are intolerable, and I cannot stand the noise of running water." '

His 'escape' is arguably a spiritual catastrophe, a disaster of lost revelation, therefore.

In the above one regard this is the most Wagnerian of Forster's images of life. Fulfilment here is associated with death: not in some morbid psychological crisis or death-*wish* but in the sense that the enigma of death is part of the central theme.

The old man, whose daughter is nicknamed 'Antigone' by the bulbs-sender, has his sole chance to be Oedipus—the self-blinded exasperated king who undergoes transfiguration at the sacred grove of Colonus. He refuses the opportunity and, I repeat, supreme narrative skill underlies Forster's presenting the company's retreat from the Khan in his aged hero's point of view while still showing us that he could have made a sterner effort nevertheless to stay; a scene in which old age itself is registered as well as moral conwardice, muddle, sloth—and yet not excused (in this respect also Forster is Austen's best heir).

The enigma of Life from any anthropocentric standing-ground is here embodied: does mortal death signalize the terminus or fulfilment of our human capacities? Hence my invocation of Wagner's work where recurrently that ambiguous issue is in question. When Brünnhilde ascends her funeral pyre (taking the old paradise, Valhalla, with her) does she extinguish herself or enter upon enhanced existence?

The tale's coherence and convincingness may signalize only what mortal imagination can perform (*homo faber, homo fictus*), not the accuracy of the sense we have from time to time that there are patterns in human experience which we are conscious of, though far from wholly able to interpret. Mr. Lucas has the option of a living death (going back to London) or perhaps of dying into life. It is as if, having achieved integrity with Nature (and thus a condition outside either age or youth), the next stage of his development must take place, like Oedipus Colonneus', in a different world altogether. Alternatively, on (say) the Hardyesque view of things, he would have been the victim of one of Existence's 'ironies'. In the fullness, at last during his advanced years, of realized livingness, of apprehended wholeness, he—and still more cruelly, the younger dwellers at the Greek country inn—would have been snuffed out; though in either case the evident superiority of the fate for this elderly English gentleman is not in question, compared to the mentality with and to which he returns. His different reactions to the sound of running water, to animal and youthful fellow creatures—beside the hollow tree-bole and in his London flat—give the measure of his abdication. But the tale gives us also the positive terminal in the whole Forster canon. In 'The Road from Colonus' we have what on this author's view, without abatement or compromise, is the goal and end of living. Mr. Lucas's experience at the Attic Khan expresses Forster's sense of the highest fulfilment possible to individual man in this world. It is ultimately to this synthesis that his vision looks and in favour of that kind of reciprocity between humans and their environment that his social comedy, ironic voice and satire operate.

Even here, however, we shall not declare we are dealing with one of the world's perfect short stories. Momentarily it does not wholly avoid being sententious: Mr. Lucas's 'desire to hang within the tree another votive offering—a little model of an entire man'—and the context, the way it is reported, are a little too morally self-conscious. Also there is the strange disconcerting use (which disfigures other of his earlier writings) of 'ere' (to mean 'before'): disconcerting because without a sufficient sense of its literary datedness. In the pages of the Brontës the word does not grate. Here it expresses the lack of historical consciousness in a full enough degree.

That comparison will serve to illustrate the big issues which depend from historical consciousness, if we press it further. Vicarage daughters that they were, and brought up on the Tory politics of a Romanticized recidivism (Patrick Brontë's coloured antique views), all three Brontë girls wrote fiction and verse which fiercely opposes the norms of their, of any historical, world: work which pleads for liberty (not least of women), new kinds of human consciousness, the liberation of the spirit itself into Nature. *Wuthering Heights* is, *inter alia*, a punishing social critique. In *The Tenant of Wildfell Hall* Anne represents Life as itself Anarchist, from an anthropocentric point of view. But all three sisters are aware of how necessary it is for any society to have traditions which bind it and operate sufficiently for its human members to find the world inhabitable at all. Forster and many of his generation (and after-comers) lacked something of this. They grew up amidst such brutal solidities that they assumed the fundamental rudiments of their social order were here to stay; with criticism, mockery and campaigns, balances could be redressed and what was wrong in it righted. So they slung bricks through the shop-window (often, leaned on an open door) till door and shop are now gone. We stand all, today, in the very cold wind of a howling empty broken arcade with little shelter of any kind.

That is not a criticism, however, there is any motive for bringing against *A Room with a View*. Our demurs there may well be different, making a serried list of headings and sub-paragraphs which in their turn ultimately prove strangely irrelevant. Possibly this novel suffers, like *Dombey and Son*, from a too-long gestation. The earlier avatars (most interestingly and helpfully available to the student in *The Lucy Novels*[8]) were Forster's first *sustained* attempt at a full-length fiction and date from his very first visit to Italy 1901–2. Like the over-germinated *Dombey*, the finished book fails quite to focus any one interest or another. Here we do have the sense of reading a *roman à clef* of which the key remains always missing.

There are four chief themes. Firstly, the author's rejection of *pensione* life abroad as a type of pettiness in many forms: the 'attributions'-game in contradistinction to a real interest in Art; social snobbery; and the trivialities of English *mores*, even at the higher levels (e.g. in Mrs. Vyse's London dinner-parties). Secondly this work is also his tribute to the happy side of Home Counties existence: the Weald, the idyll of outer Kent and of Sussex. Windy Corner enshrines the glory of that England. Thirdly there is a veiled plea for an unorthodox relation embraced in defiance of the dominant norms. George Emerson's déclassé social status does not afflict the Honeychurches when he plays tennis at their home—only when he marries Lucy. Even in 1907–8 this is not wholly convincing. Mr. Beebe supplies the homosexualism, transferred, that underlies the interest and meaning of this relation (though to suggest that Lucy is a boy *en travesti*, as is now becoming critically accustomary, is again—like the similar view of Caroline Abbott in *Where Angels Fear to Tread*—bewilderingly strained. Surely Miss Honeychurch is one of the most marvellously realized, and fresh, young women in our literature's pages. That sort of observation applies far more to the female juveniles who haunt the Balbec *plage* and the life of Albertine—whose own real name is Albert—in Proust's long documentary.)

Fourthly—if this can be seen as a distinct issue—there is the whole battle of Life seen as Art and Life Itself, actuality embraced and lived in for its own sake. Cecil Vyse regards Lucy 'as a work of art', George Emerson does not and in that aspect lives out the value which finds voice in *Where Angels Fear to Tread*:

> 'Oh, I quite sympathize with what you say,' said Philip encouragingly. . . . 'Society *is* invincible—to a certain degree. But your real life is your own, and nothing can touch it. There is no power on earth that can prevent your criticizing and despising mediocrity—nothing that can stop you retreating into splendour and beauty—into the thoughts and beliefs that make the real life—the real you.'
>
> 'I have never had that experience yet [replies Caroline Abbott]. Surely I and my life must be where I live.' (Ch. 5)

This social comedy opens at the Pension Bertolini in Florence where the young Lucy Honeychurch and her middle-aged spinster cousin Charlotte Bartlett are dismayed to discover themselves lodged in a Cockney boarding-house just when they have made a weary journey hither as tourists for the foreignness of Italy. Moreover the landlady has failed to provide them rooms with a view, as promised—instead they have back premises giving over the establishment's interior courtyard, which smells.

At this the elder of two men seated together at the general table insists on giving them the rooms occupied by himself and the son who is his companion, since theirs are at the front of the building and will answer the newcomers' needs. After much ungraciousness on the part of the prudish Miss Bartlett, and the intervention of Mr. Beebe, a clergyman of lively views also staying here, who is shortly to become the Honeychurch family's vicar at their Sussex home township of Summer

Street, the two English females do swap apartments with Mr. and George Emerson and find themselves ensconced with windows that look out on 'the lights dancing in the Arno and the cypresses of San Miniato, and the foot-hills of the Apennines, black against the rising moon'.

From here on Lucy keeps having unsettling encounters with the younger Emerson. She is present one evening in a square in Florence where a murder is committed very close by, faints and revives in the arms of George who has been standing in an arcade near at hand. During a hill-side ramble outside Fiesole these two young people unattendedly embrace—observed by the disapproving Miss Bartlett. Having fled such scenes to Rome, Lucy there accepts his third marriage-proposal from Cecil Vyse, a supercilious aesthete, and spends the rest of the summer trying to convince herself that 'She loved Cecil; George made her nervous; will the reader explain to her that the phrases should have been reversed?' (Ch. 14).

By then George Emerson has re-emerged in her life owing to one of Cecil's rather malicious little practical jokes. The local squire at Summer Street having sought genteel tenants for an ugly villa beside the Church green, Lucy has put him in touch with two elderly Miss Alans, also alumnae of the Pension Bertolini. With the aim of dismaying Sir Harry Otway (the squire) Cecil puts this scheme out of joint by pushing the Emersons, whom he has met by chance in the Umbrian Room of the National Gallery and whom he finds suitably ungenteel (the father has been 'a mechanic of some sort . . . then he took to writing for the Socialistic Press', the son is a railway clerk). This trick rebounds on its begetter for, in presence of George's frank passion Lucy breaks off her engagement. Yet it is not till, by a happy chance encounter with old Mr. Emerson, she has been made to look within and acknowledge her own real feelings, that she avoids Charlotte Bartlett's fate and the lovers are united in a marriage most of the other characters disapprove.

'Windy Corner', the name of Lucy Honeychurch's home set above the Sussex Weald, was one of the titles Forster excogitated for the whole novel,[9] and it would be an error to

underrate the degree in which the work is written to embody—
and thus to hymn—the quality of that landscape.

> The Sunday after Miss Bartlett's arrival was a glorious day, like
> most of the days of that year. In the Weald, autumn approached,
> breaking up the green monotony of summer, touching the parks
> with the grey bloom of mist, the beech-trees with russet, the
> oak-trees with gold. Up on the heights, battalions of black pines
> witnessed the change, themselves unchangeable. Either country
> was spanned by a cloudless sky, and in either arose the tinkle of
> church bells. (Ch. 15)

Stitched through the human drama of cross-purposes which is
the book's second much longer section there runs in variegated
threads the presence of the South Downs viewed under
different, though principally fine, weathers and itself constituting an important moral value. This is all part of the
novelist's intent to incarnate the character of English landscape and only his fame as a social satirist and the as yet
inextinct fashion for exalting D. H. Lawrence's insistences in
this dimension at the expense of his older contemporary, keep
Forster unrecognized for what he is—the last great Romantic
poet in English letters.

The poetry dwells in the author's noumenal sense of natural
environment—we shall see more of this in *The Longest Journey*—
not only as revealed by 'set pieces' of description (as who
should say) but through its inhabitants' existences. It is much
the more real and challenging because Forster has a sufficient
historical sense of the degree in which the English countryside
has been, let us say, not man-made but man-altered over the
centuries.

Of 'Cissie' and 'Albert', the pair of architectural blotches of
villas which 'mar' the 'triangular meadow' whereon have been
erected 'pretty cottages' and 'a new stone church, expensively
simple, with a charming spire', investing a scene which
'suggested a Swiss alp rather than the shrine and centre of a
leisured world', we have the building annals (Ch. 9) because
the book as a whole is thoroughly attentive to the either
collaborative or warring character of the process which is
mankind in Nature. Forster continually keeps in focus how
what seems to be the eternal verities of woodland and hill,

stream and plain, are indeed transient in themselves and highly transformable by their association with the species *homo sapiens*. The first paragraph of Chapter 10 makes this point in a gratifying piece of social amusement and the last of Chapter 12 illuminates it more ecstatically:

> That evening and all that night the water ran away. On the morrow the pool had shrunk to its old size and lost its glory. It had been a call to the blood and to the relaxed will, a passing benediction whose influence did not pass, a holiness, a spell, a momentary chalice for youth.

What makes Forster the last great Romantic perceiver of the English scene is that this realist's awareness of its landscape's constraints does not—in the creative phase of his career which we are presently examining—diminish; it harmonizes with the sense of Nature as an immanent power-giving deity pregnant with meaning, charged with benefic significance. This insight informs his social commentary. Just as the Honeychurches

> would descend—he knew their ways—past the shrubbery, and past the tennis-lawn and the dahlia-bed, until they reached the kitchen-garden, and there, *in the presence of the potatoes and the peas*, the great event [of Lucy's and his own, Cecil's, engagement] would be discussed. (Ch. 8, emphasis added)

so the new fiancé in conversation with their visiting vicar misapprehends an important phenomenon when he criticizes their domestic interior:

> 'I've come for tea, Mr. Vyse. Do you suppose that I shall get it?'
>
> 'I should say so. Food is the thing one does get here—Don't sit in that chair; young Honeychurch has left a bone in it.'
>
> 'Pfui!'
>
> 'I know,' said Cecil, 'I know. I can't think why Mrs. Honeychurch allows it.'
>
> For Cecil considered the bone and the Maple's furniture separately; he did not realize that, taken together, they kindled the room into the life that he desired. (Ibid.)

Generally across the loom of this book and, as the last quotation goes to show, not without a critical consciousness but rather sans sentimentalizing or other distorted discrimination, Forster is paying tribute to a part of the world, a scenic and human ambience which he cares for. Something can be and frequently is kindled into life all over the globe between mortal men and their environment which Nature and human beings 'on their own' cannot achieve. That is why the risibility on Mr. Beebe's lips is apt whenever he beholds the Honeychurch residence:

> Windy Corner lay, not on the summit of the ridge, but a few hundred feet down the southern slope, at the springing of one of the great buttresses that supported the hill. On either side of it was a shallow ravine, filled with ferns and pine-trees, and down the ravine on the left ran the highway into the Weald.
>
> Whenever Mr. Beebe crossed the ridge and caught sight of these noble dispositions of the earth, and, poised in the middle of them, Windy Corner—he laughed. The situation was so glorious, the house so commonplace, not to say impertinent. The late Mr. Honeychurch had affected the cube, because it gave him the most accommodation for his money, and the only addition made by his widow had been a small turret, shaped like a rhinoceros' horn, where she could sit in the wet weather and watch the carts going up and down the road. So impertinent— and yet the house 'did', for it was the home of people who loved their surroundings honestly. Other houses in the neighbourhood had been built by expensive architects, over others their inmates had fidgeted sedulously, yet all these suggested the accidental, the temporary; while Windy Corner seemed as inevitable as an ugliness of Nature's own creation. One might laugh at the house, but one never shuddered. (Opening of Ch. 18)

Of all imaginative writers Forster can be said to have had difficulty enough coming to terms with the kind of society 'out of which Cecil proposed to rescue Lucy' (beginning of Ch. 10); but in *this* novel he dedicates one whole side of his endeavour to acknowledging its finer flowers and more impressive blooms, human and scenic together. Lately we have learned that the model for the splendid Mrs. Honeychurch was his mutually adored grandmother Louisa Whichelo.

> She was so shrewd, downright and gay and—as Forster put it later[10]—was someone who knew how to live: no one, he said, aimed more at being commonplace or succeeded less.[11]

This sort of thing is nice to know. But all along *A Room with a View* has been evidently *inter alia* Forster's way of stating the case for the Respectable English Middle-Class ambit in which he was born and grew up and spent most of his days and which otherwise considerably tormented him.

Nevertheless it is interesting to notice how much of 'The Lucy Novels' are devoted to presenting *pensione* existence and the attributions-game in Italian-art-visiting milieux. Clearly in these earlier drafts (especially *'Old' Lucy*) Forster is not really aware of what specifically he is trying to focus. Are they to be an attempt solely at satirical comedy or can they crystallize *à travers* the silly and unpleasant snobberies—in their Italian and English environments both—larger issues of love and death? The problem is expressed in his very first note for the work,

> *Who?* Lucy Beringer, Miss Bartlett, her cousin.
> H.O.M.
> Miss Lavish.
> Miss Dorothy & Miss Margaret Alan.
> *Where?* Florence, Pension Bertolini.
> *Doing What?*[12]

and in the crudity of the following passage when it is compared with the treatment of Charlotte Bartlett in the finished book of some six years later. (In this variant a lady with a 'past', at the Pension Bertolini, is trying to launch a concert. Charlotte has instead launched the scandal.)

> Miss Bartlett had told about Mrs. Flint Carew. It is true that she proved to Lucy afterwards that it was her duty to warn people and that she had always meant to tell, whatever it might cost her, and that it was Lucy's fault for neglecting her all the afternoon. But Lucy was very disagreable [*sic*] and said so many unpleasant things that Miss Bartlett was obliged to return to the rôle that suited her best—that of the prematurely aged martyr.
>
> 'I am afraid that our travelling together has hardly been the success I hoped. I might have known that it would not do. You want someone younger & stronger & more in sympathy with you. I am too uninteresting and old fashioned and only fit to unpack & pack up your things. My only consolation is that you have found people more to your taste, and have often been able to go out without me. I have my own poor ideas of what a young lady should do, but I hope I have never inflicted them on

you. If I have, I ask your forgiveness.'

Stuff of this sort, however obviously venomous, will soon destroy the strongest nerves. Lucy soon went to her room, and strained her hands together in an agony of discomfort. (*The Lucy Novels*, p. 49)

This is very much less sophisticated than what their editor notes as 'perhaps the nicest sentence . . . that is unique to *The Lucy Novels*', the image of Miss Catherine Alan's sister 'gathering up round her little shoulders the Shawl of disapproval, which generally hung over the back of her chair' (p. 60), or indeed most of the other early drafts, inchoate and wandering— for lack of defined artistic direction—as they are.

The multiplied variety of trajectories and dénouements devised for the story in these earlier avatars—in 'New Lucy' for example (which is later than the 'Old' one) the George-Emerson character is killed in a tragic conclusion—also reflects the large number of interests their author was trying to dispose all under this one title.

What in the outcome, the completed novel, do combine are the various objects of social satire, for all are seen as co-operative in their inhibiting of free and wholesome emotion, whether it be Charlotte Bartlett's prudishness, or Mrs. Vyse's over-exposed fashionable London life or the aestheticisms of the English community at Florence. Cecil Vyse embodies in developed form the vision of art there seen in contradistinction to life, and his case extends our awareness of how malign the wrong kind of aesthetics are. Whereas visiting Italy has extended Lucy's social sympathies, it

> had quickened Cecil, not to tolerance, but to irritation. He saw that the local society was narrow, but, instead of saying, 'Does this very much matter?' he rebelled, and tried to substitute for it the society he called broad. (Ch. 10)

Likewise he does not care for Lucy as she actually is but as a lay-figure for his artistic imagination.

> Soon he detected in her a wonderful reticence. She was like a woman of Leonardo da Vinci's, whom we love not so much for herself as for the things that she will not tell us. (Ch. 8)

Patronizing and superior towards her and her family, he is also not a very passionate lover. When he kisses her, both fiancés and we the readers feel embarrassed (end of Ch. 9).

His ascetic aestheticism and critical social attitudes, in fact, are somewhere on the same spectrum of egotism masquerading as high civilizedness which characterizes the performances of the Revd. Cuthbert Eager, the English Chaplain at Florence who is, fairly self-appointedly, guardian of the city's more exclusive views.

Eager is no more really interested in Art, for all his life of constant twitterings about who painted what and where, than the other side of the Moon. Renaissance frescos are the means by which he can strike a pose and attempt to dominate others. He libels Mr. Emerson as having 'murdered his wife in the sight of God'; he is mean, shifty, ghoulish; and, in a fine little piece of dramatic irony, snubs three of his fellow visitors in the Santa Croce church before immediately proceeding there, in a lecture on St. Francis, with praise of the saint's being 'full of innate sympathy . . . quickness to perceive good in others . . . vision of the brotherhood of man . . .' (Ch. 2).

The sole difficulty with this side of the book is that Vyse and Eager and the other pretentious people—e.g. Miss Lavish the 'unconventional' novelist—are too easily seen through for the kinds of fraud they practise. They do not constitute a sufficient philosophical challenge. Anybody with some decent human feeling can put a finger on the character and motivations of their unsatisfactoriness—as the ingénue heroine herself does soon enough:

> This successful morning left no pleasant impressions on Lucy. She had been a little frightened, both by Miss Lavish and by Mr. Eager, she knew not why. And as they frightened her, she had, strangely enough, ceased to respect them. She doubted that Miss Lavish was a great artist. She doubted that Mr. Eager was as full of spirituality and culture as she had been led to suppose. They were tried by some new test, and they were found wanting. As for Charlotte—as for Charlotte she was exactly the same. It might be possible to be nice to her; it was impossible to love her.

That is as early as Chapter 5. And it is not too very long before Cecil betrays his essential selfishness once too often.

> 'My dear Freddy, I am no athlete. As you well remarked this very morning, "There are some chaps who are no good for

> anything but books"; I plead guilty to being such a chap, and
> will not inflict myself on you.'
>
> The scales fell from Lucy's eyes. How had she stood Cecil
> for a moment? He was absolutely intolerable, and the same
> evening she broke her engagement off. (Ch. 16)

Their self-imposing types of imposture having been slotted,
it remains for George Emerson and Lucy Honeychurch to
become man and wife in defiance of much of her world. But we
have a problem here too and it is that the need for this defiance
is not securely focused. I do not claim that George's social
situation would not, circa 1907–8, provoke a protest from the
middle-class family into which he marries, nor that Lucy's
engagement to him in the immediate wake of throwing Cecil
over would fail to strike them as a painful nuisance shot
through with long-indulged hypocrisy. The difficulty is that
these grievances are not (artistically speaking) corradiated
enough. Nor is one confident that the whole thing can simply
be treated as appropriately the subject for an exercise in
historical imagination.

In *The Importance of Being Earnest* for instance—which (1895)
dates from no distant epoch—the hero's suit for his beloved
Gwendolen's hand is given short shrift by her Aunt Augusta
when his antecedents are revealed as no more impressive than
'a somewhat large, black leather hand-bag, with handles to it'
left in 'the cloak-room at Victoria Station'. But the point is,
Lady Bracknell is emphatically explicit:

> You can hardly imagine that I and Lord Bracknell would
> dream of allowing our only daughter—a girl brought up with
> the utmost care—to marry into a cloak-room, and form an
> alliance with a parcel? (First Act)

By contrast, at no stage do we have a scene in *A Room with a
View* where Mrs. Honeychurch or anybody else discusses
George Emerson's disqualifications, socially or otherwise, as a
son-in-law. On the contrary Lucy's mother is heartily relieved
(in essence—herself confessing as much in Chapter 19) when
she learns her daughter has thrown 'the Fiasco' Cecil over,
and all along she has made no objection to George's coming to
play tennis with her son Freddy, to taking tea and exchanging
visits with him, or even (really) to capering about in the buff:

'Hush, dears,' said Mrs. Honeychurch, who found it impossible to remain shocked. 'And do be sure to dry yourselves
thoroughly first. All these colds come of not drying thoroughly.'
(Ch. 12)

We should not forget also that the Emersons are well-to-do
for a working-class family ('he made an advantageous marriage',
Ch. 5) and are visibly much better read (see opening of
Ch. 12) than their new Summer Street neighbours, while the
Honeychurches themselves do not rank high in the strata of
country society; the first paragraph of Chapter 10 makes *that*
deliberately plain. The newly married pair will not lack for
means ('I come into my money next year' Lucy reminds her
mother in Chapter 19) and still less plausible is it that after
they are wedded 'the Honeychurches had not forgiven them;
they were disgusted at her past hypocrisy; she had alienated
Windy Corner, perhaps for ever' (Ch. 20).

That is not the stuff of which the Windy Corner matron and
youngster are made, so that Mrs. Honeychurch not giving her
consent (ibid.) fails to be *entirely* explained either in terms of a
perennial moral grievance (as 'Lucy deceived Cecil and us
most cynically') or Edwardian social norms and expectations.

Thus we can, I think, if we care to bother, refer the essential
enigma of George Emerson's unacceptability—to Lucy early
on, to his in-laws later—or rather part of it, for some con-
cessions must be made with regard to that historical milieu, to
something authorially unarticulated. We may well feel that it
is being made to stand for some much less orthodox relation
still: and the book's dedication 'To H.O.M.', the fellow undergraduate with whom Forster had some kind of love-affair[13] at
the turn of the century may supply the tip as to what kind of
affinity is, without surfacing, here being regarded by the
author's creative impulse.

Our main concern as readers, however, should not be
artistic biographizing. The net consequence of the novel's own
procédé is that it gives slightly the impression of using a
sledge-hammer to crack a nut: a small sledge-hammer, if you
will, for a large nut, but still a moralist's proceeding where
things are out of scale.

Nevertheless it provides a very felicitous analysis of the
great Forsterian bugbear, Muddle.

The confusion at issue is in intellectual perception of moral significance. At the Pension Bertolini, in the opening of the novel, when Miss Bartlett refuses the rooms offered her in exchange by Mr. Emerson, she has no reason for replying with so ungracious a negative, with any negative at all save her dread of being, as chaperon of a younger woman, under obligation to strangers, and strangers of the male sex.

Codified into an inert normative social law, a piece of caution which in other circumstances could be intelligent and sensitive has usurped the place of good sense, charity and human warmth. Her refusal is stupid because both ladies want 'a room with a view' and neither of the Emersons is offering to seduce them; it is ungenerous because it rebuffs a genuine instance of kindness and giving; and it is ugly-uncharitable because it helps advance the process of this other pair's exclusion from any real welcome by the Pension's other inmates.

> Mr. Beebe smiled nonchalantly. He had made a gentle effort to introduce the Emersons into Bertolini society, and the effort had failed. He was almost the only person who remained friendly to them. Miss Lavish, who represented intellect, was avowedly hostile, and now the Miss Alans, who stood for good breeding, were following her. Miss Bartlett, smarting under an obligation, would scarcely be civil. (Ch. 3)

In fact they turn out to be the most feeling members of the company, given to wonderful imaginative gestures which heighten or clarify life (in the right, unhistrionic way). George leaves 'an enormous note of interrogation' scrawled on a piece of paper pinned up over the wash-stand in his room when he vacates it for Charlotte Bartlett; and when Mr. Beebe relates, further on, the Emersons' behaviour towards the two little old ladies there, we learn this:

> There was a great scene over some violets. They picked violets and filled all the vases in the room of these very Miss Alans who have failed to come to Cissie Villa. Poor little ladies! So shocked and so pleased. It used to be one of Miss Catherine's great stories. 'My dear sister loves flowers,' it began. They found the whole room a mass of blue—vases and jugs—and the story ends with 'So ungentlemanly and yet so beautiful. It is all very difficult.' Yes, I always connect those Florentine Emersons with violets. (Ch. 10)

With Charlotte Bartlett morality has become self-defeating, leading not to its own true goal—enhanced life—but to a rigid kind of automatized and deadened existence:

> at the end there was presented to the girl the complete picture of a cheerless, loveless world in which the young rush to destruction until they learn better—a shamefaced world of precautions and barriers which may avert evil, but which do not seem to bring good, if we may judge from those who have used them most. (Ch. 7)

Charlotte is a warrior in 'the vast armies of the benighted, who follow neither the heart nor the brain, and march to their destiny by catchwords' (Ch. 17), while Forster opposes to this the intelligent life of developed instinct which he finds in the Italian people.

> Phaethon had lost the game. . . .
> 'Let us go immediately,' he told them. 'The signorino will walk.'
> 'All the way? He will be hours,' said Mr. Beebe.
> 'Apparently. I told him it was unwise.' He would look no one in the face; perhaps defeat was particularly mortifying for him. He alone had played skilfully, using the whole of his instinct, while the others had used scraps of their intelligence. He alone had divined what things were, and what he wished them to be. He alone had interpreted the message Lucy had received five days before from the lips of a dying man. . . . Not so these English. They gain knowledge slowly, and perhaps too late. (Ch. 7)

If this idealizes the southern race, it does not the less for that make its point by elucidating just what the positive possibilities in human nature are—how our moral sensoria should be educated—as the author envisages them. The coachman it is who on the Fiesole hillside has conducted Lucy not to safety in the purlieus of a clergyman but to the presence and arms of her unrespectable lover.

Mr. Emerson elaborates upon the same theme when he remonstrates with Lucy later on.

> I used to think I could teach young people the whole of life, but I know better now, and all my teaching of George has come down to this: beware of muddle. Do you remember in that

church, when you pretended to be annoyed with me and weren't? Do you remember before, when you refused the room with the view? Those were muddles—little, but ominous—and I am fearing that you are in one now. (Ch. 19)

Many are the victims of the various confusions in the kind which this novel exhibits, but Lucy Honeychurch's cousin features as such *par excellence*, and indeed we can, if we wish, and profitably, regard the whole book as written round *her*. Lucy and George's fumblings towards each other across a slightly bewildering series of oppositions, the sketchy characterization of the hero, the novel's failure to combine its multiplicity of interests in a complete artistic whole; all these things fall into place if we see *A Room with a View* as a full-blown treatment of the Charlotte Bartlett kind of personality: a congeries of inhibitions and interdictions by which Forster's own world at this time was also much dominated. Of the final scene, again at the Florentine boarding-house, where the hero and heroine are united as man and wife and puzzle out Charlotte's part in the final phases of their coming together, the Abinger editor rightly remarks

> George's hypothesis—'how she kept me alive in you'—seems to be unobtrusively supported by Miss Bartlett's interjection on p. 56 [Ch. 5] 'Oh, not that way back. We can never have too much of the dear Piazza Signoria'—which Lucy was evidently avoiding because of its disturbing associations.[14]

Likewise we ought to notice how the entire work concludes with the middle-aged spinster in its focus, not the young couple.

> Youth enwrapped them; the song of Phaethon announced passion requited, love attained. But they were conscious of a love more mysterious than this. The song died away; they heard the river, bearing down the snows of winter into the Mediterranean.

What can that refer to but the thaw deep down in Miss Bartlett's being which has permitted their achieved mutuality after all? (She did not in the event stop Lucy seeing old Mr. Emerson at the Rectory, as she could have done, the final fatal day of Miss Honeychurch's provisioning for quite other foreign travel.) *A Room with a View* has arguably for its most central concern Forster's hope that while life itself remains, no individual is necessarily 'frozen, . . . withered up all through' (ibid.).

Yet to my sense the book's most signal achievement is something else again: its tone of voice. The strength of Forster's writing resides in the fact that his fiction is that of a middle-aged man written (in fact) by a young one. The prose is unself-consciously so poised. And the narrative attitude is the most valuable thing which the present work has to offer.

This is a paradox. *Why* is it that Forster's 'own' speech in his novels does not strike us merely as patronizing or pert? He interposes comments, he moralizes continuously. Yet this procedure in the main fails to irritate his reader or to disassemble his characters' identities. How?

Well for one thing the *dramatis personae* are solidly constituted by means other than the interpretative—something we find always in Jane Austen and too much lack in George Meredith. If one shears any given chapter in *A Room with a View* of its authorial metaphysics or philosophizing, the scene and the personages continue to exist in the same relief as in the complete version, because such a paragraph as the following is *added to* a fully achieved novelistic enterprise; it is not a component without which the characters' incarnations, or their *mises-en-scène*, begin to crumble:

> There is much that is immortal in this medieval lady. The dragons have gone, and so have the knights, but still she lingers in our midst. She reigned in many an early Victorian castle, and was Queen of much early Victorian song. It is sweet to protect her in the intervals of business, sweet to pay her honour when she has cooked our dinner well. But alas! The creature grows degenerate. In her heart also there are springing up strange desires. She too is enamoured of heavy winds, and vast panoramas, and green expanses of the sea. She has marked the kingdom of this world, how full it is of wealth, and beauty, and war—a radiant crust, built around the central fires, spinning towards the receding heavens. Men, declaring that she inspires them to it, move joyfully over the surface, having the most delightful meetings with other men, happy, not because they are masculine, but because they are alive. Before the show breaks up she would like to drop the august title of the Eternal Woman, and go there as her transitory self. (Ch. 4, para. 3)

As it happens there are visible weaknesses in this paragraph; and for the matter of that, plenty of individual lapses of tone or uncertain commentative gestures dotted about the book. The phrase 'She has marked the kingdom of this world, how full it is of wealth', echoes Shakespearean and Biblical rhetoric too archly. The vision of the 'radiant crust, built around the central fires, spinning towards the receding heavens' is exactly the sort of hollow poetry wherewith Edwardian agnosticism tried to hold onto metaphysic cheer in the wake of the nineteenth century's materialist demonstrations. Admirable in sentiment it may be, but it has to show for guff that begs every question under the pressure of any kind of analysis. In the upshot, however, all this hyperbole works well enough because the entire pseudo-song narrows to a fine tilt in favour of women's liberation—at a date when female suffrage was a burning issue among other features of the feminist crusade.

Yet whether it be frail or powerful, in sum, this stretch of writing nowise enfeebles the play of character or the development of plot in its context. That has been substantiated by other means. Just as the first two paragraphs of the chapter establish Lucy's frame of mind with far less partisan novelistic devices, so Lucy herself, like her fellow-personages, is still more constituted by her speech. Forster can bring his characters to life by making them talk—he does so every time—and no method else could so effectually grant them independent existence—existence independent even, as it were, of the opinions and prejudices of the mind which created them.

> 'I have been thinking, Lucy, of that letter of Charlotte's. How is she?'
> 'I tore the thing up.'
> 'Didn't she say how she was? How does she sound? Cheerful?'
> 'Oh yes, I suppose so—no—not very cheerful, I suppose.'
> 'Then depend upon it, it *is* the boiler. I know myself how water preys upon one's mind. I would rather anything else—even a misfortune with the Meat.' (Ch. 13)

This is character-creation by self-revealing prose as good as Chekhov or Ibsen's, for its sense of the play of nuance and rhythm in subtly differentiated human speech. Both Mrs.

Honeychurch and her daughter are talking somewhat abstractedly during this interchange: the mother because she has formulated a theory on her own about Cousin Charlotte's current difficulties and is ready to expound a scheme of relief; Lucy because she has been badly rattled by the contents of Miss Bartlett's letter and does not want to have to divulge them. Yet Mrs. Honeychurch's partial absence of mind expresses itself in slightly less than her usual directness of utterance; the name 'Lucy' punctuates, as a sort of caesura, her first sentence launching the topic, which she knows will be a sensitive one, and she edges towards her main idea by Socratic steps. Her child's distrait character of thought expresses itself by inattentive responses (as with the repetition of the main verb, 'I suppose').

This quality of dialogue compares favourably with the too stilted rhetoric of Forster's plays, fairly interesting thematically as those are. In *Heart of Bosnia* (1911), for instance, the characters—especially the Bosnian ones—too often address each other like Red Indians in an inferior cowboy movie of the olden days; and even in the great arioso passage given to Claggart in the libretto for *Billy Budd*, the opera Forster wrote with Benjamin Britten (1949–51), character expresses itself, the villain unfolds his motivations (in 'O beauty, handsomeness, goodness . . .'[15]) too articulately. What would remain, albeit in only a semi-realistic mode of drama, near the base of self-consciousness (I just dare to say, the *fundament* of an individual nature), is conceived—and without the one medium which would permit it, verse-speech—as capable of utterance at the very front of the personality: something which makes *that* enunciation ring stiffly out.

When we have acknowledged Forster's unflawed skill in *novelistic* dialogue and the livingness this bestows upon his stories' agents, we have not relegated material like the long divagation of commentary quoted above, from Chapter 4, as in turn independent of its surroundings and awkwardly sententious. Thematically this paragraph extends consideration of Miss Honeychurch's predicament to that of womankind in the world at large, and it also harmonizes very happily with the book's most fundamental emphasis of all, uttered by Mr. Emerson senior in Santa Croce early on:

In his ordinary voice, so that she scarcely realized he was quoting poetry, he said:

'From far, from eve and morning,
    And yon twelve-winded sky,
The stuff of life to knit me
    Blew hither: here am I.

George and I both know this, but why does it distress him? We know that we come from the winds, and that we shall return to them; that all life is perhaps a knot, a tangle, a blemish in the eternal smoothness. But why should this make us unhappy? Let us rather love one another, and work, and rejoice. I don't believe in this world sorrow.'

Miss Honeychurch assented.

'Then make my boy think like us. Make him realize that by the side of the everlasting Why there is a Yes—a transitory Yes, if you like, but a Yes.' (Ch. 2)

For the novel is directed against the fashion of philosophical despair and rather easy negation which was current as the stock-in-trade of letters then and is so yet. (Does not most of the most serious modern literature—practically all of Mr. Samuel Beckett's literary endeavour for example—feed on it as upon a very profitable udder which can never be milked dry?)

What makes us accept this sort of 'aside' is the knowledge that the novelist is not using it to press his thumb down in the scale of values since, by the descriptive passages of his enterprise no less than the dialogue, we are given full opportunity to 'trust the tale, not the teller' (D. H. Lawrence's fine figures, both). That being so, it becomes actually encouraging to be taken into the author's discursive confidence and receive from him excogitations on a wide range of human interests. On these (above-stated) terms the novel can blossom in a form as 'philosophical' as you like. But the reason why Forster is particularly felicitous in this mode of address—well, the present chapter is already long enough, and I take leave to defer that issue to the next.

Suffice it to say that *A Room with a View* is his most playful work. There is for example the main-verbless 'sentence' describing 'bumble-puppy' (Ch. 4) or the way in which all but two of the chapters have titles, some fanciful or elaborate, and those two almost cheekily are merely named 'Fourth Chapter', 'Twelfth Chapter'. He *can* be pert: one paragraph in Chapter 11 starts 'Lucy—to descend from bright heaven to earth, whereon there are shadows because there are hills', which is patronizing because as if indited from the viewpoint of an avuncular Olympian. Yet for the most part it is a measure of the extraordinary skill and value of the writer at this stage in his career that, though he is a novelist at play through most of this book, its overall tone and achievement is very far from trite or self-endorsing.

NOTES

1. *The Common Pursuit* (London, 1952), p. 262.
2. In the *Omnibus* programme interview with which B.B.C. Television signalized his eightieth birthday, 1959.
3. *Life*, Vol. II, p. 227, fn. 1.
4. *'Arctic Summer' and Other Fiction*, Abinger Edition, Vol. 9 (London, 1980), p. xxviii.
5. Ibid., pp. 240–41.
6. Id. loc.
7. Reprinted, as the second item, in *'The Life to Come' and Other Stories*, Abinger Edition, Vol. 8 (London, 1972).
8. *The Lucy Novels: Early Sketches for 'A Room with a View'*, Abinger Edition, Vol. 3a (London, 1977).
9. *Life*, Vol. I, p. 123.
10. From motives of copyright and therefore honour I cannot conclude the quotation, since Mr. Furbank charitably truncates in thus reproducing from Forster's Diary a part of the magnificent epitaph he wrote upon his grandmother following her decease: 'She knew how to live and to the end took it out of those who did not' (*Life*, Vol. I, p. 196). There we have seven-eighths of that immortal sentence; but it does not end quite at that point.
11. *Life*, Vol. I, p. 28.
12. Ibid., p. 91 and see editor's Introduction to *The Lucy Novels*, passim.
13. *Life*, Vol. I, pp. 97–8.
14. *A Room with a View*, Abinger Edition, Vol. 3, ed. O. Stallybrass (London, 1977), p. 237.
15. 'It is my most important piece of writing', he wrote to Britten, 'and I did not, at my first hearing, feel it sufficiently important musically. . . . I want *passion*—love constricted, perverted, poisoned, but never the less *flowing* down its agonizing channel. . . . Not soggy depression or growling

remorse. I seemed turning from one musical discomfort to another, and was dissatisfied. I looked for an aria perhaps, for a more recognisable form' (*Life*, Vol. II, pp. 285–86). A good criticism, I think, of the big Claggart monologue. When I talked about the opera with him—this is twenty years further on (from its composition)—he would only concede of it that it was good in parts, but not comparing with *Peter Grimes*, of the 'Sea Interludes' of which he always remained a fervent admirer.

3

The Pre-War Fiction, Part 2

Having set forth the main lines in my reading of this novelist I hope to keep the present chapter and its two successors moderately short, for it is not the pupose of my study simply to pile a fat tome onto the already fairly mountainous heap of Forsterian exegesis—rather, to offer a few different emphases and *en passant* some information.

When we consider, however, Forster's 'English' fiction from before the First World War—that is to say, the novels and tales which deal wholly in English environments or characters— we must confess to handling a body of work substantial in every sense of the term, which therefore makes brevity difficult.

1. The Longest Journey

> ... when he was a young scholer in the University, and so all his time onward, he never loved or used any games or ordinary recreations, either within doores (as Cards, Dice, Tables, Chesse, or the like); or abroad, as Buts, Coyts, Bowles, or any such: but his ordinary exercise and recreation, was walking either alone by himself, or with some other selected Companion, with whom he might conferre and argue, and recount their studies: and he would often professe that to observe the grasse, herbs, corne, trees, cattle, earth, waters, heavens, any of the Creatures, and to contemplate their Natures, orders, qualities, vertues, uses, &c, was ever to him, the greatest mirth, content, and recreation that could be: and this he held to his dying day. (*An Exact Narration of the Life and Death of Lancelot Andrewes* [1650], by Henry Isaacson[1])

In the upshot Forster's second novel becomes not so much an account of how people (like Rickie Elliot) 'join the ranks of the benighted' as his attempt—successful in my view—to take possession of the landscape of his native country.

It tells the life-story of a club-footed solitary boy whose mother has been unhappily married and who is orphaned at the age of 15. After much unhappiness at a day-school his life is transfigured by going up to Cambridge University and finding there an unanticipatedly civilized, amicable and intellectually nutritive existence. But Rickie Elliot, though heir to a competence, gains only a Second in Tripos and must earn his living in the world outside his college if he is to marry the beautiful but shallow Agnes Pembroke whom, emotionally speaking, he catches on the rebound from an engagement shattered when the bully Gerald Dawes dies in a rugby match.

Agnes's brother Herbert finds her new fiancé a job at the place of work where he is a housemaster, Sawston School (Forster's hated Home Counties township thus turns up again), and all would go well enough with the Pembrokes' scheme to draw him into a life of hypocrisy and conformity in the spiritually cramped environment of their establishment but that Rickie has dutifully contacted his aunt Emily Failing (his father's sister) and Agnes hopes to ensure his succession as her sole heir.

Mrs. Failing, the essentially mean-spirited widow of a generous-hearted man, lives at Cadover, a big estate in the middle of Wiltshire, but not alone. She has long since informally adopted an illegitimate child of Rickie's mother. Stephen Wonham, the product of a tragically brief romance in Mrs. Elliot's battered life, has grown up there half-wild, half self-educated, beside her. In an attempt to alienate Stephen's chances of inheritance the now married Agnes repeats his versified mockery of the elderly lady to her (rubbish she had learned very confidentially from Rickie who heard Stephen singing it when they went out for a ride together one day), and Mrs. Failing turns the pagan demi-god out, at the same time informing him of his true identity. Stephen rushes to visit Rickie in his Sawston school—not for charity but out of delight at having a brother. There he is turned away by the snobbish-politic Pembrokes, and Stewart Ansell, Rickie's best friend of the Cambridge time and an earnest philosopher, angrily denounces the shabby *ménage à trois* in front of the whole assembled Dunwood House.

It is the consummation of a tragic period in Elliot's life, most marred of all by the fathering no less than the early death of a badly lame little girl. Rickie rebels against his moral incarceration and, having first been blinded as to his wife's faults, now invests entirely in the person of his half-brother Stephen, with whom he lodges at the Ansells, as the basis of a new *credo* for living. His wholesale idealism receives a bad blow therefore when, having extracted a promise of temperance from this companion, who is visiting Cadover again with him against his will, he discovers Stephen drunk at a dangerous crossing over the local railway line. He himself is fatally wounded as he intervenes to save the other from an oncoming train and dies disillusioned, a heart-broken man.

The stories he has written, however, begin to sell and to be valued; Mrs. Failing leaves her manor to his worthy cousins the Silts; and Stephen Wonham is a married man with a child in the conclusion, a successful yeoman farmer who has given up his flirtation with alcoholism.

This novel is generally regarded as a failure or at best a very partial success, and I cannot see why. Because (to take up one complaint) it is misogynistic—at least towards Woman as Spouse? But why may it not be, if that helps articulate other themes than merely a temperamental antipathy to marriage? Agnes Pembroke is a bad lot who gets treated fairly unsparingly by the author, but to jib at that is artlessly to criticize the plot-*données* of the work, across whose structure is stitched its fine image of far more important things.

Forster is on top form here, first of all, as a social critic in the profoundest sense: an analyst quite exceptionally close in perceiving the falsehoods and malignities which breed about the human will. Mrs. Failing, for instance, is an extraordinary achievement: a character anatomized, seen all round and through as very much possessed of all but unforgivable faults, even exasperatingly horrible, yet never dismissed or degenerating into simple villainesshood.

She rang the bell twice, and her maid came with her candle and her walking-stick: it was her habit of late to go to her room as soon as dinner was over, for she had no one to sit up with. Rickie was impressed by her loneliness, and also by the mixture in her of insight and obtuseness. She was so quick, so clear-headed, so imaginative even. But all the same, she had forgotten what people were like. Finding life dull, she had dropped lies into it, as a chemist drops a new element into a solution, hoping that life would thereby sparkle or turn some beautiful colour. She loved to mislead others, and in the end her private view of false and true was obscured, and she misled herself. How she must have enjoyed their errors over Stephen! But her own error had been greater, inasmuch as it was spiritual entirely. (Ch. 34)

That comes later than her verdict on Elliot as an artist.

'Mrs. Failing—' said Agnes, who had not expected such a speedy end to their chat.

'Call me Aunt Emily. My dear?'

'Aunt Emily, what did you think of that story Rickie sent you?'

'It is bad,' said Mrs. Failing. 'But. But. But.' Then she escaped, having told the truth, and yet leaving a pleasurable impression behind her. (Ch. 11)

The response that little interlude evokes is characteristically complex. Time and again we have the passion of a great young man's vision and the compassion of a great middle-aged one's charity shining as arc-lamps do upon a theatre-stage, to illuminate and give perspective both together to an actor or troupe by focusing from different angles upon one and the same spot.

Then there is the value of the *leit-motifs*, as Peter Burra has happily named them,[2] which in this book operate still more richly than such things do even in any other of the Forster novels: articulating the work's central themes and amplifying, qualifying them on every re-appearance.

The tale starts with an undergraduates' informal parley on the nature of reality: whether it is an objective fact or a subjective appearance. 'They were discussing the existence of objects. Do they exist only when there is someone to look at them? or have they a real existence of their own?' (para. 6).

Next we may note how Ansell, on their first encounter, refuses to acknowledge Agnes Pembroke's existence; that this philosopher friend of Rickie is preoccupied through much of the story with a thesis 'About things being real' (Ch. 15) and has the backing of his family for being so, in these terms:

> Mr. Ansell was not merely a man of some education; he had what no education can bring—the power of detecting what is important. . . . So when Stewart said, 'At Cambridge, can I read for the Moral Science Tripos?' Mr. Ansell had only replied, 'This philosophy—do you say that it lies behind everything?'
> 'Yes, I think so. It tries to discover what is good and true.'
> 'Then, my boy, you had better read as much of it as you can.' (Ch. 3)

Some of Rickie Elliot's estimable quality as a human being comes from his ability not only to 'see the best in' other people but to idealize them—by *not* 'detecting the beautiful from the ugly, the interesting from the dull, the tragic from the melodramatic' (in Ansell's exasperated words, Ch. 6). But it also makes his tragedies.

Possessed of the idea that Miss Pembroke and Mr. Dawes are heroic lovers, divinely inspired ('It was the merest accident that Rickie had not been disgusted. But this he could not know') upon seeing them embrace in their Sawston garden (Ch. 3), he insists to the young woman, when her fiancé dies, that she should hold to the worth of what she has lost:

> He panted, 'It's the worst thing that can ever happen to you in all your life, and you've got to mind it—you've got to mind it. They'll come saying, "Bear up—trust to time." No, no; they're wrong. Mind it.' (Ch. 5)

and he has a leavening influence. *Pro. tem.* Agnes does so and briefly becomes an honest impressive lady:

> 'We are not leaving Sawston' she wrote. 'I saw how selfish it was of me to risk spoiling Herbert's career. I shall get used to any place. Now that he is gone, nothing of that sort can matter. Every one has been most kind, but you have comforted me most, though you did not mean to. I cannot think how you did it, or understood so much. I still think of you as a little boy with a lame leg—I know you will let me say this—and yet when it

> came to the point you knew more than people who have been all
> their lives with sorrow and death.'
>
> Rickie burnt this letter, which he ought not to have done, for
> it was one of the few tributes Miss Pembroke ever paid to
> imagination. (Ch. 6)

The point is that in reacting finely to the demise of her
betrothed, she confers greatness on their relationship retroactively, even if that quality was missing in the historical case.
Yet it is by taking the Agnes who is a 'goddess' *in potentiâ* as
actually so valuable that Rickie makes his wretched marriage.

Likewise it is right enough of Ansell to react in the following
way to Stephen Wonham's presence:

> A silence, akin to poetry, invaded Ansell. Was it only a pose
> to like this man, or was he really wonderful? He was not
> romantic, for Romance is a figure with outstretched hands,
> yearning for the unattainable. Certain figures of the Greeks, to
> whom we continually return, suggested him a little. One
> expected nothing of him—no purity of phrase nor swift-edged
> thought. Yet the conviction grew that he had been back some-
> where—back to some table of the gods, spread in a field where
> there is no noise, and that he belonged for ever to the guests
> with whom he had eaten. (Ch. 26)

Yet he *is* made of mortal clay, not a celestial perfection and
Rickie, in turning to this half-brother as the principal repository
and guarantee of his renewed values-system, is only too likely
to find that crashing down, upon an hour of need—as in the
event he does.

Nevertheless, the reference to the Elysian field is all-relevant.
For all his own self-deprecation in the matter (end of Ch. 6),
we can see that Rickie with his stories which celebrate these
very idealities of imagination, is far nearer the heart of what is
essentially worthwhile in living than the prudential calculations
of a Herbert Pembroke who 'for all his fine talk about a
spiritual life . . . had but one test for things—success: success
for the body in this life or for the soul in the life to come'
(Ch. 17). Elliot's imaginative writings hymn, like Plato, a
world more real than the world of appearances because,
fantastic as they are, they pick upon the best latencies in
humankind and its environment and extrapolate these for
their own sakes.

Burra speaks finely about two other *motifs*.

> In *The Longest Journey* there are several examples—the star
> Orion is one of them, and recurs somewhat like violets in *A
> Room with a View*. A more structural *motif* in the former book is
> the level-crossing near Cadover. When Rickie and Agnes arrive
> at Mrs. Failing's, Stephen tells them accusingly that their train
> ran over a child at the crossing. There follows some futile
> badinage as to what has happened to the child's soul, which
> Stephen cannot endure. '"There wants a bridge," he exploded.
> "A bridge instead of all this rotten talk and the level crossing."'
> It appears later that a second child had been rescued by
> Stephen himself. The crossing is passed and repassed by Rickie
> later in the book, each time with the memory of death. At the
> end he is killed there himself, wearily saving Stephen, whom he
> finds drunk across the line. And in the concluding chapter we
> learn in a casual remark from Stephen that the railway has been
> bridged. A train is heard passing across the final darkness. The
> sense of completion is extraordinary.[3]

Yes; and this, I think, not solely by reason of some contrived
'aesthetic effect' that could have been worked up by other
means but, again, because the circumstances give voice to a
key issue: who will inherit Cadover and manage the estate (at
last) properly; or, to put the matter on a larger basis, what is
the use of a Rickie Elliot in this world?

This question also operates like a theme in a piece of music,
recurrently reappearing in partly altered form. From the
drama's human agents the first comment it evokes is Mrs.
Aberdeen's, Rickie's bedder at Cambridge: 'His one thought is
to save one trouble. I never seed such a thoughtful gentleman.
The world, I say, will be the better for him' (Ch. 1); and the
last is Mrs. Failing's:

> She wrote of him to Mrs. Lewin afterwards as 'one who has
> failed in all he undertook; one of the thousands whose dust
> returns to the dust, accomplishing nothing in the interval.
> Agnes and I buried him to the sound of our cracked bell, and
> pretended that he had once been alive. The other, who was
> always honest [Stephen], kept away.' (Conclusion of Ch. 34)

That verdict is as inaccurate as it is brutal. Rather, Rickie
Elliot's fate parallels that of Mr. Failing, his uncle-by-marriage:

Perhaps the Comic Muse, to whom so much is now attributed, had caused this estate to be left to Mr. Failing. Mr. Failing was the author of some brilliant books on socialism—that was why his wife married him—and for twenty-five years he reigned up at Cadover and tried to put his theories into practice. He believed that things could be kept together by accenting the similarities, not the differences of men. 'We are all much more alike than we confess' was one of his favourite speeches. As a speech it sounded very well, and his wife had applauded; but when it resulted in hard work, evenings in the reading-room, mixed parties, and long unobtrusive talks with dull people, she got bored. In her piquant way she declared that she was not going to love her husband, and succeeded. He took it quietly, but his brilliancy decreased. His health grew worse, and he knew that when he died there was no one to carry on his work. He felt, besides, that he had done very little. Toil as he would, he had not a practical mind, and could never dispense with Mr. Wilbraham [the nasty bailiff who punishes the local tenantry]. For all his tact, he would often stretch out the hand of brotherhood too soon, or withhold it when it would have been accepted. Most people misunderstood him, or only understood him when he was dead. In after years his reign became a golden age; but he counted a few disciples in his lifetime, a few young labourers and tenant farmers, who swore tempestuously that he was not really a fool. This, he told himself, was as much as he deserved. (Ch. 11)

One of the finest and most moving features of Forster's art is his ability to convey, in full, the beauty of a benevolent personality and the way it reverberates beneficially through, and beyond, its lifetime, even athwart all its own real failures and the world's very delimiting incompetencies; so that the perception of it—as benefic—is not at all sentimentalized, i.e. distorted. (We get this again for instance, famously, with Mrs. Moore in the later chapters of *A Passage*, soured for all that her nature has been during its more recent days by the Cave-experience.)

It is significant that Forster is one of our few twentieth-century novelists whose work is really devoted to charity, affection, kindness—I refer to the best of his tales. Such a devotion inhabits all of Henry James's pages and, at one remove, those of Joseph Conrad, but so many of the other major talents writing fictive prose in English from, or based within, the shores of the British Isles during this age, have been busy proving themselves unsentimental, unfooled, ironic, detached: a much lesser achievement.

Rickie Elliot in fact bequeathes the world several legacies of import: a witness which his half-brother, in the wake and shock of his death, takes seriously; a series of narratives which hymn the ideal in humanity and landscape (and do so to increasing critical applause); and possibly the motive whereby Mrs. Failing dies intestate, in consequence of which Cadover passes to the conscientious Silts, not the wholly unfitted, griping Pembrokes. 'They'll do,' Stephen says. 'They've turned out Wilbraham and built new cottages, and bridged the railway, and made other necessary alterations' (Ch. 35). These alone are sizeable accomplishments on the part of a not very extended life; yet all are perhaps of no more than equal significance with the quality itself of his consciousness up till his marriage and then late in his days, his humble attentiveness to the nature, the living form of English scenery.

The Longest Journey's hero is awake to the chalk-pit outside Madingley, 'the brief season of its romance', and knows that 'it was not by preciosity that he would attain to the intimate spirit of the dell' (Ch. 2). He is in sympathy with the *genius loci* of the Cadbury Rings.

> [Mrs. Failing] nodded, and he asked her what kind of ghosties haunted this curious field.
>
> 'The D.,' was her prompt reply. 'He leans against the tree in the middle, especially on Sunday afternoons, and all his worshippers rise through the turnips and dance round him.'
>
> 'Oh, these were decent people,' he replied, looking downwards—'soldiers and shepherds. They have no ghosts. They worshipped Mars or Pan—Erda perhaps; not the devil.' (Ch. 13)

He responds to the magic hour of disappearing light on the winter afternoon where he and Wonham drive through the very heart of the Wiltshire scene between Salisbury and Cadover, and where the wonderfully full evocation of the outer demesne is so actualized for not being in the least 'written up' (the episode begins with 'The direct road from Salisbury to

Cadover is extremely dull', Ch. 33). But still more apprehensive than the senses of his leading character are the novelist's towards the natural environ which is not only Wiltshire but by implication—by extension—all of England's rurality at this climacteric date (1907). It is stitched through every chapter; it is present no less when Stephen Wonham wanders homelessly through various unwelcoming London districts (Ch. 30) than when Forster's own eye delivers to us the Cadover scene in full. Yet there—in Chapters 11–13—though to do so itself gashes the unitary fabric of the whole, we can most point to the novel as incarnating the essential quality of English countryside at its last historical moment of equipoise between Nature and Man, the latest epoch in which 'the wildness of our island, never extensive was' not yet 'stamped upon and built over and patrolled'[4] and before Forster felt obliged to write 'the moment nature is reserved . . ., she is an open air annex of the school room'[5] in his *Commonplace Book* entry of 7 April 1928.

The Longest Journey is the last great Romantic perception of our landscape. The novel celebrates—and with a fidelity, a perception, as keen as Wordsworth's—that era in which Man had reduced the English terrain from its primordial savagery (even in the eleventh century very much of the country was still wild boars and endless swamps) to a 'civilized' organum which yet held its own 'against' the powers of its human inhabitants. Forster's thought on the topic, here as later, is capable of being muddled. When in the same *Commonplace Book* entry, already referred to, he says 'The sort of poetry I seek only resides in objects Man *can't* touch—like England's grass network of lanes 100 years ago, but today he can destroy them',[6] he is overlooking the fact that the grass network of lanes was itself the consequence of a very thorough collaboration between men and Nature during a given historical period. As J. H. Plumb has pointed out 'Between 1750 and 1780 [owing to the enclosure movement] the English countryside became the countryside we know, a countryside of hedges, fields and scattered farms'[7]; something which our author himself acknowledges later in 1928 under the 8 August heading *Evening Walk* when he wails:

> I waddle on under a ruck-sack of traditional nature-emotions and try to find something important in the English countryside—

man-made, easily altered by man. The knowledge that I use statements that I've seen through paralyses me. I am condemned to old-fashionedness and insincerity. George Meredith, my predecessor on these downs, could upset himself with a better conscience. What a pity the poetry in me has got mixed up with Pan![8]

Yet as is so often the case, it is the earlier man who is more visionary, his later older avatar has drunk from 'the teacup of experience' (LJ, Ch. 7, para. 2) and maybe Experience *is* the Mother of Illusion. With regard to his hopes at that time for a happy future balance of the vegetable, animal and mineral theatre and its *homo sapiens* agents, the young writer of his pre-First-World-War fictions may be already anachronistically inspired, 'a Pagan suckled in a creed outworn', but in this novel he conveys matchlessly the supreme value of a Natural order which is sufficiently humanized yet not overdominated by the technological skills and commercial appetite man has since then so developed.

The fineness of Forster's treatment we can perceive the more clearly if we compare these three chapters with another novel's handling of the theme at no distant date, D. H. Lawrence's *The Rainbow* (published 1915 but begun earlier): specifically the first section of the latter's Chapter 1. Both sequences offer an account of a rural landscape and the life within it led by folk who make their living there. Yet Forster's human and natural scenery is all individualized as Lawrence's is not.

All the features of Lawrence's farming family the Brangwens' way of life are generic. They all have the same look in their eyes (paras. 2 and 3), they have the same reactions, identically, to thrift (apple-peelings—para. 5) and 'the rush of the sap in spring' (ibid.). The men share the same insights into Nature's workings and all do the same things exactly as one another when the seasons turn through the year.

Their womenfolk are similarly identical to each other, though their interests and yearnings are different from their males'. They experience the appeal of 'the road and the village with church and Hall and the world beyond', and 'saw themselves in the lady of the manor, each of them lived her own fulfilment in the life of Mrs. Hardy'.

Admittedly Mrs. Brangwen surpasses these in ambition.

> Looking out, as she must, from the front of her house towards the activity of man in the world at large, whilst her husband looked out to the back at sky and harvest and beast and land, she strained her eyes to see what man had done in fighting outwards to knowledge, she strained to hear how he uttered himself in his conquest, her deepest desire hung on the battle that she heard, far off, being waged on the edge of the unknown. She also wanted to know, and to be of the fighting host.

and she asks herself of her children how they can get into the larger world of 'cities and governments and the active scope of man'. Yet this but extends the trajectory of feeling which lances through her sister-wives of the local community, and indeed well may she be known throughout this introduction as, simply, 'the woman' or 'the Brangwen wife of the Marsh', for she and all the other agricultural toilers here are clods— creatures only animated by an instinct-life, who move and have their being shorn of such real individuality as indeed animals in flocks do possess (I speak as, erewhile, a small-time poultry-keeper myself)—and unloveable clods at that. With these initial 1,700+ words they are already shaping up to being, like almost all of Lawrence's personages, mortals un-interested in empathy for its own sake who only consult their own feelings, the movements of self-will from moment to moment, and live each deafly in a walled tower of petty egotism.

In sum, this author characteristically is being too reductive in his portrayal of human psychologies and missing out of account all the dimension of natural affection, of Caritas and Philadelphia, which (thank the Lord) is part of most men and women's birthright along with their noses or their teeth. That unsuccessful section of 'East Coker' (in *Four Quartets*), where Eliot subsumes the country folk of a former century to his theological purposes and wholly fails to individualize *them*, is actually slightly preferable, I think: in a vague weak way, given that they are at least (allegedly) dancing and having an unself-conscious good time.

By contrast the behaviour of the 'homely Nurse' Earth's 'Inmate Man'[9] in the Cadover vicinity is shown for born out of the environing world yet fully individualized. Flea Thompson, a shepherd, who breaks his word and keeps Stephen waiting for him more than four (not the pledged two) hours upon the Rings with his flock, while he kisses his girl at Wintersbridge, is slighter built than the man he has thus wronged and 'Podge' Wonham expects to floor him when next they encounter.

> He rode up to the culprit with the air of a Saint George, spoke a few stern words from the saddle, tethered his steed to a hurdle, and took off his coat. 'Are you ready?' he asked.
> 'Yes, sir,' said Flea, and flung him on his back.
> 'That's not fair,' he protested.
> The other did not reply, but flung him on his head.
> 'How on earth did you learn that?'
> 'By trying often,' said Flea.
> Stephen sat on the ground, picking mud out of his forehead. 'I meant it to be fists,' he said gloomily.
> 'I know, sir.'
> 'It's jolly smart though, and—I beg your pardon all round.' It cost him a great deal to say this, but he was sure that it was the right thing to say. He must acknowledge the better man. Whereas most people, if they provoke a fight and are flung, say, 'You cannot rob me of my moral victory.' (Ch. 12)

At Sunday church we are given Mrs. Failing's view of the local tenantry in the congregation:

> The rest of the congregation were poor women, with flat, hopeless faces—she saw them Sunday after Sunday, but did not know their names—diversified with a few reluctant plough-boys, and the vile little schoolchildren, row upon row. (Ch. 13)

but that that is a hopelessly crude slander upon them, for all that the village does some vicarious living through her, like Lawrence's female peasantry through *their* squire's lady of the Hall,[10] is clear from her lack of proper appreciation of others present: for instance Rickie, whom she wholly underrates, and the vicar's wife who has already figured, with her husband, as not dull, or at least as individual, in Mrs. Failing's own conversation.

> The vicar of Cadford—not the nice drunkard—declares the name is really 'Chadford', and he worried on till I put up a window to St. Chad in our church. His wife pronounces it 'Hyadford'. I could smack them both. (Ch. 11)

95

Whenever we meet the 'locals' they do or say something independent. At the cattle market in Salisbury Wonham

> met and made some friends. He watched the cheap-jacks, and saw how necessary it was to have a confident manner. He spoke confidently himself about lambs, and people listened. He spoke confidently about pigs, and they roared with laughter. He must learn more about pigs. He witnessed a performance—not too namby-pamby—of Punch and Judy. 'Hullo, Podge!' cried a naughty little girl. He tried to catch her, and failed. She was one of the Cadford children. (Ch. 12)

Likewise later in the tale in the same city when he and Rickie Elliot find 'outside the station a trap driven by a small boy, who had come in from Cadford to fetch some wire netting', the little incident that follows is alive with instinctual life, yes, but not that of reduced generalizations (Ch. 33).

More important is the whole identity of the Wiltshire landscape as very inhabitable womb, home and tomb of Man. This, again, is not romanticized in the sentimental sense. Forster begins his survey with the undistinguished aspect of the house at Cadover which itself answers to the characteristic 'failure' of the Wiltshire scene at large to be picturesque.

> A valley, containing a stream, a road, a railway; over the valley fields of barley and wurzel, divided by no pretty hedges, and passing into a great and formless down—this was the outlook, desolate at all times, and almost terrifying beneath a cloudy sky. The down was called 'Cadbury Rings' ('Cocoa Squares' if you were young and funny), because high upon it—one cannot say 'on the top', there being scarcely any tops in Wiltshire—because high upon it there stood a double circle of entrenchments. A bank of grass enclosed a ring of turnips, which enclosed a second bank of grass, which enclosed more turnips, and in the middle of the pattern grew one small tree. (Ch. 11)

Yet Wiltshire is moving all the same and as Forster etches in first one feature of the scene, then another, we do experience ('Looking into the heart of light, the silence'[11]) the not-anthropocentric but neither alienated nor antipathetic Nature which is England's finest glory—compare the Indian sun in *A Passage*; or which, rather, was at this epoch but can hardly be said to dominate amongst us any more in our late-twentieth-century, so much more technologized and megalopolized day. Organized religion or a criticism of organized religion becomes irrelevant in the midst of the apperception available here.

Stephen overthrew the Mosaic cosmogony. He pointed out the discrepancies in the Gospels. He levelled his wit against the most beautiful spire in the world, now rising against the southern sky. Between whiles he went for a gallop. After a time Rickie stopped listening, and simply went his way. For Dido was a perfect mount, and as indifferent to the motions of Aeneas as if she was strolling in the Elysian fields. He had had a bad night, and the strong air made him sleepy. The wind blew from the Plain. Cadover and its valley had disappeared, and though they had not climbed much and could not see far, there was a sense of infinite space. The fields were enormous, like fields on the Continent, and the brilliant sun showed up their colours well. The green of the turnips, the gold of the harvest, and the brown of the newly turned clods, were each contrasted with morsels of grey down. But the general effect was pale, or rather silvery, for Wiltshire is not a county of heavy tints. Beneath these colours lurked the unconquerable chalk, and wherever the soil was poor it emerged. The grassy track, so gay with scabious and bed-straw, was snow-white at the bottom of its ruts. A dazzling amphitheatre gleamed in the flank of a distant hill, cut for some Olympian audience. And here and there, whatever the surface crop, the earth broke into little embankments, little ditches, little mounds; there had been no lack of drama to solace the gods.

In Cadover, the perilous house, Agnes had already parted from Mrs. Failing. His thoughts returned to her. Was she, the soul of truth, in safety? Was her purity vexed by the lies and selfishness? Would she elude the caprice which had, he vaguely knew, caused sufferings before? Ah, the frailty of joy! Ah, the myriads of longings that pass without fruition, and the turf grows over them! Better men, women as noble—they had died up here and their dust had been mingled, but only their dust. These are morbid thoughts, but who dare contradict them? There is much good luck in the world, but it is luck. We are none of us safe. We are children, playing or quarrelling on the line, and some of us have Rickie's temperament, or his experiences, and admit it.

So he mused, that anxious little speck, and all the land seemed to comment on his fears and on his love.

Their path lay upward, over a great bald skull, half grass, half stubble. It seemed each moment there would be a splendid view. The view never came, for none of the inclines were sharp enough, and they moved over the skull for many minutes, scarcely shifting a landmark or altering the blue fringe of the distance. The spire of Salisbury did alter, but very slightly, rising and falling like the mercury in a thermometer. At the most it would be half hidden; at the least the tip would show behind the swelling barrier of earth. They passed two elder-trees—a great event. The bare patch, said Stephen, was owing to the gallows. Rickie nodded. He had lost all sense of incident. In this great solitude—more solitary than any Alpine range—he and Agnes were floating alone and for ever, between the shapeless earth and the shapeless clouds. An immense silence seemed to move towards them. A lark stopped singing, and they were glad of it. They were approaching the Throne of God. The silence touched them; the earth and all danger dissolved, but ere they quite vanished Rickie heard himself saying, 'Is it exactly what we intended?'

'Yes,' said a man's voice; 'it's the old plan.' They were in another valley. Its sides were thick with trees. Down it ran another stream and another road: it, too, sheltered a string of villages. But all was richer, larger, and more beautiful—the valley of the Avon below Amesbury. (Ch. 12)

Here we have much of the book in epitome. The Nature of the English scene is neither tidied up nor glamourized but shown for pregnant of a meaning which, though it cannot be put into words, can be intuited: a significance which is felt as it impinges on such occasions as this and with which, for all they cannot finally identify or characterize it, men can in gladness accommodate themselves.

There are crudities in the text, precisely where the author tries to verbalize this heart of the matter. 'Throne of God' is a bit too portentous. Forster again works in (oh dear!) 'ere' without any sufficient sense of how the word has by 1906, and well before, accreted necklaces of inverted commas around it. Yet most of this passage is immensely strong.

Rickie's conscious mind occupies much of its ride in worry-ing about his concerns in the social world. *Et pour cause.* It is the case that Mrs. Failing produces a thunderbolt for his wife before they quit Cadover, a branding shock which does illuminate the 'frailty' of their 'joy' and indeed blasts the same. Yet though his aunt tells of Stephen Wonham's relationship to them, as illegitimate half-brother, and speaks out of 'selfishness', what she utters is not a 'lie' (paragraph two of the quotation). The lie is in their marriage itself, to which Agnes has brought Herbert Pembroke standards of value and ambition. The revealing of Rickie's kinship with Stephen acts as a catalyst, first in the degeneration of Elliot's character and then in his re-ascent out of the Limbo of spiritual inertia and dishonesty where the Pembrokes have belayed him. The reason why acknowledging his blood-tie and making the most of it (Chs. 31–4) produces this rescue is that (a) it is a piece of honesty in a household given over to the deceitful and (b) it puts the hero back 'into touch with Nature' through Stephen who has remained a child of the same by birthright and by upbringing all along; and who therefore thinks any such phrase is 'cant' (end of Ch. 12).

We see that process at work, at an explicit level, in the drive they take between Salisbury Station and Cadover near the end of the novel (Ch. 33). But it has been implicit in Rickie's feeling for the Madingley Dell early on, in his stories, and in his response to the rural environments all along.

The book as a whole endorses his view of the fragility of human fates within this organum, and aptly enough, since a novel which reproduces Nature in its pages, albeit a civilized English Nature, ought surely to represent not only her fecund friendliness but her character too as an extravagant murderess (compare the large number of deaths in Wordsworth's narrative poems). A mystic apprehension of the power in question is at work throughout *The Longest Journey* and is heightened by the author's sense of the brutality intrinsic also: 'We are none of us safe . . .'—with the reference to the children who have been killed on the local branch railway line, which in turn echoes Rickie and Ansell's near-fatal accident in the tram at Cambridge earlier on.

Yet human life here is set over against the natural scene in which it arises without being reduced thereby: 'all the land seemed to comment on his fears and on his love.' And the quantity of violent sudden deaths in the work assist in constating its balanced account of Man-in-Nature. Over against all the continuities, of season and weather, rural life and new development—the various positive legacies and outcomes Rickie Elliot leaves behind—they set the insecurity of the individual human tenure.

Hence the appositeness of so much reference through the text to the Greeks, enlisting their attitudes to the circumvallating order of things. The reality Ansell is after lies neither in a worldscape wholly untamed nor in a *mise-en-scène* entirely man-ordered—like the systematization of behaviour and beliefs at Dunwood House—but in a creative play of humans and Nature together as partners not subordinates, a marriage of instinct and intelligence between them. Reality is proportionable, in sum. Not man-centred, nor inimical to man, it is a bright light behind the actual which shines in the kenning of such creatures as ourselves where the correct balance between *homo sapiens* and his great Earth-Mother is happily achieved.

The novel handles a large cast of characters, and incidents no less varied, with a poise we hardly notice. There are bits of callow writing, though I don't think the notorious passage in Chapter 3 where Rickie catches sight of the two lovers embracing (' "Do such things actually happen?" and he seemed to be looking down coloured valleys . . .' etc.) counts for one of them. The very uncertainty that begets in us—is this straightforward reporting or is it ironic? does it mediate the hero's or the author's thoughts to us?—seems to me a felicity. The experience of carnal passion, even at one (innocent) remove, cannot be docketed and ticketed neatly. Getting it into focus may take a lifetime and longer. We can never know whether Elliot overrates what he has seen; he does not, cannot, himself. Generally the book's effect is of the action having been lived through by the narrator before he wrote it—to say which is not discordant with Forster's avowal to the Woolfs that 'he made up his novels as he went along'.[12] Nor is the tone patronizing. Indeed the style is less sly than in the other novels, there is less (though no lapse) of the quietly comic commentary, the voice of as it were Austenian irony; and this befits what is so passionate a revelation of the positive values in Nature which the author has here decisively got down on paper.

Rickie Elliot idealizes his half-brother Stephen for bearing their mother, especially her voice, in his identity (see conclusion of Chapter 33). Like his idealization of the Gerald-Agnes relation this is shown for partly fruitful, partly a mistake. Wonham may or may not be hard to believe in, according to one's own experience of our species. He is by definition a sport and therefore hard to focus as a type. Yet this is not a major problem, nor his defection, in the lists of artistic probability—if it be so (I find him credible enough)—a serious wound in the fabric of the whole, because he is not the centre of the novel.

When one submits to the way *The Longest Journey* so articulates England as Nature at a special moment of equipoise between Man and his rural or semi-rural environment, and to Forster's blending with this his voice of moral percipience and social analysis—the way the novel is so worldly-wise *and* shot through with the last great Romantic perception of our landscape—one looks in vain for such an achievement else-where in twentieth century British fiction; because this work embodies a comprehensive vision rare in life or art. We are not here dealing with the observation of an Austen and the kennings of a Hardy, as it were, patchwork-quilted together. Something far more integrated and therefore substantial than that offers. It is one of the few complete treatments of Man-harmoniously-in-Nature which ever have been done; it is the last that was possible in the context of our society[13]; and these things are wholly accomplished in their integrity.

2. *The Pre-First-World-War Shorter 'English' Fiction*

The wholeness of view which there finds expression we shall not discover in the briefer pieces of fiction—those set in English environments this is to say—which Forster wrote before the First World War; whether we look at the tales he published in *The Celestial Omnibus* collection (1911) and *The Eternal Moment* (1928) or the fragments unprinted during his life but posthumously issued of late.

Ironically however, perhaps the most mature of these is the earliest, the torso beginning 'They are Nottingham lace!', Forster's first attempt at a novel, composed 1899–1901. Here in the account of a bullied sensitive adolescent called Edgar

Carruthers, who finds in Sidney Trent, a slightly lower-caste newcomer to his district teaching at his cousins' school nearby, the focus and means of rebellion, the main Forsterian themes of the ensuing decade are already operative.

The author himself was unnecessarily severe upon this accomplishment in later time: ' "This wasn't writing," Forster said, looking back on it. "The apparatus was working, not inaccurately, but feebly and dreamily, because I wasn't sure it was there." '[14] For what is remarkable, rather, is how little the gush and wholesale enthusiasms, the unself-aware yearnings of adolescence feature in a creative intelligence not much older than the fragment's hero. This social satire—upon the Tonbridgean middle-middle class values—is very amusing, very strong (has a painful cutting edge) and is far from simple-minded.

> During one of their walks Trent abruptly said 'it's all over the town about pappa being a draper.'
>
> Edgar said 'oh'. 'I'm very sick,' he continued.
>
> 'Why do you mind? You're always trumpeting that you think yourself vulgar.'
>
> 'Because I can't conceal that, but I can conceal my ancestry. It'll do us a lot of harm. It's the one thing to our credit that we made money by our own efforts, and yet the one thing that we daren't let get about. It'll choke off people calling on us. They're none too eager as it is. I'd like to wring the neck of the people who let it out.' (Section VI)[15]

Indeed a principal recognition running through what we have of this abandoned novel is the inescapability of society, the individual's need of a nourishing place inside it, and the whole question of what terms one is to make with one's social reality

> Not in Utopia,—subterranean fields,—
> Or some secreted island, Heaven knows where!
> But in the very world, which is the world
> Of all of us,—the place where, in the end,
> We find our happiness, or not at all![16]

For Edgar's existence in the Manchett household is all but intolerable given the degree in which his uncle bullies him there.

Forster's exhilarating quality as a social ironist derives from his ability, like Jane Austen, to show us most earnestly 'all the sordid petty personal crushing oppression' which characterizes too many human relations, 'the impinging of family pressure, the impinging of one personality on another, all of them in highest degree damn'd, loathsome, and detestable',[17] yet by doing it in a mode of slily comic insight to reveal also (1) how ludicrous in the limitedness of their imaginations are the malign of the world and (2) how, therefore, they are far from indefeasible or beyond defiance. We have an example in *Mansfield Park*. Fanny Price's senior aunt is terrifying, yes, but also laughable:

> The winter came and passed without their being called for; the accounts continued perfectly good;—and Mrs. Norris in promoting gaieties for her nieces, assisting their toilettes, displaying their accomplishments, and looking about for their future husbands, had so much to do as, in addition to all her own household cares, some interference in those of her sister, and Mrs. Grant's wasteful doings to overlook, left her very little occasion to be occupied even in fears for the absent. (Ch. 4)

Already *aet. suae* 21–3 Forster is pretty good as observing the difficulties as well as advantages suffered by the bad in the performance of their cruelties.

> Mr. Manchett was feeling low. He had hardly recovered from the effects of the crossing, and before him at the breakfast table were seated some fellow passengers who had seen him being ill. And he did not like Dublin. As Mrs. Manchett had often told him 'Ireland was not the same as England.'
> He disliked the transparent flattery and the brogue. It was not straight: it was a halfway-house to the continent.
> To his surprise he found among his letters one from Edgar. It was an excuse for delaying the evil moment of breaking the top off his egg, and he opened it. But it left him with still less appetite. 'Impertinence!' he muttered. 'Open mutiny.' But why? He could give no reasons for his indignation, but felt it was just. At all events he must reply at once. He would give anything not to write. His personality, like himself, did not travel well. If he could talk to his nephew face to face he would soon get the upper hand. A few remarks like 'don't stoop, my boy; you're as round as an old woman' inserted into the

conversation would make his opponent nervous and compliant. But to write 'don't stoop' by letter was impossible.

He could write in many ways. First, a round reproof for impertinence. He longed to do this, but had no handle for it. Secondly, acknowledgement that he did disapprove the friendship, and permission to Edgar to show his letter to Trent. This he also wished to do, and it would have been the wisest course. But he was not himself: he was on alien shores and feeling unwell. He dared not do it. The third course was not to compromise himself, and to write a jovial breezy letter, laughing at his nephew and wife for the way they fretted over trifles. This he prepared to do, and sat down after breakfast with an aching head to write. It is impossible to be breezy to order, and the letter was not a success. It betrayed irritation, and also betrayed hostility against Trent together with timidity to avow it. However he sent it, and spent the rest of the morning regretting he had done so.

'I've heard from Uncle George,' said Edgar, when the letter arrived. 'He doesn't mind me knowing Trent.'

One can guess however at the reason for which this was abandoned. Edgar's breakaway from his emotionally tyrannous uncle and aunt is either too slight or too large a subject for Forster to handle on a novel-length canvas at that time. Yet before we quit '*Nottingham Lace*' it is worth noticing how even this social comedy set in suburban villas and shops is imbued with landscape, how the vales and woods of Surrey function continuously through it—as backdrop, as beckoning visionary horizon, and as a mainspring to the language, action and morality of the work. Messages from Valhalla inhabit the hills upon which Edgar's bedroom window looks out, and the more truly in that the Surrey scene is reported *sui generis* in and for its own character.

Seeing life steadily and whole is, by contrast, not a strong enough feature of the otherwise very fine short story 'Ansell' written not much later (circa 1902–3).[18] A wry treatment of academic versus natural open-air life, it overlooks the question of ways and means at an important level. The likeable eponymous hero gets his living—in every sense of that word—by being a factotum on a country estate. But if the other major character, the half-unnamed narrator, has at the end lost his hoped-for employ as a Fellow at his university college (and the

£80 per annum which goes with that position) on what material basis will *he* live in future?

The moral of 'The Celestial Omnibus' is that the young boy travelling therein, entirely unnamed—as if names do not count, only realities—has stepped into the heart of what poetry and philosophy are about and offer. The self-importantly literary man (artfully nomenclatured) cannot bear such a consummation: 'Mr. Bons—he could not resist—crawled out of the beautiful omnibus. His face appeared, gaping horribly.'

'Other Kingdom' is a reworking of the Apollo and Daphne story, and appears indeed as one of Rickie Elliot's efforts in *The Longest Journey*. From a domineering young businessman whose bullying is cleverly disguised as sophisticated opinions, his fresh young fiancée with her serious and true commitment to Nature escapes by transfiguration into tree-life and leafhood. In the Faun and Wessex-ism of 'The Curate's Friend' Forster expresses his feeling of this epoch about the English country-side, the spiritual nourishment it offers for those properly awake enough to receive the same, and identifies—a recurrent theme in this author—self-confident inaccuracy with moral inanition of the kind which is not awake: '. . . and a few Roman earthworks. (I lectured very vividly on those earthworks: they have since proved to be Saxon.)'

'The Other Side of the Hedge' is a parable against 'progress' and pleads for humanity to 'rest upon the earth'. 'The Machine Stops', 'a reaction to one of the earlier heavens of H. G. Wells',[19] is likewise a remonstrance in prophetic form against the linear forward development of the Earth's mech-anization and technologico-industrializing. In this futuristic science-fiction the whole planet has become a honeycomb of automated life which finally breaks down and returns to Nature her proper sway. 'Mr. Andrews' expresses the imposs-ibility of imagining anything infinite and therefore (though this is surely a logical fallacy) the impossibility of 'anything infinitely good or beautiful' existing 'excepting in my dreams'. Would not even the fullest-developed embryo in its mother's womb find it impossible to imagine a world of colour?—but that does not prove that a world of colour does not exist.

'The Point of It' I fail to understand, though evidently it is parabolic too; in saying which we at once identify a limitation of these pre-War stories, their all-but-homiletic nature as sketches with precepts, narratives for maxims, diagrammatic embodiments of the main items in the author's ethos rather than attempts at fully incarnating life. Thus it is that some of them are too anecdotic: not a comment on their length (though such as 'The Rock' and 'Co-ordination' *are* very short) but on their emblematic characterization of human individuals.

Nevertheless in their kind these allegories are delicately done. 'Other Kingdom' for example is rich and full in ironies—which are nutritive, far from merely mocking hints—about scholarship, nature-worship, freedom and love: the real as opposed to traditionally or diplomatically received purpose and direction of these things. And if we are required by these fantasies (in Forster's own words on this branch of fiction) 'to pay something extra',[20] I think we are ready to subscribe the fee for all that it *is* more than usual suspension of disbelief. While we accept their supernaturalist conventions we take on a pagan world's way of thinking, with what that, out of (say) the Greek dramatists, implies. (Not for nothing is the boy Ford studying *Oedipus Colonneus* at the end of 'Other Kingdom'.) Time and again we are shown a human dimension invaded by Nature with something She is trying to say. For enjoyment this compares favourably with Forster's later commitment to wholesale Hobbesian materialism, as registered in the *Commonplace Book*.

He has of course every right in 1960 to agree with Gaudier-Brzeska that 'Christians and Pantheists may insist that the soul is separate from the body, but this is not true. There is a live body, that is all',[21] or in 1956 to anticipate 'death as a permanent anaesthetic' and find any other possibility quite unreal,[22] but in that case I deduce the appropriate 'literary report on life' (Henry James's phrase[23]) is—in the domain of imaginative writing—simply silence.

The matter is worth some explicitness.

Dichtung, poesis—whatever you want to call it—has for its most fundamental basis the assumption that more strictly functional modes of utterance ('The bus stop you want to reach is 103 yards away at the second turning after the third one on the left', 'You can claim Family Income Supplement at this office on Thursday afternoons') do not meet the whole human case; that we mortals live under a dispensation of things which we do not and cannot sufficiently understand, and upon which (it follows) we need to bring all the parts of our intelligence to bear which automotive activity can enlist.

The materialism developed between the sixteenth century and the present day is distinct from earlier non-theological views of the world in that it shuts out agnosticism far more completely than any religion. The cosmogony has varied in the period, but in broad crude terms we can say that Hobbes, H. G. Wells and a body of scientific opinions now are like enough in seeing the Universe as an organum in a state of continuous becoming, where our planet and the accident of Life (as we mean the term) are trivial by-products, miniscule marginalia of a Drama very alien to anthropocentric considerations, and where the death of an individual, as in the longer term of the human species, means the absolute termination of consciousness.

Now the Occident currently has much in common with Corinth's cultural situation at the time it was visited by St. Paul, a territory in a state of wholesale philosophical bewilderment. Yet the difference is, those first-century Greeks felt their options upon the mystery of life were open, as was symbolically shown elsewhere in the peninsula:

> Then Paul stood in the midst of Mars' hill, and said, Ye men of Athens, I perceive that in all things ye are too superstitious.
>
> For as I passed by, and beheld your devotions, I found an altar with this inscription, TO THE UNKNOWN GOD.[24]

Agnosticism of the Ancient Greek kind can hold itself close to a severely bleak view of things. Homer's poems, like Proust's novel in our age, for all the golden aureole of language in which they are realized, are visions of life on earth as Hell really, and Sophocles is dialectically unanswerable when he ends the cruel doings in *The Women of Trachis* with the rider 'You have seen many things here today terrible and strange: and not one of them that is not Zeus.'[25]

Still to find the Universe—or the conditions under which *our* lives go on—mysterious is something other than to have become certain it is ultimately just an executioner. The latter

107

view, the foremost concomitant of our modern materialism does quite simply, if one is willing to face the matter straight, invalidate all living entirely.

You and I experience reality successively, through time. Unless the possibility exists, therefore—however dimly entertainable, however vague and unlikely—that in spite of appearances we continue to be after our mortal demises, all our days, retroactively no less than prospectively, will be voided of significance. If Death be ultimate and final annihilation for the individual, then his life is not worth taking seriously—all of it, and the same must be said for the species as a whole.

Inevitably it will be more convenient and comfortable meanwhile, for all parties, if we have lived decent well-behaved lives rather than the opposite. If we have to be temporarily marooned in a state of existence, it is preferable not to share the flitting scene with a Bedlam of maniacs. But 'the greatest happiness of the greatest number' itself becomes a formula all but emptied of real import when we reflect that so very soon that greatest number—in a mere two ticks of the carbon clock—will itself be eternally insensible and beyond the reach of hurt or help. If Gaudier-Brzeska's view is accurate, then what we are dealing with here in this world is the Condemned Cell, and all our strivings or thinkings in it are mere brief attempts at re-arrangement of its furniture.

For the same reason the game is indeed too trivial for the candle of artistic treatment. That seeks to elicit deeper than everyday wisdom and wholly conscious intelligence out of the human mind, by the strange indirect processes which are a poem's, a play's, a novel's (etc.) way of constituting its thought. Forster himself puts this well in his fine essay of 1927 'Anonymity: an enquiry'.[26] But if at the best we are occupied, whether writing or politically engaged, farming or making love, simply in assays at making more homelike conditions in an Abattoir, what is the point—especially of the more complicated and abstruse human dealings, such as the artistic?

While men remain *in doubt* about what Destiny will permit them, as individuals, all these activities are potentially worthwhile; and intimations from the 'lower personality', the one 'deeper down' below the 'surface' of S. T. Coleridge or William Shakespeare[27] are well worth appropriating for extensions of our own habitual outlooks. But if decisively and exclusively we are convinced that all that awaits the lot of us is 'a permanent anaesthetic', I cannot see the virtue of bothering. Yes, reading *The Winter's Tale* or attending a performance of *King Lear* will give me a couple of brief thrills now, but in view of the coming blotter, so what? One cannot take the sketchy caperings of a house-fly,[28] the very transient excitement of its nervous system between two endless voids, all that seriously, surely?

In sum, an agnostic position makes sense of getting interested in 'all the choir of Heaven and all the furniture of earth'; the (modern) materialist one, by which my own personality is imbrued (for I am of course, like everyone else, a child of my time) and unconvinced (for I have a thinking mind also and see too many flaws in it), does not.

The distinction I am seeking to make can be drawn *viâ* the posthumously published tale *'Ralph and Tony'*[29] (beginning 'After dinner Margaret . . .') written also very early in the century (1903). Largely an untransmuted piece of personal aching (Forster's frustrated longing for a lover) it lacks the edge and bite of *'Nottingham Lace'* in being almost entirely devoid of authorial detachment and humour. The significant features, its character as a plea against Muddle and for Justice, or its embodiment of Tony's paganism—important this, in filling out for us the picture of the kind of paganism Forster was committed to at this time—are almost submerged in the too personal *cri de coeur* which the story but thinly veils. Yet the narrative does not wholly set its face against a view of things as mysterious, in favour of peremptory and absolute materialism. The possibility of the soul's existence—though it sees this as improbable—is allowed.

> He had not asked questions, because he knew everything—knew from the moment that he fell on the slope that he would never climb the mountains again. And with the knowledge all his life broke up. Nothing mattered now he was diseased. And such a fiendish disease, which left him in appearance unchanged, young, vigorous, hard in muscle and bone, full of the will to live, yet fearing to use and enjoy lest his heart should stop and he and his body altogether.[30] Religion he hardly considered, though to use his own phrase 'he had never thrown it over'. But even if its most favourable account was to [be] believed, he

would not have his body again for some time, and from his experience of the dissecting-room he doubted much whether that account was true. He was in fact a pure pagan, all the more complete for being unconscious, living the glorious unquestioning life of the body, with instinct as a soul. Intellect he had, and also that nameless residue which some suppose will be immortal, but it was still far in the background, and he had made only the physical parts truly his own. (Section IV)

The pre-First-World-War E. M. Forster has not sealed up these possibilities one way or the other; and that is another reason for not being surprised at his ability to create before he was middle-aged in contradistinction to his lapse of novelistic power thereafter. The short stories of this period and indeed all his writings up to (including) *A Passage to India* are about a world it is worth taking seriously, though the last-named work is transitional. The later tales have to suffer *inter alia* from addressing themselves to an areopagus which is, at an ultimate if unconscious level, apprehended as not being so.

3. Howards End

Not taking its own debate seriously enough, however, is the fatal flaw in *Howards End*, which otherwise is so full of individual good things that we turn to it—those of us who are Forsterians at all—again and again during a lifetime as to a warehouse packed with all manner of treasure trove and nutritive wisdom. But the book fails as a whole because though on the philosophical plane Forster may have got his antithesis right—weighing death against money[31]—on the level of action it is stillborn. The Wilcox family with whom the Schlegel sisters take up is from first to last a sitting duck, so that when the novel takes close aim, prods it with its rifle-butt and then shoots it straight through the breast, the bird's inertia during the course of the whole operation confirms what we had guessed from the beginning: that it has been dead all along, indeed a stuffed ornamental trophy mounted on the shelf of Radical Opinion.

*   *   *

Margaret and Helen Schlegel, half British, half German, live in London with their young brother Theobald. Now in their twenties and having managed their lives alone over the sizeable period since their parents' death, these girls encounter an English business family while sightseeing in Germany, and Helen accepts an invitation to stay with it at its rural retreat 'Howards End'. There she meets and is kissed by Paul, the youngest son of the clan. An engagement is not the consequence however. Paul has just been momentarily flirting. The thing is broken off as soon as begun. Life resumes its usual tenor. Yet their paths *have* tempestuously crossed and it makes indirectly for a renewed relation again in London later when the Wilcoxes move into a flat opposite the Schlegels' Wickham Place apartment. For Mrs. Wilcox, a shadowy yet inspired presence, finds in Margaret a spiritual heir for the Hertfordshire house and on her deathbed, a very short while later, in a pencilled note bequeathes this her property to the elder of the Schlegel women.

The 'legacy' is ignored, perhaps rightly, by her kinsfolk. But again the acquaintance does not end there, because the middle-aged Mr. Wilcox after a couple of years of widowhood gets attracted to Margaret and, proposing to her, is accepted: to Helen's horror, who sees the Ducie Street family as repositories of the most benighted attitudes. Such a mistake is exacerbated in Helen's estimation by the fate of one Leonard Bast, an insurance clerk she and her siblings have met at a Queen's Hall concert earlier.

Leonard, a youngster who is unhappily married, has struck the two sisters—in spite of his half-baked literary talk out of Ruskin, Borrow and Thoreau—as striving after profound experience in a way that really is original; and when they have mentioned his case to Henry Wilcox, the latter has told them to advise their new friend to clear out of the Porphyrion, his employing company, as it is liable to collapse. The advice is passed on, taken, and ruins Bast because the bank where he gets work instead then reduces its staff. Helen comes to the wedding-breakfast of Margaret's prospective step-daughter Evie, in Shropshire, with the Basts in tow, when she finds them impawned and starving. The appearance of Leonard's wife however, left alone briefly on the lawn while rooms are negotiated at the local hotel, is not happy for with this lady Henry has had a liaison years before, in Cyprus. Confronted by her, Wilcox supposes his fiancée to be intent on exposing him. But Margaret, who thus learns of his infidelity to his dead wife, neither breaks off her engagement nor finds herself able to wring a new position for Leonard from the man who shortly does become her husband. Helen meantime debunks to Germany, having unsuccessfully tried to send Leonard half her fortune (£5,000); and as the months lengthen her sister is harrowed by her resolute avoidance of any personal contact. Only their aunt's near-fatal illness brings her to England and gives a handle for getting a *viva voce* interview. She is lured to Howards End on the plea that their Wickham Place books and furniture are stored there with a charwoman solely in attendance.

Margaret now discovers that Helen is with child. So does her husband; and her husband's bully of a son Charles Wilcox discovers the identity of the baby's father: Leonard Bast. While Henry revolts his wife by hypocritical condemnation of Helen's condition, expressed most obtusely of all in his refusal to let her sleep that one night at Howards End, Charles decides to thrash the 'culprit' within an inch of his life. In this purpose he is assisted by Leonard's visit to the old small country farmhouse, for the latter has traced the current where-abouts of the new Mrs. Wilcox, to whom he wants to confess and apologize. Margaret and Helen have already decided to go to Germany together and have no more dealings with the Wilcoxes; but Charles's punishment proves fatal, Leonard dies of his diseased heart's failure, and the consequences are severe.

> Charles was committed for trial. It was against all reason that he should be punished, but the law, being made in his image, sentenced him to three years' imprisonment. (Ch. 43)

Overwhelmed by catastrophe Henry turns to his wife's man-agement unconditionally. Abandoning the sterile blue-stocking scheme Margaret takes her 'invalids' back down to Howards End to recruit; the temporary shelter becomes their permanent home; and the novel closes with the house being settled—the Wilcox family giving their, albeit in some cases grudging, consent—firstly upon Margaret and then after her lifetime upon her nephew, Helen's baby who is romping in the field outdoors. Alongside these testamentary dispositions—'It does seem curious that Mrs. Wilcox should have left Margaret Howards End, and yet she get it after all'—is expressed the hope that the child in the meadow will inherit and advance a harmony, not the

> craze for motion [which] has only set in during the last hundred years. It may be followed by a civilization that won't be a movement, because it will rest on the earth. All the signs are against it now, [says Margaret] but I can't help hoping, and very early in the morning in the garden I feel that our house is the future as well as the past. (Ch. 44)

I offer no apology for the inadequacy of that bald synopsis because no *compte rendu* can do the story-telling of *Howards End* justice. It is one of the most skilfully organized of fictional actions, one of the major masterpieces of Narrative art. The laudatory portion of Forster's own note on the book in 1958 is itself but faint praise beside what is due: 'Very elaborate and all pervading plot that is seldom tiresome or forced, range of characters, social sense, wit, wisdom, colour.'[32]

The marvel is, firstly, how the novelist introduces so large a world, and then maintains its existence through the course of so much activity at the level of personal relations.

We should note how, starting with one sister's confidential and indeed confessional letters to another—that other with whom she has the most cherished intimate relation in her life, who is in some degree an alter ego—the presented scene expands and its human population increases as we move from page to page in the early chapters. Helen's communiqués from Howards End evoke herself very much, Margaret slightly, the Wilcoxes in considerable measure and the house as a fully realized picture. Her final missive in this mode

> *Dearest, Dearest Meg,*
> *I do not know what you will say: Paul and I are in love—the younger son who only came here Wednesday.*

takes us inevitably to the Wickham Place breakfast-table where not only do we observe Margaret and their aunt Mrs.

Munt but also hear the first notes sounded characterizing Germany and England—those countries in themselves, and in relation to each other. Then on the journey to King's Cross Station, preparative of Aunt Juley's disastrous trip to Howards End, the brief initial signs emerge of the novel's treatment of London—its spreading suburbia, and encroachment on the countryside. Chapter 3 launches us forward again into the thick of the immediate drama—without undue delay, for the meditations in the preceding page or two have accompanied our seeing Mrs. Munt aboard her train for Hertfordshire; and she proceeds to entangle matters—in a first-class scene of social comedy—with Charles Wilcox and his family in consequence of a disastrous misprision. Chapter 4 more spaciously than hitherto considers the issues which have been evoked: passion, its nature and value; Wilcox as against Schlegel principles; Germany's more recent history and current political attitudes; England's; the Schlegel girls as individuals.

The narrator weaves in and out of each other particular fates and important generalities; thus the book develops. The British nation is thematically enlisted—and its continental rival (in a lesser degree, to be sure, but sufficiently for certain purposes)— Music—the English metropolis—the Poor ('not . . . the very poor. They are unthinkable . . .', Ch. 6); and the whole is more substantial from the fact that action and commentary are so intertwined. For the author's philosophizings, as in his other works, do not take the place of solid character-creation. His personages are individuated in and for themselves—not least by their idiosyncrasies of talk and speech-rhythm. Commentary is very plentiful but additional to, not a substitute for this primary, accomplished portion of the novelist's task.

Yet in its very plenitude it extends the novel's range. The extraordinary talent which so weaves its image of life that we keep entering deeper and farther into an expanding human world as the first half of this relatively lengthy book unfolds, also finds expression in the way, across the work's progress, the life of Nature is apprehended as going on all the time. This was more modestly the case in *A Room with a View*. It happened on every page of *The Longest Journey*. Man's vegetable and mineral environment is continually fore- or background of the human agents' experience in *Howards End*. The scene in which

Margaret announces to her sister Mr. Wilcox's proposal and her inclination to accept him is prefaced, for example, by an account of England's topography. Mrs. Munt and Helen have taken the German cousin 'Frieda Mosebach, now Frau Architect Liesecke . . . to these heights [of 'the final section of the Purbeck Hills'] to be impressed' and there the physical 'system of our island' is expatiated upon, then individual details of its geology (' "And your English lakes—Vindermere, Grasmere—are they, then, unhealthy?" ' Ch. 19).

This is characteristic in a tale which also represents the non-Natural life of the world as going on within and behind its human doings:

> And the conversation drifted away and away, and Helen's cigarette turned to a spot in the darkness, and the great flats opposite were sown with lighted windows, which vanished and were relit again, and vanished incessantly. Beyond them the thoroughfare roared gently,—a tide that could never be quiet. . . . (Ch. 5)

> The city herself, emblematic of their lives, rose and fell in a continual flux, while her shallows washed more widely against the hills of Surrey and over the fields of Hertfordshire. This famous building had arisen, that was doomed. Today Whitehall had been transformed: it would be the turn of Regent Street tomorrow. And month by month the roads smelt more strongly of petrol, and were more difficult to cross, and human beings heard each other speak with greater difficulty, breathed less of the air, and saw less of the sky. Nature withdrew: the leaves were falling by midsummer; the sun shone through dirt with an admired obscurity. (Ch. 13)

The two sizeable paragraphs which in the text follow that last quotation are quintessentially representative Forsterian commentary; and we welcome so much of it, surprisingly, because it is not the tedious or nagging moralizing which under another novelist's hand it could easily be (even many of the other Great Novelists would go disastrously wrong if they admitted so much philosophizing into their projects), but rather advances the book's action and its character-portrayals.

The passage in question, extended as it is, addresses itself directly to one of the subordinate themes in which the novel's principal issues are embodied: the restless and technological development of modern life as expressed in the rising, falling and spreading architecture of London, its representativeness as an increasingly mechanized and homogenizing influence.

It does moralize, very intelligently; 'The Earth as an artistic cult has had its day, and the literature of the near future will probably ignore the country and seek inspiration from the town' is by way of prophecy a direct bull's-eye hit for something written 1908–9, when we consider the major poetry produced during the next fifteen years. But the moralizing itself, like the orchestral interludes in a good opera, develops the life of the story and its personages. By the time it has had its say we know what new revelation has visited Margaret Schlegel with the expiry of her Wickham Place lease: the loss of that home is an exile, spiritually a more serious one than she had anticipated; further, the impending extrusion itself has made her wake up to the (for her) unsatisfactory nature of contemporary London as (she now sees) no milieu of a true home for anybody. Here we watch the vision and therefore part of the character of this heroine alter, as her options both widen and narrow; and observe the movement of Time's inaudible and noiseless step as it begins to impinge upon Margaret's own sensoria in a new way. The very generalizing of the two paragraphs drops into the mixture of her fate a couple more grains of concern—elevated, philosophic, yes, yet increasingly urgent—which make her all the more receptive later to Mr. Wilcox's marriage-proposal, for gradually she now begins to fear that she too will be, like Jacky Bast

> On the shelf,
> On the shelf,
> Boys, boys, I'm on the shelf. (Ch. 6)

Part of what Henry Wilcox appears to offer her, in the next phase of the tale, is a home instead of a rootless life which suddenly has discovered itself as rootless.

Thus, though neither she nor the narrator ever explicitly say so (at least in the terms of the popular song just quoted) a woman's anxiety at approaching what Jane Austen called 'the years of danger' is aggravated by her perceptive mind's new awareness of the current scene around her as exceptionally changing and foundationless, even for the basis of a life in our transitory human courses; and all this is actualized by means as apparently indirect as the meditation on London and modern civilization at the beginning of Chapter 13.

Yet the first of these two paragraphs (beginning 'To speak against London is no longer fashionable') does not offer itself as indirect reported thought solely from inside the world of the book's action but rather the fruit of the narrator's excogitations in his own voice upon his own experience of life, though these mediate to us considerations which lie at the very heart of Margaret Schlegel's new disconcertment.

> Certainly London fascinates. One visualizes it as a tract of quivering grey, intelligent without purpose, and excitable without love; as a spirit that has altered before it can be chronicled; as a heart that certainly beats, but with no pulsation of humanity. It lies beyond everything: Nature, with all her cruelty, comes nearer to us than do these crowds of men.

In consequence of this sort of rhetoric (wholly integral as it is with the work's drama) the novel gains a scale out of all proportion to its numerical word-count, feels half-way as spacious as *War and Peace* in fact as the image of a world. So much has been taken within its purview, the particular has so been related to the universal, by the time its tale is done.

Forster's genius throws out other kinds of fine-nerved reticulations as well. For one thing the minor characters are not lost sight of—i.e. given to lead only intermittent lives, to exist merely when they are needed, wheeled on for the story's purposes, and otherwise unimaginable.

Theobald ('Tibby') Schlegel, for instance, starts in our acquaintance as 'an intelligent man of sixteen, but dyspeptic and difficile'—traits which are illustrated in the two chapters immediately following (5 and 7) where he appears. When next we glimpse him, briefly in Chapter 12, a year and a half later, he has 'just been up to try for a scholarship at Oxford'. His talk is entirely of this experience and, for all that it is reported speech, very indirectly presented, the fact that he has sustained one topic without lapsing into boredom, as earlier was his wont, and has been enthusiastic on a single subject—'he gave a description of his visit that was almost glowing'—gives us a sense of new development having taken place in this personality, though not real new maturing. Two years more are reported as going by (opening of Ch. 13) and when we encounter him now, 'in his second year at Oxford, [and] down for the Easter vacation', he has become a very detached undergraduate—which we deduce not from authorial allegation but his converse. It is that of someone on the threshold of full adulthood. He is self-confident and worldly enough to ask his elder sister about her unmarried status in ironic tones— 'Has nobody arst you?'—and to sprawl uninvited at his full length 'so far back in his chair that he extended in a horizontal line from knees to throat' (cap. ibid.)

In *Aspects of the Novel* Forster pays a finely-judged tribute to George Meredith's power of construction:

> A Meredithian plot . . . resembles a series of kiosks most artfully placed among wooded slopes, which his people reach by their own impetus, and from which they emerge with altered aspect. Incident springs out of character, and having occurred it alters that character. (Ch. 5)

But a still finer tribute is due to the later writer. On each occasion that we meet Forster's characters afresh, we find they have subtly developed, if only in that aspect which is the passage of Time; and this is every bit as true of his minor as of his principal personages. Whether conscious or otherwise on the creator's part, the achievement derives from that abnormally alert attentiveness to other human beings, their physical movements and speech-patterns no less than their ethical codes or professional habits, which is the fictionist's most desirable piece of equipment; and it powerfully assists in creating our sense of a solid whole world between the covers of *Howards End*, not a series of vignettes, however cleverly contrived or judiciously observed, between spaces open and empty of phenomena.

Yet another feature of his so-much-substantiating art which conceals art is the harmony of the book's metaphors with its human life. The poet and social historian behind this work are at one and perceive through their separate eyes, and though finding different modes of expression for them, the same truths. We have the natural and very unstrained appearance and reappearance of Leonard Bast (with his predicament-in-indigence) cropping up exactly in the manner of the goblin's footfall as perceived by Helen Schlegel over the third movement's course of the Beethoven Symphony. Likewise there is Margaret's search for a home. Recurring as these things do, like *motifs* in a music-drama—each time a renewal of the theme in question, yet modified by a different context of surrounding concerns and enlarged by their own accretions of reference—they express the work's major themes in the other sense, the sense of moral preoccupations. *Howards End* poses the life of commercial and imperialist action against that of imagination, Death versus Money, and—which is its deepest as well as most successful accomplishment—constitutes an evolutionary apprehension of human society.

This is Forster's 'condition of England' novel agreed—his 'condition of Europe' one, as one may say, in so far as the frequent involvement of things and people, cultural and political references German bring in that other Empire as Britain's strange Continental mirror-image: in rivalry, jealousy, emulation, and with that the problem of international peace:

> Oh, yes, it was a nuisance, there was no doubt of it. Helen was proof against a passing encounter, but—Margaret began to lose confidence. Might it reawake the dying nerve if the family were living close against her eyes? And Frieda Mosebach was stopping with them for another fortnight, and Frieda was sharp, abominably sharp, and quite capable of remarking, 'You love one of the young gentlemen opposite, yes?' The remark would be untrue, but of the kind which, if stated often enough, may become true; just as the remark, 'England and Germany are bound to fight,' renders war a little more likely each time that it is made, and is therefore made the more readily by the gutter press of either nation. (Ch. 7)

But the novel has an even wider margin of reference. Margaret Schlegel's search for a home parallels Humanity's in a civilization where our species has not yet found a way of settling down to be peaceful, happy and quiet upon the earth's surface. Pacific, rooted living is embodied in the unique instance of Ruth Wilcox—who significantly has come of Quaker stock and has wished the rector's sermons would shine with 'a more inward light' (Ch. 11). For her, places are more important than people because she sees the primacy of a proper home-base and home-centredness in the construction of an individual life's value.

> Then she said vehemently: 'It is monstrous, Miss Schlegel; it isn't right. I had no idea that this was hanging over you. I do pity you from the bottom of my heart. To be parted from your house, your father's house—it oughtn't to be allowed. It is worse than dying. I would rather die than—Oh, poor girls! Can what they call civilization be right, if people mayn't die in the room where they were born? My dear, I am so sorry—'
> Margaret did not know what to say. Mrs. Wilcox had been overtired by her shopping, and was inclined to hysteria.
> 'Howards End was nearly pulled down once. It would have killed me.' (Ch. 10)

In the larger process of the book as a whole, as we move from scene to scene, house or apartment to apartment or house while the heroine seeks an appropriate abode and way of life within them ('Oniton was to prove one of her innumerable false starts', Ch. 25) we are made to develop, like her, a barely suppressed impatience at the flaw in her society whereby endemically and of its essential dynamic it fails to 'rest on the earth'. These false starts cumulatively evoke wakeful exasperation at the lack of settled and focused living all around the cosmopolite Schlegels, as on their own part.

> 'Curious mounds,' said Henry, 'but in with you now; another time.' He had to be in London by seven—if possible, by six-thirty. Once more she lost the sense of space; once more trees, houses, people, animals, hills merged and heaved into one dirtiness, and she was at Wickham Place. (Ch. 24)

The motor-car constantly invades the scene over the course of this story and is always associated with some failure in discrimination and morality. At the beginning it is practically as much provocative as mere backdrop of the quarrel between Mrs. Munt and Charles Wilcox; a motor-smash brings the noisy family back to London from their northern tour prematurely (Ch. 10) just when Mrs. Wilcox is about to take Margaret Schlegel down to Howards End; on the way to Oniton the car in which the latter is travelling runs over a cat, whose owner 'screamed wildly at them'.

Margaret felt their whole journey from London had been unreal. They had no part with the earth and its emotions. They were dust, and a stink, and cosmopolitan chatter, and the girl whose cat had been killed had lived more deeply than they. (Ch. 25)

One day when I called on the author he told me he had just been dipping in *Howards End*. He could no longer remember the book as a whole but did recall 'the scene where they run over a cat and don't mind because it isn't a dog!' (It was assumed by some during his last years, simply on the ground of their tally being so advanced, that Forster must be senile. This was the very opposite of the truth. His *memory* was impaired and he had other difficulties, but as a thinking being he was 100% as competent as ever; and occasionally, in a very gentle charitable way, would run rings round visitors a half or one-third of his age who had come to be patronizing or pompous.)

Logic tells us that the process epitomized by the motor-car in this novel is inexorable and irreversible. Forster faced up to the grim prospects for our civilization increasingly as the years went by after 1910 and the *Commonplace Book* records his progressive disillusion, so that even the fall of a brutal régime in his beloved Italy prompts a general lament about the world's future at large.

Rec[*euillement*[33]]. *cont. next day.* It is 11.0. again [on Monday 26 July 1943]. Musso has resigned and disturbed me by superficial hopes. I know that there will be no betterment in my lifetime—or that betterment like worsement is something too deep to be observed at any particular moment. What I do see and this morning hear is machinery used for evil. And machinery will be used increasingly. That is the knockout first intercepted by Ruskin and Baudelaire, as Butler, now by Gandhi and by punies like Barbe Baker, Lionel Fichter, William Plomer & myself. I cannot rid myself of the theory that men will one day stop making and using machines, and revert with a tired sigh to the woods. But who will start the stopping? The Managerial Class? My dears, is it likely? Bombless anarchy? Honester in my thinking than most people, I fake the remoter future instead of the present, to help myself to bear the present. If I pursued my conclusions, I should let down my friends [i.e. have a nervous breakdown, commit suicide?]. I *do* love several people and want to help them. Don't know why and am incapable of asking why and bored by the answers pasted on me by psychoanalysis. I may read Barnham's Managerial Revolution disingenuously, but can't read Freud at all.

This then is the falsity in my outlook: 'I say chaps—don't let us develop machinery any more—let's be less organised.' Is it likely that the decay of human energy, which may come about, will take this congenial form?

What would the world be, once bereft
Of wet and of wildness? Let them be left
O let them be left, wildness and wet;
Long live the weeds and the wilderness yet.

Wildness and Wet are being removed, and if they do return we shall be too degraded-feeble to appreciate them.

This receuillement has proceeded too long.

And by 10.0.P.M. I have done no work. Have just heard a helpful sincere and untrue talk from Priestley; man the master of his future (isn't); young wouldn't have fought as they have without believing in a better future (they fought to save their skins and their homes).[34]

For long decades now it has looked as if weeds and wilderness will successively be ever more edited out of the geosphere by the dominance of man's will commercially and politically to exploit it. (Yet it should not be said this *will actually* happen. Anything is possible in the hearts and destinies of men, and perhaps the human species, just before it has eliminated too many game 'reserves' and all-but-extinct species will suddenly itself be speedily thinned to a scant remnant by a plague-massacre of its own scientific development's creation. Will this be AIDS[35] or a bacterium turned monstrous by our heavy abuse of antibiotics, crops and soil, our rape of Nature in the cause of too-easy farming and medicine? AIDS looks like a proleptic signal. In that case mankind will continue, but in a few scattered steadings on the globe incapable of too much dictatorship again over organic life for a very lengthy era. To say as much is not to recommend the release of viruses from Porton Down, or wherever, by crank conservationists; that might trigger off universal destruction of all life-forms; murder is murder and its wages worse still than death of the body;

122

'It must needs be that offences come; but woe to that man by whom the offence cometh!' and anyway it means working for a deeper, more thorough, abiding and creative victory over ourselves and for our terrene environment when we strive for a change of direction through spiritual rather than microbial assaults.)

Inevitable as a future seems with 'roads full of cars, skies full of aeroplanes, and the very heart of night throbbing with little noises that man has made',[36] the strange and wonderful thing is that, without recourse to apocalyptic shifts or scientifictional foresquints, *Howards End* is redolent of a sense of human evolution that is benign. The opening of Chapter 31 expresses the tone of this.

> Houses have their own ways of dying, falling as variously as the generations of men, some with a tragic roar, some quietly, but to an after-life in the city of ghosts, while from others—and thus was the death of Wickham Place—the spirit slips before the body perishes. It had decayed in the spring, disintegrating the girls more than they knew, and causing either to accost unfamiliar regions. By September it was a corpse, void of emotion, and scarcely hallowed by the memories of thirty years of happiness. Through its round-topped doorway passed furniture, and pictures, and books, until the last room was gutted and the last van had rumbled away. It stood for a week or two longer, open-eyed, as if astonished at its own emptiness. Then it fell. Navvies came, and spilt it back into the grey. With their muscles and their beery good temper, they were not the worst of undertakers for a house which had always been human, and had not mistaken culture for an end.

That is elegiac but not only so. The Wickham Place apartment, scene and repository of the best Schlegel days, appears to 'mulch down', as we may say, into the London soil after the fashion of leaf-mould in a garden, for the fecundity of spiritual life in the future. And this fertilization we see in practice when Helen carries to their logical conclusion her father's principles while dealing with the Basts, or more generally across the trajectory of the whole tale Margaret finds she has 'charged straight into these Wilcoxes and broken up their lives' (Ch. 44).

Henry's family are trade and Empire; Paul is a type of English colonialism in Africa; and we feel that this is wobbling, that an inner emptiness makes their sorts of enterprise at home and abroad not only hollow but also frail. The youngest son is, for example, like his brother, hardly very intelligent, subtle or adept at manipulating matters:

> Paul rose to his feet. He was accustomed to natives, and a very little shook him out of the Englishman. Feeling manly and cynical, he said: 'Down in the field? Oh, come! I think we might have had the whole establishment, piccaninnies included.' (ibid.)

Cumulatively we are infused with the feeling that life is developing and developing to a goal. This comes to us from a thousand touches and traits; sometimes individual items in the story's plot, sometimes from the novelist's open philosophizing, pointing the moral and adorning the tale:

> To Leonard, intent on his private sin, there came the conviction of innate goodness elsewhere. It was not the optimism which he had been taught at school. Again and again must the drums tap, the goblins stalk over the universe before joy can be purged of the superficial. (Ch. 41)

> At such moments the soul retires within, to float upon the bosom of a deeper stream, and has communion with the dead, and sees the world's glory not diminished, but different in kind to what she has supposed. (Ch. 43)

> . . . the chaotic nature of our daily life, and its difference from the orderly sequence that has been fabricated by historians. Actual life is full of false clues and sign-posts that lead nowhere. . . . Life is indeed dangerous, but not in the way morality would have us believe. It is indeed unmanageable, but the essence of it is not a battle. It is unmanageable because it is a romance. . . . (Ch. 12)

Howards End offers, then, for its deepest achievement, a visionary sense of life—in its totality, the entire human organum—as evolving toward a goal of great fulfilment: creative, pacific, contented, this-worldly. In the very fact that by the end the heroines across all their stumblings have discovered a home where they can know tranquillity, we would be willing to see the theme properly epitomized and to hope that mankind's muddling and fumbling is the means whereby the key is being turned in the lock of its technologico-industrialized fate. To laugh at any intuition of the approach of an Earthly Paradise is otiose; so much intelligence is required, in the first place, to imagine a living version of the like, quite apart from the fact that on this side of its accomplishment Forster's fourth novel puts together its mosaic of ameliorist hints and hopes with tremendous skill.

The book fails to convince as a whole, however, because its antitheses are not equitably worked out. It is all very fine to oppose Death against Money and the life of imagination against that of action but it is a lampoon, not a fair debate, where the representatives of commercial, imperialist and other derring-do are so easily contemptible. Margaret Schlegel keeps putting the case for the private-free-enterprise spirit, trading development and so forth, but in the nature of his fable and its characterizations the author entirely fails to put flesh upon the bones of her argument.

> If Wilcoxes hadn't worked and died in England for thousands of years, you and I couldn't sit here without having our throats cut. There would be no trains, no ships to carry us literary people about in, no fields even. Just savagery. No—perhaps not even that. Without their spirit life might never have moved out of protoplasm. More and more do I refuse to draw my income and sneer at those who guarantee it. (Ch. 19)

Well stated, but that is just how the performance of the family she marries into is never allowed to strike us. Confronted by any actual instance of Wilcox deed or speech we can only feel how unnecessary, vulgar and antipathetic it is. Henry's dealings in rubber are unspecified. 'The genial, tentative host disappeared, and they saw instead the man who had carved money out of Greece and Africa, and bought forests from the natives for a few bottles of gin' (Ch. 34). Early and late his conduct and utterances are only exploitive or dishonest. He turns out to have cheated his first wife, to want his second in a subordinate unchallenging role; to manipulate property as investment not as spiritual homes; and his children and their spouses are considerably cruder. They disparage those who do not agree with them and patronize the poor but not the arts; they are bullying and greedy merely, and one can scour the novel in vain for one generous impulse finding birth or expression amongst them. In short, the Opposition (to the life of fine consciences) has not been given a fair hearing, whereas in *A Passage to India* the novelist is fair, one may say deadly fair, to both sides, Indian and Anglo-Indian.

This is typified in the central plot-hinge on which the story turns. We are supposed to see the Miss Schlegels' scrupulosity as moral sensoria set over against their incompetence in the 'outer life of telegrams and anger'; *vice versa* in the Ducie Street household. So logically Margaret and Helen should have sensitive ideas about Leonard Bast, his needs and outward-reachings, while giving him bad career-advice when exigent issues come to the point. In contrast Henry Wilcox, for all his political attitude towards the insurance clerk's class being unhandsome, should make them pause in their free-thinking tracks by giving him a good employment-tip and thus alone of the different extraneous persons who take an interest in Bast's future being of practical use and solid help.

> 'Walking is well enough when a man's in work,' Leonard answered. 'Oh, I did talk a lot of nonsense once, but there's nothing like a bailiff in the house to drive it out of you. When I saw him fingering my Ruskins and Stevensons, I seemed to see life straight real, and it isn't a pretty sight. My books are back again, thanks to you, but they'll never be the same to me again, and I shan't ever again think night in the woods is wonderful.' (Ch. 27)

Instead it is, if anything, the other way about. As well as embodying the worst sides of commercial imperialism and the ruling classes' thought, Wilcox senior proves a bruised reed exactly when it comes to City-talk, investment tips (Bast's investment of his labour) and practical action; as does his son Charles near the end, in being so impetuous, passionate and uncalculating that he gets himself into jail for homicide. Contradistinctively the two sisters from Wickham Place with their serious attempts to regain employment for Leonard, Helen's payment of his debts and her offer of half her fortune, show for the active agents of material aid in the outer world of adventurous doing which is supposed par excellence to be the Wilcoxes' sphere.

The sexual psychology of the book would anyway be vapid in a degree, because it simply is not part of E. M. Forster's equipment to be able to represent convincingly attraction between male and female persons. But this is weakened still further, rendered yet more implausible by his failure to show the Wilcoxes as having—Mrs. Ruth Wilcox of course excepted—any real positive quality or competence at all. Margaret Schlegel's interest in the head of the family would just begin to be credible if we beheld him, through her eyes, as a man who gets necessary things done while women like herself with political opinions dither to fatuous effect; but that dichotomy is never truly enacted. Of the two of them, she is the one palpably shown for the practical disposer and gainer (his money-makings all take place offstage). Likewise her sister with Leonard Bast. We think rather of his 'fatal forgotten umbrella' as having fathered Helen's child than the now destitute insurance-clerk (Katherine Mansfield's cruel *bon mot*) all the more readily because Helen has not been squashed into a philosophical tight corner by Wilcox proficiency and virtues. Their alleged strong points she has seen through by the end of Chapter 2 *et pour cause*. Bating again their mother, this family *has* no significant values or capabilities.

To make that complaint is not to write off *Howards End* as an approved literary collapse. Forster does keep bashing away at a somnolent duck of a target whose ethics never were defensible. 'The Great North Road should have been bordered all its length with glebe. Henry's kind had filched most of it' (Ch. 43). But there is much else in the novel beside the crudity of the Wilcoxes as representatives of Business and its behaviour. The treatment of poverty here is wholly unfalsified, and exactly on this account I agree with D. H. Lawrence in finding the portrait of Leonard Bast a success,[37] shot through as it is with painful subtle ironies.

There is his heart-complaint, though he is the grandson of sturdy yeoman-farmers: a malady which convinces and signifies no less at the physical than symbolic levels (he is rarely represented as getting a square meal and always as trying to live beyond the foreshortened strength his dietary gives him).

Even the somewhat embarrassing reference to 'the keenest happiness he had ever known' being 'during a railway journey to Cambridge, where a decent-mannered undergraduate had spoken to him' (Ch. 14) crystallizes the pathos of a mind caught between two sorts of living and failing of both of them just because our society has ceased to 'rest on the earth' in an agrarian modality and the modern alternative city-existence falls short of providing the very fulfilments, of spirit, of intellect, with which its urban industrialized aggregations have enticed men to join them.

> Hints of robustness survived in him, more than a hint of primitive good looks, and Margaret, noting the spine that might have been straight, and the chest that might have broadened, wondered whether it paid to give up the glory of the animal for a tail coat and a couple of ideas. . . . She knew this type very well—the vague aspirations, the mental dishonesty, the familiarity with the outsides of books. (ibid.)

Of course this idealizes the old feudal type of society, something which as to any generosity of spirit between its human members is in my own experience quite appalling to inhabit. Yet in this and other ways the novel does present very livingly the question, how much are we what our income makes us? Is there a residue of quintessential selfhood, or is that fashioned out of our material circumstances?

Generally the book is informed by tremendous humanity. Time and again Forster elucidates the most fugitive failures or penetrations of loving-kindness in mortal creatures' intercourse and in so doing wakes up our moral nerve-ends, makes our own discriminations more articulate and thereby operatively more capable.

> 'Are you the boy whom I saw playing in the stacks last week?'
> The child hung his head.
> 'Well, run away and do it again.'
> 'Nice little boy,' whispered Helen. 'I say, what's your name? Mine's Helen.'
> 'Tom.'
> That was Helen all over. The Wilcoxes, too, would ask a child its name, but they never told their names in return.
> 'Tom, this one here is Margaret. And at home we've another called Tibby.'

'Mine are lop-eareds,' replied Tom, supposing Tibby to be a
rabbit.
'You're a very good and rather a clever little boy. . . .'
(Ch. 37)

It is also in a relaxed way exhilarating. As when reading
Jane Austen, we rustle with continuous quiet shocks of perception for page after page the gaps between the publicly
presented, inwardly acknowledged and actual motive for a
given action are slily noted by one of the closest observers of
human behaviour.

> 'The facts as they touch Meg are all before you,' she added;
> and Tibby sighed and felt it rather hard that, because of his
> open mind, he should be empanelled to serve as a juror. He had
> never been interested in human beings, for which one must
> blame him, but he had had rather too much of them at
> Wickham Place. Just as some people cease to attend when
> books are mentioned, so Tibby's attention wandered when
> 'personal relations' came under discussion. Ought Margaret to
> know what Helen knew the Basts to know? Similar questions
> had vexed him from infancy, and at Oxford he had learned to
> say that the importance of human beings has been vastly over-
> rated by specialists. The epigram, with its faint whiff of the
> eighties, meant nothing. But he might have let it off now if his
> sister had not been ceaselessly beautiful. (Ch. 30)

Thus the book's account of Theobald Schlegel's inhumanity,
which is always shown in this wise. Indeed it is not too much
to say that the whole novel is one of the supreme dwelling-
places in our literature of two of the Four Loves, Caritas and
Philadelphia, loving-kindness and fraternal affection. Tibby is
thoroughly placed, if you will, and drastically—as in Tom's
comment, unwittingly apt, above; but his coldness is traced to
its origins and understood even if it cannot ultimately be
forgiven.

Moreover I know of few other novels where things seem so
thoroughly—and yet so interestingly—a slice of life, uncoerced
by the needs of onward-propelling story. Is this because the
characters moralize as much as they do—that is to say, as
frequently as a certain class of people do in real life, more
frequently than the Novel-form has up to our own century
confessed—though the trick is not overplayed; or is it because

Forster activates such considerable and various masses on his canvas, brings in so many entities, they appear non-plot-impelled even while all adds up in fact to a closely-stitched tapesty of a narrative?

Either way it is a major work on anybody's scale, and while we may demur at this element or that,[38] we cannot do without the nutriment it affords. This author is not among those who put forth all their strengths together in one book which is to be considered as a perfect enterprise. His virtue is scattered across. his *oeuvre* as a whole and *Howards End* enriches our lives with experiences the other fictions do not offer.

NOTES

1. His amanuensis as well as biographer.
2. From his essay 'The Novels of E. M. Forster' (*The Nineteenth Century and After*, November 1934), reproduced with the Everyman editions of *A Passage to India* (1942, 1957) and most recently the Abinger text of the same novel, the term here quoted being locatable on p. 319 of this last-named volume.
3. Ibid., pp. 319–20.
4. From the author's Terminal Note to *Maurice*, last paragraph of section headed 'Notes on the three men'.
5. *Commonplace Book* (London, 1978), p. 49.
6. Id. loc.
7. J. H. Plumb, *England in the Eighteenth Century (1714–1815)* (Harmondsworth, 1950), p. 82.
8. *Commonplace Book*, p. 51.
9. I quote here from stanza 6 of Wordsworth's Immortality Ode, and for the same reason that I enlisted the tenth line of the sonnet 'The world is too much with us' two pages back. To say that *The Longest Journey* is Wordsworthian is about as 'de-naturing' of its achievement as it would be to remark of Wordsworth's great poems that they are Forsterian-in-the-character-of-*The Longest Journey*. My point is, these great *opera* have an equivalent and related value, are all-important testimonies flowering upon the same tree.
10. 'Sunday church was a function at Cadover, though a strange one. The pompous landau rolled up to the house at a quarter to eleven. Then Mrs. Failing said, "Why am I being hurried?" and after an interval descended the steps in her ordinary clothes. She regarded the church as a sort of sitting-room, and refused even to wear a bonnet there. The village was shocked, but at the same time a little proud; it would point

out the carriage to strangers and gossip about the pale smiling lady who sat in it, always alone, always late, her hair always draped in an expensive shawl' (Ch. 13).

11. *The Waste Land*, line 41.
12. *Life*, Vol. II, p. 57.
13. By 'our society' I mean the planet at large. A poet in, say, Tonga or the African Sahel, possessed by a vision similar to that which Forster has embodied in this novel would nowadays be too much aware of it as o'ercrowed by the triumph of the Machine. Such regions would seem harmonious on sufferance, not titanically so with the voice of adamantine Fate. *The Longest Journey* was written in the last trembling of the balance before all tilted into technology's shaping. Thence, plus its own genius as a literary work, arises its distinction.
14. *Life*, Vol. I, p. 75.
15. In *Arctic Summer and Other Fiction*, Abinger Edition, Vol. 9 (London, 1980).
16. Wordsworth, *The Prelude* (1850 version), Book Eleventh, 'France (*concluded*)', conclusion of the fourth verse-paragraph.
17. I quote these words from Ezra Pound's, as it were obituary, tribute to Henry James in *The Little Review* for August 1918 (pp. 6–9). He is commenting on the 'pettiness talked about Henry James's style. The subject has been discussed enough in all conscience, along with the minor James. What I have not heard is any word of the major James, of the hater of tyranny. . . .'
18. Published in *The Life to Come and Other Stories*, Abinger Edition, Vol. 8 (London, 1972).
19. Forster's own words in his Introduction to the Collected edition of his short stories (London, 1947).
20. *Aspects of the Novel*, para. 7 of Ch. 6.
21. *Commonplace Book*, p. 240.
22. Ibid., under the heading 'Book' at the very end of the volume (unpaginated portion of the whole).
23. Leon Edel & Gordon N. Ray (eds.) *Henry James and H. G. Wells [A Record of their Friendship, their Debate on the Art of Fiction and their Quarrel]* (London, 1958), p. 267, from item 70 in the volume, James's final letter to Wells, of 10 July 1915.
24. *Acts of the Apostles*, Ch. 17, vv. 22, 23.
25. *This* I take to be the Atheist's crunching Ace of a debating-point; and matchlessly it is expressed by Sophocles too. The question 'Is there a God?' answered however affirmatively, I suppose such a philosopher to waive. 'The Universe logically must have a first cause,' he may remark, 'and it is probable, since intellective mind seems creatively superior to that which it observes, that first cause has something in the nature of a Personality as our genus recognises the phenomenon. But all this is trivialized by the conditions under which sentient life is carried on. They are so painful and absurd, one can only deduce this first cause ("God" is far too loaded a term) is either malefic—a rather petulant and therefore silly point of view (why should It go to any trouble just to put *our*

miniscule noses out of joint?)—or It is interested in achievements and goals quite other than anything with which human beings (for instance) can identify.'

To this argument Christianity, otherwise tongue-tied, responds by alleging that It has participated, in fullest measure and on the same terms as members of the animal and vegetable creation, in 'the horror and the boredom' as well as 'the glory' (T. S. Eliot's phrase) it has begotten—that is to say, in Christ's Passion.

No answer, if you do not believe the Gospels' records to be true, or to be aptly interpreted by the churches. And not a complete answer anyway, in an ethical debate conducted on logical principles solely. But it gives the whole aspect of the cosmos a different character, if one *be* convinced. I make this point here because it will be relevant when we come to discuss *A Passage to India*.

26. *Two Cheers for Democracy*, Part 2, under 'Art in General'.
27. From ibid., p. 82.
28. I adapt thus Forster's own image in one of his *Commonplace Book* entries; this, after reading Eddington and his *Nature of the Physical World*: '. . . The seriousness of a large housefly can't be taken very seriously' (p. 57).
29. To be found in the *Arctic Summer and Other Fiction* volume.
30. The Abinger editor represents this phrase as: 'and he [die] and [lose] his body altogether'. But is not the verb 'stop' qualifying the rest of its sentence? (op. cit., *proximo supra*, p. 84.)
31. *Life*, Vol. I, p. 198.
32. *Commonplace Book*, p. 218.
33. I.e. collection or gathering-together of himself in peaceful contemplation.
34. *Commonplace Book*, p. 167.
35. The new Acquired Immune Deficiency Syndrome 'first noted in 1979 in New York, San Francisco and Los Angeles, although a case was identified in Cologne in 1976 which is little mentioned.' For more information see, *inter tanta alia* being currently published on the subject, the article by Duncan Fallowell in *The Times* of London for Wednesday 27 July 1983, p. 8, from which the above quotation is extracted.
36. *Commonplace Book*, p. 52, an entry of 1928 under the heading *Death an escape into the non-human*, which begins 'That, if consciousness survives, will be an adventure worth attempting after roads full of cars', etc.
37. See *Life*, Vol II, p. 10.
38. The creative act here is shot through with paradox. Just as one thinks of *Howards End* as a supremely humane utterance even though it is so jejunely unfair to the Wilcoxes, so one finds in a novel fashioned with evidences of unusual control, authorial skittishness which does not really know what it would be at. The book has its couple of 'in-house jokes' as one may say, little jests which Forsterians are to enjoy from having read the earlier works of the same writer. In Chapter 13 Margaret says to her brother, on the subject of his gaining a profession, 'I was thinking of Mr. Vyse. He never strikes me as particularly happy.' and it turns out that this latter (almost certainly Cecil from *A Room with a View*) is the type

Tibby most likes. Then she compares him with an unlovely kind of opposite: 'Look at the Wilcoxes, look at Mr. Pembroke.' These references give us bits of authorial coy cleverness in exactly a manner that the wholesale inclusion of Forster's own short story 'Other Kingdom' into conversation and the fabric of *The Longest Journey* or the hilarious pointed, even slightly poignant, mention there of 'a certain Miss Herriton' (*LJ*, Ch. 16) whom Mr. Pembroke but briefly thinks of proposing to, do not. Traditional theories about the organic nature of a great artist's inspiration and his material's *disponibilité* as it grows count for little in face of this book which exemplifies total mastery and unintegrated creative impulses by turns.

4

Maurice, Other Stories, *Arctic Summer*

Forster's career in 1913 illustrates two golden rules which ought to be inscribed upon every creative artist's conscience: (1) Repress yourself, encourage your themes to come forth in sublimated form, and (2) Don't hold your breath. Once enticed by a compelling idea-emotion toil at it as fast as possible, for the night may come in which no man can work— not merely your own death but a war, plague, famine or revolution that leaves your scheme disorientated—and unnecessary delays now will likely have you kicking yourself afterward.

'So here I am with 3 unfinished novels on my hands' laments a diary-entry of 17 December that year. The three were his Indian novel, *Arctic Summer,* and *Maurice.* The first he managed to complete after the European conflict that came the following August. His editor has notably remarked of this fulfilment

> Perhaps we should even regard *A Passage to India,* gratefully, as a magnificent rearguard action, initiated before the turning-point came with *Maurice,* and completed with the aid of a theme that relegated sex to a minor role.[1]

Fair enough, and it may have proved no disadvantage to that novel that the Great War intervened between its conception-beginning (1912) and completion (1921–24). Forster's Anglo-India is arguably the more representative of itself for spanning both sides of the convulsion and not being so strictly located *in*

134

time that the Marabar Case looks like some now dated reworking of contemporary circumstances surrounding the 1911 Durbar or the Amritsar Massacre, say, of a decade later, but becomes type of the whole Raj's administrative relationships and tensions. In any event, India was not so drastically transformed by the aftermath of Sarajevo in the way—I mean to say, immediately—that the consciousness of a Western intellectual had to be. Forster visiting Dewas State Senior in 1921 was a whole lot more altered—any Briton had to be— than his environment there in the intervening nine years.

But that he began *Maurice* with 'exaltation' and, overcoming various checks, wrote that novel 'during the following Spring . . . at speed'[2] rather than sublimating its material into *Arctic Summer* seems to me a first-class disaster.

Since its publication in 1971 *Maurice* has had so bad a press that I feel churlish for lobbing one more brick. Yet the worst of it is not the book's sentimentality and lack of control; rather, that there is no subject there, no treatment of a central issue. It is a novel so thoroughly void of a theme it fails even of being a *roman à thèse* Campaigning for Homosexual Equality, as an established organization in Britain nowadays does. For essentially it is just a personal yell from one particular individual declaring his sexual loneliness and crying out for a bed-partner; to which the only response ever can be 'oh dear'. Authors can make great literature out of solitariness and emotional hunger. Frequently they do; perhaps even usually. 'Lips only sing', one of our poets has told us, 'when they cannot kiss.' But *Villette* is a great book as *Maurice* is not because Charlotte Brontë had at least enough understanding of the character of sexual appetite to know it can only become interesting and illuminated in a literary ado where *relationship between personalities* can be envisaged.

Forster seems to have been incapable of this in regard to homosexual affinities in his writings and—some of the time at least—in his life. 'Lust and tenderness bring relief': the *Commonplace Book* thus enunciates his position on the whole business at one point.[3] Well, it is a view, but not one with which imaginative writing can do anything. *There* we have to feel the reality of two characters in the quality of their appeal to each other. Individually the three main personages of the suppressed posthumously published work come off in an intermittent way: Clive Durham, Maurice Hall, Alec Scudder; but the kinds of needs in Maurice's nature which Alec's personality (or body) satisfies are never elucidated. We are just told that the two men want to go to bed together and do, and we have to take the magnetism between them as a *donnée*. It merits the same strictures Forster himself made upon younger fictionists' treatment of sexual love at large:

> *No sensuousness* in contemporary novels. If lust is described it is with contempt or scientifically. No effort to involve reader in toils. Contrast Silvia's Lovers (p. 136): how attractive, and to each other, are Silvia & Charlie.[4]

Solider ground has given way under our feet by the time this very immaterialized relation has emerged. The Clive of Cambridge days, whose own transmutation into a hetero-sexual and squirearchical 'jolly old boy'[5] is itself artistically pretty thoroughly unaccomplished, is imaginable as a mate for the Maurice of their early confederacy together: his intellec-tualism and bodily delicacy appeals to the other's athleticism and robustness and *vice versa*. Their beings are shown to be complementary and to attract (e.g. second half of Ch. 16).

But we are not then given the logic of this relationship *either* working through to a 'durable fire' *or* going off its own rails *or* being thrown by social invasion. Clive's temperament is switched by his creator so that the issues which the affinity has begun to focus—should such love be 'platonic' or physically expressed; can it survive in any known society; can such affections in men so young develop, etc.?—are left standing just where the book ought to begin to explore them.

Instead, the novelist attempts a legerdemain. We are to see Maurice as 'saved' from 'Suburbia' and its values (in the terms of the 'Terminal Note' to the book that Forster furnished in 1960) by a class-conflict's involvement in Alec's sex-appeal.

Yet this is a red-herring, as Lytton Strachey was moved to remonstrate at the time (when shown the novel after its accomplishment in 1914).[6] The problem of Maurice's snobbery and false social values generally never comes alive in the way that, for instance, the Herritons' do in *Where Angels Fear to Tread* or Herbert Pembroke's in *The Longest Journey*. The book is too much concerned to dramatize the need of an individual to break out of sexual orthodoxy and society's constraints in that dimension. Having chopped up the camel of *that* moral law, Maurice is not going to strain at the gnat of social distinctions. Nor does he. He invites his new comrade, on the contrary, to toss everything away—both their careers (and sources of income), all connections, relatives (how?), the lot—like confetti in a world well lost. And indeed the novel's weakest element of all is its handling of the social framework, especially in the conclusion. By what manner, even in a perpetuated 1913 and 'an England where it was still possible to get lost'[7] could two men of such dissimilar background, speech-accents and the rest of it, do that? They would surely have stood out, amid any surroundings, however remote, like a beacon. It is of a piece with the book's whole day-dreaming weakness, its intellectual and emotional inchoateness, that it fails to engage with that major issue as well.

I write thus ungraciously about this work (for it has incidental felicities) because I strongly suspect its begetting made still-born *Arctic Summer*—of which we have enough to be pretty sure that the latter was a far superior birth. One intuits that had Forster continued to force his unpublishable sexual desires down the channel of respectable fiction-writing, he would have found an objective-correlative means for doing so with the relation between Martin Whitby and Clesant March. Having instead brought off a happy-ever-after homosexual story, no wonder that the creative thrust failed in him to identify a 'solid mass ahead, a mountain round or over or through which . . . the story must somehow go'; that he 'had not settled what is going to happen and this is why the novel remains a fragment'.[8]

Arctic Summer, started in the Spring of 1911, six months after the very successful publication of *Howards End*, has a theme which has been well summarized by Mr. Furbank as an extension of the predicament staring its creator's own life in the face at that time:

> To work, nevertheless, was the necessity. But to work in what spirit, or supported by what desires? As usual, he broadened the question and made it a general issue of human conduct. Some of his friends, like Dickinson and George Trevelyan, Russell and the Sangers, worked very zealously at public

causes, such as education, Fabianism, women's suffrage and
international understanding. To work in their fashion, and to
make this the goal of one's middle age, was a dignified and
attractive ambition, but it had its dubious aspect too. It might
make life better for humanity, but might it not also make it
greyer? This antithesis preoccupied him and began to offer the
subject for a novel. In *Howards End* he had weighed death
against money; in his new novel . . . he would oppose battle to
work. He would contrast the civilized and socially useful man,
who longs for an 'arctic summer', a long cool spell in which to
carry through worthwhile work, with the chivalrous man, the
knight-errant, who wants not to work but to fight for his faith.
It was a promising theme, and he addressed himself to it
hopefully—suffering more seriously now, however, from fears
of 'going smash'.[9]

Martin Whitby, a civil servant with a promising career and
enlightened 'modern' wife Venetia, goes travelling with her
and his mother-in-law Lady Borlase in Northern Italy. There
they meet and somewhat exasperate a very different type of
compatriot, Clesant March, a young soldier with antique
notions of heroism and of chivalry towards women. The
Whitbys would be able to pigeonhole him as a reactionary
Tory with outdated principles (Venetia does so) but for a
sequence of events. The story begins with March saving
Martin's life as, in a jostling crowd on Basle station, the elder
man is nearly pushed under the wheels of the oncoming train
which the mêlée of tourists are fighting (in an amusing piece of
Forster comedy) to enter. (All the British are calling upon one
another to be 'Gentlemen', i.e. let Number One get aboard
first, for the vehicle is heavily overbooked.) Further, March's
instinctual kind of behaviour in that crisis—the heroic
unthinking pounce practically under the locomotive—contrasts
very favourably with what Martin finds out about himself later
on during the trip: his own physical cowardice. Whitby has
taken his Italian chauffeur, who is lame, to the cinema one
evening. Suddenly the temperamental celluloid bursts into
flame, the little theatre is engulfed in smoke and fire and
Martin next discovers himself, in the uproar's trice, as out in
the street having fled and left his hobbled companion to fend
for himself. The fact that the chauffeur has also escaped
unharmed, in the event, is not the point.

Whitby confesses the whole thing that night to his wife and rejoices that in her Fabian intellectualism she thinks nothing of the episode, whereas a 'womanly woman' might forgive but would never forget it. Yet his system of values, hitherto so secure and thought-out in their civilizedness, is shaken.

The antithesis between March and Whitby is further illustrated, however, by their attitude to women. On a visit in Milan, preparatory to making a recommended trip to the neighbouring castle of 'Tramonta', the two men encounter a minx who keeps house for her father the castle's owner and who attempts to exploit them, during his absence, rather in a sinister version—certainly morally and perhaps even financially blackmailing—of the romantic absurdities of Flora Finching in *Little Dorrit*. She tries to make a lot of having been alone with them in the house while her father is away, but Martin simply and decisively stamps on this by declaring exactly what has happened when he returns; and Lieutenant March is shocked at such candour. The young Clesant assumes that a woman's good name should always jealously be guarded by any gentleman at whatever cost.

But the novel further vindicates Martin's view. Clesant hero-worships his elder brother and greatly aggravates the latter's sufferings at Cambridge precisely because they have been brought up on 'extravagant notions of man's duty to women'[10] by their northern matriarch and, still more, her stern brother (their father has died early in their lives, in some disgrace). Lance, the brother, is to be sent down from his college for sexual misdemeanour with a woman. His sibling cannot believe the charge and, in becoming disillusioned when its truth is confessed, so curses his former hero that Lance commits suicide.

Now there are weaknesses in the fragments as they stand; we are dealing after all with an unrevised and uncompleted masterpiece. There is, maybe, a little too much 'interior moralizing' as one may call it on Martin Whitby's part at the novel's opening, derived from the Italian scenery; and we need a more solidly constituted reason for something which looks borrowed rather heavily out of Henry James's ghost stories:

Lieutenant March's appearance, in the portrait of an heroic military ancestor, in a big mural at the Tramonta castle. This is a decisive moment in Whitby's moral education. Once again I avail myself of Mr. Furbank's unimproveable summary:

> Visiting a castle near Milan, where there is a fresco of the battle of Lepanto, he notices, with strange emotion, that one of the warriors in the painting resembles Clesant March. He notes in his journal: 'Very moving: warriors about to fight for their country and faith,' and is amazed at what he has written, 'so little resemblance did it bear to his usual art-criticism'. The vision, for this is what it is, stays with him, and gradually it develops into a *malaise*.[11]

As a plot-aid and as it stands that episode is too much like a useful coincidence in a spooky tale; and Henry James had anyway already used up the idea in such tall stories as 'Owen Wingrave'. Likewise the suicide at this literary torso's ending is a little too pat, melodramatic and therefore sentimentalized in its emotive charge. It has not been quite sufficiently worked up to—or at least would need more retroactive substantiation than the fragment, there breaking off, provides.

When we have named those minor blemishes, however, we have catalogued all the faults of what promises to have proved, *had* it been pushed through (however recalcitrantly—Forster laboured against the grain with misgiving and distaste, after all, through most of *A Passage to India*[12]) a better novel still than *Howards End* or *A Passage*, perhaps. For *Arctic Summer* articulates a central predicament of human living, for the individual and the community, for the individual-in-the-community, which even two great wars and the possibility now of global extinction in a third, have not outdated. Should we strive for 'the millenium towards which all good citizens are co-operating' (Section or Chapter 1) or should we be individualist, heroic and instinctual in reaction to our mortal apportionment?

The author very lightly touched up his mss. to their fifth chapter's conclusion and delivered these at the Aldeburgh Festival of 1951, explaining to the audience at the end of his reading why the book had not been completed and why he was not then uttering even the whole of what had been originally accomplished: '. . . there is about half as much of it again—

. . . but . . . it now goes off"[13]; and supplementing the standard
account of the novel's fundamental failure in conception (no
transforming 'major event' towards and through which the
tale could move). He had dealt competently with the Whitbys,
including, I may add, Venetia's very enlightened and likeable
sister Dorothea, and would have done so no less with her
father than with her mother (the Borlases); and he had
realized well Martin and his background. But the other family
were inadequately provided:

> I think I know about March. He is first and foremost heroic, no
> thought of self when the blood is up, he can pounce and act
> rightly, he is generous, idealistic, loyal. When his blood is not
> up, when conditions are unfavourable, he is apt to be dazed,
> trite and sour—the hero straying into the modern world which
> does not want him and which he does not understand. Part of
> his idealism takes the form of fantastic chivalry towards women.
> How should such a character be presented? Impressionisti-
> cally—that is to say he should come and go, and not be
> documented, in contrast to the Whitby's [*sic*] and Borlase's who
> can't be documented too much. I managed that a little in the
> chapters I've read. March does gleam on the walls of Tramonta,
> I think. But in the unread chapters I equipped him with a
> complete family circle which made me shudder when I re-
> examined them the other day—a lofty mother in a Northum-
> brian eyrie, an elder and sunnier brother, knight-errantresses of
> sisters, an uncle who was a Tory publisher. No more, no more.
> The only way to present this hero was to root him as little as
> possible in society, and to let him come and go unexplained.
> T. E. Lawrence, whom I did not then know, offers a hint. . . .[14]

At the risk of *lèse-majesté* I have to say that this is rubbish, all
too typical in its obtuseness. Usually, though not invariably,
Forster was somehow a perfect fool of a commentator upon his
own work.

One can conceive revision improving the chapters in which
the March family figures, if you will, but for the novelist's
deepest purposes they are excellent as they stand. For they
broaden out the theme of Forster's antithesis 'between the
civilized man, who hopes for an Arctic Summer and the heroic
man who rides into the sea'[15] to incorporate a specifically
twentieth-century dilemma. Does a tolerant, because secular

materialist society prove its own undoing? Do royalism, religion, the old more primitive tribal values (as it were) make for doom—or their opposites? Here is the March boys' uncle at the Northumbrian eyrie anatomizing what Martin Whitby stands for:

> 'Whitby's the age,' he said rather sententiously, 'or what gets termed the age, though it's made of sterner stuff really, thank God.'
>
> Lance, still upon the wrong track, murmured, 'How beastly.'
>
> 'I don't think Uncle Arthur means that.'
>
> 'Exactly,' said Mr. Vullamy, again much pleased. 'Nothing as definite as beastliness, Clesant. I object to him really as an example of a type which is poisonous and spreading. Poisonous is too strong a word for it. Every word is too strong for it— that's the trouble. Mind, boys, you mustn't repeat this, for I know nothing against Whitby, who is an industrious and honest government servant. I wouldn't mind him if he didn't propagate the type and its ideas with such rapidity. He's against morality—but quietly, mind you, quietly; against religion, but quietly; against the Throne and all that we hold dear in the same way. Lance's Socialist on Bramley Down is open: we know where we are with him. The country's real danger is these crawling non-conformist intellectuals. A big war will clean them out—but till it comes—'
>
> 'Uncle Arthur,' said Lance, 'you'll get put in chokey. That'll be the end of you!'
>
> 'Not I! That isn't Whitby's line. He fights no one. His aim is to modify, till everything's slack and lukewarm. You agree, don't you?'
>
> Clesant nodded.
>
> 'And when he has modified, then the real forces of evil—of which he has no conception—then they'll come in and take their turn. Oh, I'm wasting too many words on the fellow, but I've lately heard him hold forth at a debate against National Service. He argued in effect that if human nature was feebler, there'd be no more wars, and he wanted to enfeeble it. We were at the South London Institute, which was founded to produce better citizens, but the atmosphere has become socialist; his sort of talk goes down there. I got up and said Mr. Whitby was perfectly right: if human nature was feebler there would be no more wars: merely envy, hatred, malice and all uncharitableness.'
>
> 'Man must be a coward,' said Lance.

Mr. Vullamy could not grant this either. Besides, he wanted to sketch Martin's character to his nephews. They would have to reckon with the type soon, and it was rather difficult: their young eyes, trained to see only light and darkness, might misunderstand it unassisted. Whitby was neither coward nor villain: he was a man without faith and infinitely dangerous. 'He won't fight,' he complained. 'It isn't that he can't or daren't, but he won't. He declares it unnecessary. Life will of course prove him wrong.'

'Yes indeed!' chorused the boys. . . .

Their uncle watched them, smiling. Yes, Clesant was shaping, and with the touch of Romance that puts the last edge on steel. He would make a fine younger son. He had scented the enemy by instinct, and his queasiness at following where they trod evinced the race in him. Lance, dear Lance, one had always known what he was—the joyous knight of the sabre who slashes and roars. But the rapier—may we not need that too in Armageddon?— and Clesant showed signs of proficiency. (Section VI)

The distinction here is that Mr. Vullamy is not too easily answered. You can set down the First World War, if you like, to outdated dynasticisms and militarisms of a kind he seems to be recommending (though even that would be a pretty crude account of its contributive factors), but after all the Martin Whitby sort of values have dominated in European (and I include European Russian) thought since this was written. Yet we have had a Second World War and the international crisis seems scarcely less chronic now than in 1911–12. By that date the March family are already defending heavily besieged and weakened moral positions. Have the Whitbys therefore been given, since the eighteenth century, too much their head—or too little? Did Wilhelmine Germany, or the relatively civilized Hapsburg Empire—in comparison with what has obtained since in most of the Austro-Hungarian map—perish of its feudalism or its modernity? The nationalisms of the Balkans sparked all that 'Armageddon' off and have only served to bring disaster upon their peoples. Were they forward- or backward-looking things along the Whitby-Vullamy polarity of values?

The names here of their very selves help to express these complex dichotomies. Whitby's evokes that centre of civilization, book-learning, scholarship which studies the past for the sake of the future—counting on a long 'arctic summer' for fruition of elaborate social progress—*and* (significantly) a religious tradition, that (most famously under the Abbess Hild in Caedmon's day) illuminated Northumbria itself in one of England's darkest times. 'March' suggests Spring, vitality and military movement. But movement not necessarily well-directed, vernal energies that may boisterously just destroy. *Where* are 'Lance' and his brother striding in their soldierly tradition?

This is a novel which had to get written before August 1914. After that it could, to its creator, only seem out of date since, as Forster remarked in his 1951 commentary, his two heroes would have lived on into a world neither of them could have endorsed or made sense of. The chance of Civilization having an Arctic Summer would have appeared all but paralysed to a Whitby, the value of individual heroism all but cancelled to a Clesant March given that T. E. Lawrence's Arab revolt in that epoch seemed 'the last effort of the war-god before he laid down his godhead, and turned chemist' (*Abinger Harvest*, Part II, 'T. E. Lawrence').

Now there may well have been some underlying homosexual interest which Forster had in the two men's relationship and which he did not see his way to clarifying, articulating, with his material as it stood. But the *Maurice* project, begun and pushed through the next year, effectually disposed of that, of the creative tension's need which, left to itch, like grit in an oyster, might have irritated into existence a transforming event for the story to go through in the fashion of his other novels. For, as he made clear at the end of his Aldeburgh address, the author had only been interested in his scheme on the condition that it had a happy outcome: that Clesant March and Martin Whitby in the upshot helped, did not destroy each other.[16] It is a tragedy that Forster went ahead with *Maurice*, not this vastly superior work, its immediately-begun predecessor. The issues of *Arctic Summer* are all too livingly with us today, and we desperately could do with the Forsterian insight putting forth its full strength across their ample range, which here is embodied with such genius.

The whole business provides a further gloss on the mis-direction of his artistic career and positively invokes, let alone permitting, commentary upon its decomposition. First of all, the more Forster acknowledged his homosexuality and sought direct expression of it in life and letters, the more the creative gift was withdrawn from him. His love-affair with Mohammed el Adl (in Egypt 1917–22) seems to have been more amply avenged in loss of artistic power than any but the most vindictive moralist could wish. As he felt increasingly attuned to living and writing about this sort of affinity, so all the fundamental kinds of literary *intelligence* deserted him. Of his surviving ' "sexy stories" (Forster's own phrase)'[17] the puta-tively earliest—'The Life to Come', 'Dr. Woolacott' and 'Arthur Snatchfold'—though very sufficiently depressing in that like the others they leave one just feeling dreary and desiccated, are at least well written. Each hangs together with an intrinsic logic which, I have already argued, is missing from the drama of 'The Other Boat'. But by the very end of his creative life, circa 1962, when with J. R. Ackerley's help he is writing the tale 'Little Imber',[18] every deepest thing one means by the phrase 'literary tact' has been lost sight of. Already long before (1927) in an amusing passage in the *Commonplace Book*, he has noted that 'my ability to write fuck may preserve me from too close contact with H.[enry] J.[ames]. . . .'[19] But the ability to write 'fuck' is exactly a feature in his equipment which the fully awake kind of imaginative creator will never use and for the inexorable reason that in no culture known to Man, certainly not our own Occident, has language ever been devised to describe sexual intercourse or the bodily organs most imme-diately concerned which is other than clinico-medical or (as it were shamefacedly) slangy—i.e. pseudo-pornographic. The matter is of great philosophical interest and suggests that there has been, at some primordial date, something remarkably like a Fall from Innocence ('And the eyes of them both were opened, and they knew that they were naked; and they sewed fig leaves together, and made themselves aprons'). For why is our race able to talk of hands and cheeks, noses and eyes—I mean, use words for these members—which are neither bleached of half their significance nor loaded with louche connotation; yet if we talk of sexual organs or congress we must use terms either too coldly scientific for certain contexts or too haplessly gamey; *or* too inapt (e.g. 'love-making' of occasions where simple lechery is in the case)?

Whatever be the rights and wrongs of all this, it reflects no

145

credit upon Forster that he loses progressively all sense of these inescapable discriminations. 'Little Imber' is all through silly and disgusting, a portentous illustration of how everything degenerates, including its prose style, when a great mind is held in thrall by an unintegrated appetite. Subject-matter, treatment, language are all here equally a sordid botch.

Generally indeed, the homosexual stories he has left behind represent major failures of intelligence; whereas intelligence is what we have in full in all the parts of *Arctic Summer* which are bequeathed to us.

Take the treatment of its tributary theme, the roles permitted to women in the modern world. Dorothea Borlase, Venetia's blue-stocking sister, brief as is her appearance in her London flat, is a still more rounded, likeable and in that regard more realized version of both the Misses Schlegel. Her female parent is maternal, warm, necessary; but in being complacently traditionalist as to all her views for women, limited. No mere Earth-Mother figure either, Lady Borlase is very perceptive, 'sharp'. But though she represents the best of the old wisdom about what womankind can be and do, though she is hugely likeable, enjoyable, respect-worthy, we shall not (I think) just endorse her positions flat out. Venetia Whitby, her other daughter, is a liberated feminist of a more unimaginative sort than her sibling, and something there is dried-up which we reject, yes; yet there is a freshness, an innocent openness to argument, reason, intellectual appeal in her which gives her identity as modern Shavian textbook-Socialist woman a lot more value and substance than easy old mumblings about the life of instinct, the *ewig weibliche* and the rest of it can comfortably slot. In the wake of Martin's fiasco at the Italian cinema she and her mother are discussing whether or not he is too much in the company of women, and she asks

> 'What could a man do that we don't do?'
> 'He could be a man, my dear.'
> 'Well, as you know, I don't agree at all, and no more does Martin. He hates what we call "smoking-room civilisation". He's as anxious as I am that Hugo shouldn't be taught all the rubbish about "little girls do this" and "little boys do that". If he likes people—that's all he cares about.'
> 'No doubt that's the correct attitude, but I has my feelings.

He'd be happier if there was another man.'

'Well, there's the chauffeur. Or did you mean a gentleman?' she added with a touch of scorn.

'Heaven help me, but I did mean a gentleman.'

'Oh.'

'Be it how it may, I'm afraid he's not enjoying motoring as much as we are. Don't you think he isn't as merry as usual?'

'Everyone has these ups and downs,' said Venetia. 'Sometimes I'm not merry.'

Lady Borlase gave a clap of laughter.

'What is it mother?'

'Dearest Nettie, nothing.'

'I believe you're laughing at me. Did I say anything odd?'

It was at moments like this that Lady Borlase saw the unalterable candour of her soul.

Forster's treatment of womanhood is far less superficial in this novel than his later thought (for example his essay on Cambridge and its attitude to women there[20]); and here his homosexual's inability to present erotic interest between the different genders tells for a strength. In *Arctic Summer* the novelist's failure to register, or at least realize, the physical appeal to Martin Whitby of his wife, only serves to focus the March family principles the more fairly: i.e. *that* household's view that men and women will lose their way emotionally as well as politically if females are not the objects of male chivalry, if the sexes do not lead lives apart, if civilization means a watering-down of these barriers, too, so that maleness is not stimulated by masculine companionship nor femininity developed by its exaltation in home-centred rôles. Yet the intent to set every woman on a courtly pedestal—the March scheme of chivalry—is at its most exposed when Clesant and Whitby visit in Milan the Tramonta minx; or when we compare the fixed ethos, mechanical utterances and cold nature of Clesant's mother with the values and personalities of the younger Borlase women.

Almost certainly the inspiration of the human ado in *The Longest Journey* is homosexual—if we are to be bothered, this is to say, with seeing it in an authorial-biographic way at all. But there, in sublimating that impulse, Forster has found a creative role for it. His hero Rickie Elliot's relation to the pagan athlete

E. M. Forster: Our Permanent Contemporary

Stephen Wonham is not saddled with any explicit avowal of such a basis and is therefore able to assist in something far more important: the evocation of the landscape of England and its worth.

He wanted a happy outcome for the two heroes of this later substantial work, and it seems that *Maurice*, by being openly an 'Uranian' love-story with a happy-ever-after ending, drained off the creative irritant of the major book, as we may say. I find it a catastrophic loss to our literature, never having read anything of this author's with greater excitement than *Arctic Summer*, albeit that it is a fragment.

Of Forster's biggest projects it is the one he handles, as far as he takes the work, with greatest equity and in that sense success.

NOTES

1. Introduction to *The Life to Come and Other Stories*, second section.
2. *E. M. Forster: A Life*, Vol. I, pp. 257, 258.
3. *Commonplace Book*, p. 67.
4. Ibid., p. 161.
5. *Life*, Vol. I, p. 258.
6. *E. M. Forster: The Critical Heritage*, ed. Philip Gardner (London, 1973), p. 430 [letter of 12 March 1915]: 'The Maurice-Alec affair didn't strike me as so successful. For one thing, the Class question is rather a red herring, I think. One suddenly learns that Maurice is exaggeratedly upper-classish—one wouldn't at all have expected it in the face of things—and then when the change comes it seems to need more explanation.'
7. 'Terminal Note' to *Maurice*, penultimate paragraph.
8. Interview with P. N. Furbank and F. J. H. Haskell: *Paris Review*, Spring 1955, pp. 30–1: 'The novelist should I think always settle when he starts', he there remarks, 'what is going to happen, what his major event is to be. He may alter this event as he approaches it, indeed he probably will, indeed he probably had better, or the novel becomes tied up and tight. But the sense of a solid mass ahead, a mountain round or over or through which . . . the story must somehow go is most valuable and for the novels I've tried to write essential.' Forster uses almost the same terms in his Aldeburgh address on the subject four years previously.
9. *Life*, Vol. I, pp. 198–99.
10. Ibid., p. 208.
11. Ibid., id. loc.

12. See Editor's Introduction to the Abinger Edition of *A Passage to India* (London, 1978) *passim* and especially pp. xiv–xix.
13. *Arctic Summer and Other Fiction*, Abinger Edition, Vol. 9 (London, 1980), p. 160.
14. Ibid., p. 161.
15. Ibid., p. 162.
16. Ibid.
17. *The Life to Come and Other Stories*, editor's Introduction, second section.
18. In *Arctic Summer and Other Fiction*.
19. Op. cit., p. 42.
20. *Two Cheers for Democracy*, Part 2, under 'Places'.

5

A Passage to India

Forster's last novel has become, since the very hours of its first publication, the Trojan Horse of a critical conspiracy—not always intentional—to cover his *oeuvre* as a whole with left-handed compliment. Early documents in the case, including Leonard Woolf's review, can be seen in Philip Gardner's *The Critical Heritage*[1] and show how soon this orthodoxy was invested in. *A Passage* is exalted into a classic, a completely successful major novel, the one work in the canon deserving such praise; and by that concession opinion is able to warm to its task of itemizing all the faults of the pre-War fictions and very thoroughly depreciating them. For if you are seen to praise one of his books unreservedly, you cannot be accused of blindness or ungenerosity in 'placing' the other offerings of a given author, can you?

It is a plausible ploy and has worked effectively. It took in the artist himself. One day when I called on Forster near his ninetieth birthday he told me he had just been reading, and was convinced by, an article of V. S. Pritchett's which demonstrated that the pre-First-War novels had all dated badly and would not last.

I yelled with vexation.

'He points out all their servants and class-conflicts that are no longer current. . . .'

'But Shakespeare's plays are not held to have dated because they deal in kings and princesses and aristocratic court life.'

He was not very budgeable *in situ* and the discussion ended with him saying, anxiously, 'But I do think *A Passage* will live, don't you?', to which I heartily averred agreement.

Nevertheless the tenor of our talk had exasperated me. I rushed back to my college room and penned an essay of a long letter arguing that his earlier novels were the kind of 'news that stays news'.

When next I called, a week later, a conscious smile appeared on the old man's face. 'Thank you for your letter' was his amused greeting.

Perspective needs restoring. *A Passage to India* is indeed a very major work but it is not free of serious flaw, any more than its predecessors are significantly inferior to it.

A political novel, a critique of colonialism and of relations between different races or societies in juxtaposition, it also reticulates, as one may say, around the question 'Will The God (Shri Krishna, Lord of Creation) come?' Or, to put it more specifically, can we ever hope so to get into relation with the Unseen that the cause of the universe being as it is is perceived in our own lives and they are invested with meaning, with absolute value? For once in his days Forster spoke aptly about his own achievement when in the Programme Note to Santha Rama Rau's dramatized version of the book, written for the original production by the Meadow Players at the Oxford Playhouse, January 1960, he said 'I tried to indicate the human predicament in a universe which is not, so far, comprehensible to our minds.'[2]

The place is British India, the time somewhere in the first quarter of the present century. Adela Quested, chaperoned by her possible mother-in-law Mrs. Moore, has come to Chandrapore to see her prospective fiancé Ronny Heaslop the City Magistrate there, on a sort of visit of self-reassurance prior to their engagement. She is earnest, gawky, and 'desirous of seeing the real India'. 'Try seeing Indians' is the riposte of Mr. Fielding, Principal of the Government College, who goes on, as good as his word, to arrange a tea-party for the two English ladies with Dr. Aziz, the local Deputy Surgeon and Professor Narayan Godbole, a Hindu assistant in his school.

On the spur of a moment's characteristic impetuosity Aziz invites them all to tea at his bungalow, realizes with horror that their acceptance will mean total discomfiture and shame—'It

was a detestable shanty near a low bazaar. There was practically only one room in it, and that infested with small black
flies'—and changes the plan to a trip to the Marabar Hills and
their famous Caves some miles outside the city.

This scheme is persisted in, despite quiet disapproval from
the British officials of the place and the effectual moral failure of
a 'Bridge' Party put on by the chief of them, the Collector Mr.
Turton, where Indians come and are given hospitality which is
far from attentive or warm-spirited enough at the English club.

On the morning of the picnic Godbole is late and Fielding
who awaits him, being delayed, misses by a fraction their train.
Aziz does the honours of the tour, however, happy in the
sympathetic company of his adored Mrs. Moore. He and the
ladies escorted by a party of servants visit the Caves and, when
the Englishman at last joins them, makes up the excuses which
he himself finds plausible for the fact that Adela has quit the
scene suddenly alone. Separated from the rest of them she is
reported as going back to Chandrapore in the same car driven
by Miss Derek (an English P.A. who has stolen both *congé* and
motor from her employer the Maharani of Mudkul) which
brought the belated Fielding to the bottom of the hill.

> 'It is quite natural about Miss Quested,' he remarked, for he
> had been working the incident a little in his mind, to get rid of its
> roughnesses. 'We were having an interesting time with our
> guide, then the car was seen, so she decided to go down to her
> friend.' Incurably inaccurate, he already thought that this was
> what had occurred. He was inaccurate because he was sensitive.
> He did not like to remember Miss Quested's remark about
> polygamy, because it was unworthy of a guest, so he put it from
> his mind, and with it the knowledge that he had bolted into a
> cave to get away from her. He was inaccurate because he desired
> to honour her, and—facts being entangled—he had to arrange
> them in her vicinity, as one tidies the ground after extracting a
> weed. Before breakfast was over, he had told a good many lies.
> (Ch. 16)

The situation turns out much more serious in fact, for when
the rest of them return to Chandrapore (minus their guide
who has bolted, having been struck in the face by Aziz at the
time he temporarily lost Adela), the host of the party is
arrested on a charge of attempted sexual assault.

Ranks close. The British community is all for vengeance under the merest forms of law. The Indians see Adela's allegation as an infamous slander used to enhance justification of their politically subservient status. In the fierce divided days which follow, Fielding throws in his lot with his Indian friend—and is vindicated during the electric proceedings of the trial when Adela, whose memory has been, like Mrs. Moore's, much possessed by her experience of a special echo in the Caves, withdraws her charge unconditionally (Ch. 24).

The expectable disaster of serious rioting is averted—just—though Aziz, in the wake of his experience, remains at first bitter and implacable. Eventually, however, he is persuaded to acquit his detractress of the heavy damages he could claim—a piece of generosity which wins him, as he predicts, no admiration amongst the British. Fielding works him round to this abdication of revenge by invoking the name of his beloved Mrs. Moore: rather a necromantic proceeding, in that Ronny Heaslop's mother has been packed off back to England before the trial—partly on the grounds of her ill-health and the ever-mounting temperatures of the Hot Season, partly because she is no asset to her people's 'side', believing in Aziz's innocence instinctively and cantankerously all along—and she has died during the voyage home.

But a coolness begins between the English schoolmaster and the Indian doctor. Aziz has had his nerve broken:

> the English. . . . had frightened him permanently, and there are only two reactions against fright: to kick and scream on committees, or to retreat to a remote jungle, where the sahib seldom comes. (Ch. 34)

He takes the latter course and goes off with his three young children to a career of semi-poverty and very compromised medical professionalism in the employ of a Hindu prince in the Native State of Mau, ever more convinced at the same time that his once absolutely loyal friend Cyril has gone back to London to marry Miss Quested and gain the money he was persuaded to waive.

The story resumes in its third section, 'Temple', two years later. We are introduced to the festival of Gokul Ashtami at Mau, wherein a leading celebrant is Professor Godbole—also living and working here and through whom Aziz was originally recruited to the palace staff. Stitched in and out of these religious manifestations, the relationship of Aziz, Fielding and their respective families moves to an amicable close. Fielding is on an educationist's visit, on behalf of the Government of India, and Aziz is made to discover his mistake; Cyril has met and married Mrs. Moore's daughter Stella, not her onetime daughter-in-law elect, though it is through Adela's good offices that the couple have encountered. Stella's brother accompanies her and her husband on *this* 'passage to India' and has a catalystic effect:

> 'I must go back now, good night,' said Aziz, and held out his hand, completely forgetting that they were not friends, and focusing his heart on something more distant than the caves, something beautiful. His hand was taken, and then he remembered how detestable he had been, and said gently, 'Don't you think me unkind any more?'
> 'No.'
> 'How can you tell, you strange fellow?'
> 'Not difficult, the one thing I always know.'
> 'Can you always tell whether a stranger is your friend?'
> 'Yes.' (Ch. 36)

Mr. Furbank tells us that this is

> Forster's profoundest portrait of his young self . . .—Ralph, whose brief apparition at the end of the novel is so moving and central to the book's design. Aziz gets the impression, at first, that the timid, strange-looking Ralph is 'almost an imbecile'. But . . . with his sureness over spiritual and human matters he is the agent of such reconciliation as there is in the book.[3]

Fielding and Aziz go for one final ride together in the hills nearby, aware now that they are on opposite sides of an as yet unbridgeable divide, culturally and politically, yet parting with friendly mutual respect.

As a political tractate the book is very even-handed. The good and bad qualities of both sides are well illustrated over the course of a novel which, in *Howards End*'s unhurried unforced manner, presents many aspects of the large scene and problem it is concerned to anatomize. The Indians are shown for almost hopelessly at odds and incompetent among themselves but very living; the British as much better at administration yet unacceptably unlovely in their role of master-caste. Indian incompetence is evidenced as early as Chapter 2. At Hamidullah's small evening gathering the meal is late in preparation—and obviously not for the first time;

> He raised his voice suddenly, and shouted for dinner. Servants shouted back that it was ready. They meant that they wished it was ready, and were so understood, for nobody moved.

The topic of conversation, *Is it possible for an Indian to be friends with an Englishman?* (one of the novel's main themes), keeps being clouded, obscured by emotional wool-gathering on its disputants' part which, as well as being comic in a beguiling way, implies a fearful indisposition to hard logic on the part of a subject race:

> '. . . They entrusted all their children to me—I often carried little Hugh about—I took him up to the funeral of Queen Victoria, and held him in my arms above the crowd.'
> 'Queen Victoria was different,' murmured Mahmoud Ali.

Members in a single family cannot behave with easy frankness towards one another on even the simplest occasions so that life may move along with all-round comfort and ease.

> A servant announced dinner. They ignored him . . . and . . . spent twenty minutes behind the purdah. Hamidullah Begum was a distant aunt of Aziz, and the only female relative he had in Chandrapore, and . . . It was difficult to get away, because until they had had their dinner she would not begin hers, and consequently prolonged her remarks in case they should suppose she was impatient.

Nor is food-taking on the part of an Hindu necessarily less complicated. Professor Godbole's participation in Fielding's tea-party is unproblematic if you like.

> The Brahman . . . took his tea at a little distance from the outcastes, from a low table placed slightly behind him, to which he stretched back, and as it were encountered food by accident; all feigned indifference to Professor Godbole's tea. (Ch. 7)

But hardly as much can be said for his involvement in the Marabar picnic. Indeed the expedition as a *plan* is fraught with irrational difficulties, let alone as an achieved event.

> Then there was the question of alcohol: Mr. Fielding, and perhaps the ladies, were drinkers, so must he provide whiskey-sodas and ports? There was the problem of transport from the wayside station of Marabar to the caves. There was the problem of Professor Godbole and his food, and of Professor Godbole and other people's food—two problems, not one problem. The Professor was not a very strict Hindu—he would take tea, fruit, soda-water and sweets, whoever cooked them, and vegetables and rice if cooked by a Brahman; but not meat, not cakes lest they contained eggs, and he would not allow anyone else to eat beef: a slice of beef upon a distant plate would wreck his happiness. Other people might eat mutton, they might eat ham. But over ham Aziz's own religion raised its voice: he did not fancy other people eating ham. Trouble after trouble encountered him, because he had challenged the spirit of the Indian earth, which tries to keep men in compartments. (Ch. 13)

Nor do Hindus shine at organization and good sense. At the 'Bridge' Party a married couple, the Bhattacharyas, acquiesce most blithely, even insistently, in the proposition that Mrs. Moore and Adela should visit them the next Thursday morning—when they are due to be in Calcutta—(Ch. 5) and in the event the English ladies are more than a little bewildered and pained, fearing they have offended against 'some point of Indian etiquette' when the carriage promised for them has never come (Ch. 7).

Yet while that incident may express a social difficulty which is not amenable to easy handling, less can be said in excuse of the fact that by the end of the tale the high school which Godbole is returning to his birthplace in Central India to start 'on sound English lines' (Ch. 19) has

> been converted into a granary, and the Minister of Education did not like to admit this to his former Principal. The school had been opened only last year by the Agent to the Governor-General, and it still flourished on paper; he hoped to start it again before its absence was remarked and to collect its scholars before they produced children of their own. (Ch. 37)

The issue has its very serious sides, as Ronny Heaslop is moved to remonstrate with his mother:

> She forgot about Adela in her surprise. 'A side-issue, a side-issue?' she repeated. 'How can it be that?'
> 'We're not out here for the purpose of behaving pleasantly!'
> 'What do you mean?'
> 'What I say. We're out here to do justice and keep the peace. Them's my sentiments. India isn't a drawing-room.'. . .
> He spoke sincerely. Every day he worked hard in the court trying to decide which of two untrue accounts was the less untrue, trying to dispense justice fearlessly, to protect the weak against the less weak, the incoherent against the plausible, surrounded by lies and flattery. That morning he had convicted a railway clerk of overcharging pilgrims for their tickets, and a Pathan of attempted rape. He expected no gratitude, no recognition for this, and both clerk and Pathan might appeal, bribe their witnesses more effectually in the interval, and get their sentences reversed. (Ch. 5)

This has a gloss further pointed when Aziz at Fielding's tea-party discourses upon justice, prisons and law-giving and proves quite incapable of conceiving a proper justiciary role (Ch. 7).

Over the course of his novel Forster also shows that the Indians are disunited and corrupt as well as incompetent, but he is not writing a lampoon. People retain their individuality and we are not affronted by the image of a subcontinent whose human inhabitants and various cultures are merely imbecile. Mr. Das proves a very effective magistrate; and the jeer about Aziz's missing collar-stud (Ch. 8) is all upon the rude Englishman who mockingly makes it. (I had a sense of 'double take' one morning when, calling at a late hour, I was asked by Forster to tie up his top shirt-button for him, the vinculum which clasps a modern collar about its wearer's neck and which he was having a struggle in fastening himself. Clad to fullest formality otherwise, he stood in the middle of the carpet in front of his fireplace, the pair of us illumined by the full noontide strength of a very bright midday, while I did so, and the tiny episode for me irresistibly recalled Aziz's first encounter with Fielding—with therefore an odd sensation of its own. It was as if on a visit to Stratford circa 1614

Shakespeare should get you to spend quarter of an hour with him searching round his room for a missing handkerchief.) Yet the effectual picture *A Passage* presents as a whole is of a land where people cannot be expected to make a sufficient success of self-direction and for whom, therefore, a British Raj is necessary.

In this regard the novel remains wholly topical. When we consider the desperate poverty that characterizes India today and the corruption which, thew and sinew of all government since Independence, only aggravates the hunger and the squalors, it is solely the wilfully blind among us who refuse to ask the question, *What good did Ghandi bring to his people?*

He may be supposed to have brought some good to the race he helped demote and extrude. Ronny Heaslop's character deteriorates with every month he spends as City Magistrate in Chandrapore and it is plain to see why. He is part of an 'Army of Occupation', a ruling class, and only the saintliest of the saintliest in any mortal species are uncorrupted by that sort of position. It puts one in mind of Jane Austen's Sir William Lucas in *Pride and Prejudice* who

> had been formerly in trade in Meryton, where he had made a tolerable fortune and risen to the honour of knighthood by an address to the King, during his mayoralty. The distinction had perhaps been felt too strongly. (Ch. 5)

except that Sir William's vanity, thus elevated in his own country, is not tainted to boorishness, whereas the Brits, as a social stratum, in their eastern Empire are condign churls. The 'Oppressors of India' (phrase from Heaslop's letter to Fielding near the end) is an inept term, but we can perceive how it has come to be coined, for the Raj's administrators—as Forster sees them and (again) as they *were*—are exploitive, racist, rude, begetting flunkeyism in their subject peoples and, as little tin gods allowed too much importance, behaving much too high-handedly.

What is more they are also victims of their situation since, though they bring unity—or at least peaceful coexistence—to India and administer the territory competently making things work, their role encourages them to be soured charmless creatures who do not know how to live.

> The Collector had watched the arrest from the interior of the
> waiting-room, and throwing open its perforated doors of zinc,
> he was now revealed like a god in a shrine. . . . 'I have had
> twenty-five years' experience of this country'—he paused, and
> 'twenty-five years' seemed to fill the waiting-room with their
> staleness and ungenerosity—'and during those twenty-five
> years I have never known anything but disaster result when
> English people and Indians attempt to be intimate socially.'
> (Ch. 17)

But what is there to enjoy in a life spent up at the Club or
otherwise avoiding Indians? The conversation in that sanctuary
is as out-of-date, phoney and 'bullety' as the bottled peas
served with its 'menu of Anglo-India' (Ch. 5). Practically all
the people we meet there (the Principal of Government
College and the two ladies visiting from England excepted)
have turned themselves into walking human clichés and they
rarely do anything that brings them or other folk the least real
satisfaction. One of the few occasions which prove this rule
by its infrequency is when the stray subaltern (who later
denounces his opponent-in-play unbeknownst) practises polo
against Aziz on the maidan outside Chandrapore (Ch. 6).
Forgetful of nationality for a little while the Englishman enjoys
himself as much as the Indian. But this is unusual. Most of the
time most of the British are locked up in a dire lack of
imagination, induced by their compromising political rôle in
this alien and subjugated land; and with that they lack not
only kindness, affection and respect but also that AWE which is
appropriate in presence of the other (foreign) person just
because she or he *is* other and all human beings, when you
come actually to look at or think about them for two minutes,
are miraculous.

> He spoke sincerely, but she could have wished with less
> gusto. How Ronny revelled in the drawbacks of his situation!
> How he did rub it in that he was not in India to behave
> pleasantly, and derived positive satisfaction therefrom! . . . His
> words without his voice might have impressed her, but when
> she heard the self-satisfied lilt of them, when she saw the mouth
> moving so complacently and competently beneath the little red
> nose, she felt, quite illogically, that this was not the last word on
> India. One touch of regret—not the canny substitute but the

159

true regret from the heart—would have made him a different man, and the British Empire a different institution. (Ch. 5)

This has been censured as inadequate by way of analysis or criticism for one of the world's major colonialisms, but it seems to me exactly right and for the same reasons that the book remains only too topical in our own day. All its political side or vision is wholly up-to-date in application to, say, Hong Kong or modern Black Africa.

The Chinese in many other dimensions leave us British standing—for hard work, first-class family life, courtesy, cuisine, sense of humour (constant friendly *intelligent* giggling) and personal good looks—let alone being fully any Occidental society's equals in landscape, artwork, poetry, ceramics and fabrics of course. But they have pretty well decisively proved themselves a tragic disaster from generation unto generation in the political sphere, and the last two centuries in the Middle Kingdom have been a catastrophe of human government: what time they have 'tried' their old-fashioned absolute monarchy, local feudalist warlord rule, a modern western-style republic and a Communist state. They seem incapable of thinking in civic terms, and indeed their political and economic thought has for its boundaries the frontiers of the social micro-unit, the household and its immediate relatives. In consequence nepotism and corruption are the middle names of all administrative dealings where a Chinese is in a position of authority. An instinctive overwhelming urge to employ the members of his family, whether in the chief political rôles of the country or the management of a large business, dominates his behaviour and soon enough produces venal inefficiency. In the free Chinas today—Taiwan, Singapore, etc.—people without power and wealth are wild to work for companies of which the chief executive is, for instance, a Briton, on the ground that promotion in those enterprises will go by merit not blood-kinship—and the productivity and morale within such corporations are equally high: something which would not be the case if they were staffed by British workers, so many of whom, even in these recessive days (1983), still want high salaries and big perks without the actual bother of anything in the nature of real toil.

Accordingly, even if Hong Kong can resolve the 1997 problem of its Lease (in the direction of a maintained *status quo*), it is still an open question how much the community will continue to prosper there if and as more and more Chinese people occupy its leading positions, in business and government. (Huge fortunes will go on being made by individuals but that is not the same point.) In the past the ethnically local persons were almost invisible on a commercial or administrative board. Now 70% of all senior posts are filled by them; and not before time, one would cry, in a community which is 98% Han or Hakka and an enclave where in former years, still more scandalously, the indigenous population were made actually to enter public banks and bureaux by the back door in proof of their third-class citizenship. There has been a long day during which the British in that territory treated their coolie servants much too much *de haut en bas*; and anyway it is still more depressing that the Chinese are not apt at self-government and flourish only under a foreign flag. The twenty decades of awful famines (for lack of good administration in Peking), of humiliations and suicides, which have demoralized this great and beautiful nation, culminating recently in the supremely horrible years of the 'Cultural Revolution', are too frightful a price to pay, on the individual citizen's part, for that foreign flag's removal—though other tendencies in our century have made the big-nosed bug-eyed 'foreign devils' from distant islands far oversea much less insulting there now than once upon a time, unwittingly as often as deliberately, they tended to be. Yet while we may not have many Turtons and Burtons left in our remaining colonial and quasi-colonial outposts, all the other problems *A Passage to India* treats of, in its political dimension, remain unresolved.

In Black Africa the choice for a long time has been between two very unhappy options: indeed, I think, it antedates the White Man's first visits and exploitations. From its prehistory that portion of the globe has been populated by a multitude of different tribes most of whom are so much at variance with their neighbours as only to desire opportunities of genocide. After the butcher Idi Amin was finally dethroned in Uganda, the new

Kampala government which the world with relief had seen installed in his mass-murdering place proceeded to attempt to starve one of its northern populations to death. Now that Rhodesia is Zimbabwe and Europeans no longer hold the ring there, the Shona (majority) are sharpening up their weapons for a showdown with their old rivals the Matabele, many of whom have already been slaughtered. The heart-breaking terrifying thing in Black Africa is not the incidence, pretty well ubiquitous, of one-party states gripped by dictators, or fairly corrupt oligarchical rule—what was Sir Robert Walpole's ministry in Great Britain 1721–42? It is the uses to which power is put, once (invariably) seized by one man or a caucus. Extermination of other racial groups comes high on the list of priorities, and is accompanied by or alternates with quelling incompetence in the management of an economy, a political rhetoric and behaviour of bottomless hypocrisy and the goading of half-famished populations to frenzy in specious causes designed to keep their thoughts off the catastrophic decline of everything at home. Most of them countries very rich in minerals or agricultural potential, most—like Tanzania for example—have managed to bankrupt themselves with these methods of self-government.

To say 'Well, it is all the white man's fault. He should not have disturbed the balance of things by interfering in the Dark Continent in the first place', is to utter three errors. First, that statement constitutes no policy—except one of despair—for the amelioration of matters *now*. Second, there was ever only balance in the sense that it was a continent of warring tribes who had assegais rather than gunpowder and repeating rifles; and the third point follows, that Black Africans would in course of time anyway have learned about modern weaponry and have traded with entrepreneurs for it, howsoever aloof, as a principle, the European and other extraneous nations had kept from their affairs. Effectually this happened in the Far East. The Chinese shut their minds to the barbarism of the 'foreign devils', the Japanese, entirely self-governing, did not; and from the end of the nineteenth century till 1945, Japan, as a first-class up-to-date arsenal, wreaked havoc upon her defenceless neighbour.

The only thing that would have sufficed on these last two counts, would have been for Africa to be situated on another planet across innavigable space; and to wish that is possible but useless. We live in one world and have to make the best of it together.

The choice all along in that region therefore has really been between leaving Black Africa's peoples to their own devices—as in recent decades has been accomplished by various Independence movements and treaties—so as insouciantly to watch a terrible age of murder, terrorism and famine stalk the bush and its cities; or the establishment of the kinds of polity, colonialist in essence, which characterizes currently the Republic of South Africa. Those are the only options; there is not a happy third; for anyone who believes that were there majority rule in the hinterland of Johannesburg, Natal or the Cape there would not be a bloodbath— not of whites but among the various nations of blacks—is made of the stuff of incorrigible sanguinity upon which revolutionists prey and against whose heads all experience beats in vain. Black Africa is, when self-governing, a very bloodthirsty, hypocritical, demoralized and hungry-because-incompetent place to be.

Yet who can fall in love with the humiliations implicit in apartheid or the fact that 'Democracy' (on a one-man one-vote basis) works so vildely in that area of the world that a dominant, culturally alien master-caste *is needed in it*?

In other respects than the political these subject peoples have very much to offer that Westerners lack and need; yet is a true interchange in the spirit of real friendship possible where civic status is so unequal?

If feckless in certain ways, some of the Indians we encounter in Forster's novel are charming after a fashion that few of the British people ever manage to be.

This is not only in superficial things; as when, at the Collector's 'Bridge' Party Mrs. Moore and Adela Quested leaving the Bhattacharya group, do so

> among a flutter of compliments and smiles, and three ladies, who had hitherto taken no part in the reception, suddenly shot out of the summer-house like exquisitely coloured swallows, and salaamed them. (Ch. 5)

Indians' aptitude for actually putting something big into life and getting something big out of it (the terms are tautologous) is typified by the scene at Aziz's bungalow where fellow-citizens visit him in his sickness and he recites a poem by Ghalib. Those of us who inhabit Western circles, which would writhe with embarrassment in such circumstances, can only envy—intensely—the others' response on the occasion:

> It had no connection with anything that had gone before, but it came from his heart and spoke to theirs. They were over-whelmed by its pathos. . . . The squalid bedroom grew quiet; the silly intrigues, the gossip, the shallow discontent were stilled, while words accepted as immortal filled the indifferent air. . . .
>
> Of the company, only Hamidullah had any comprehension of poetry. The minds of the others were inferior and rough. Yet they listened with pleasure, because literature had not been divorced from their civilization. The police inspector, for instance, did not feel that Aziz had degraded himself by reciting, nor break into the cheery guffaw with which an Englishman averts the infection of beauty. He just sat with his mind empty, and when his thoughts, which were mainly ignoble, flowed back into it they had a pleasant freshness. The poem had done no 'good' to anyone, but it was a passing reminder, a breath from the divine lips of beauty, a nightingale between two worlds of dust. Less explicit than the call to Krishna, it voiced our loneliness nevertheless, our isolation, our need for the Friend who never comes yet is not entirely disproved. (Ch. 9)

The same moral holds good of Aziz's sudden rushes of emotion and friendship throughout the book. They are value-less, if you will, as a human foundation, a basis for society or its rule of conduct, but wonderful as an achievement of life's very *goals*.

> 'Mrs. Moore, Miss Quested, our expedition is a ruin.' He swung himself along the footboard, almost in tears.
>
> 'Get in, get in; you'll kill yourself as well as Mr. Fielding. I see no ruin.'
>
> 'How is that? Oh, explain to me!' he said piteously, like a child.
>
> 'We shall be all Moslems together now, as you promised.'
>
> She was perfect as always, his dear Mrs. Moore. All the love for her he had felt at the mosque welled up again, the fresher for

forgetfulness. There was nothing he would not do for her. He would die to make her happy. (Ch. 13)

Being an Oriental in spirit (as diagnosed by Aziz in Chapter 2) the elder English lady has also these vitalizing accessions of feeling which transfigure.

> He looked at her now as she sat on a deckchair, sipping his tea, and had for a moment a joy that held the seeds of its own decay, for it would lead him to think, 'Oh, what more can I do for her?' and so back to the dull round of hospitality. The black bullets of his eyes filled with soft expressive light, and he said, 'Do you ever remember our mosque, Mrs. Moore?'
> 'I do. I do,' she said, suddenly vital and young.
> 'And how rough and rude I was, and how good you were.'
> 'And how happy we both were.' (Ch. 14)

In comparison, the non-'Oriental' British—like Mrs. Turton—are always 'saving themselves up': for an occasion which eventually therefore never really comes. (It is ironic that when at last the Collector's wife does actually shed tears, they are, in the light of Adela's subsequent recantation, as it were 'misplaced'.) The foreigners in this tale are seen to instil much-needed structures and efficacies into the Indian scene. Even when mad with anger Mr. Turton functions as an effective and responsible administrator.

> Terminating the interview, the Collector walked onto the platform. The confusion there was revolting. A chuprassy of Ronny's had been told to bring up some trifles belonging to the ladies, and was appropriating for himself various articles to which he had no right; he was a camp-follower of the angry English. Mohammed Latif made no attempt to resist him. Hassan flung off his turban, and wept. All the comforts that had been provided so liberally were rolled about and wasted in the sun. The Collector took in the situation at a glance, and his sense of justice functioned though he was insane with rage. He spoke the necessary word, and the looting stopped. (Ch. 17)

Yet this efficiency, without which life would be—and in self-governing India now largely is—a swamp, is the good side of a spiritual inhibition on the part of the English which makes them adept at the mechanics of living (very important) but missing from year to year the point of being in a state of existence at all.

A friendliness, as of dwarfs shaking hands, was in the air. Both man and woman were at the height of their powers— sensible, honest, even subtle. They spoke the same language, and held the same opinions, and the variety of age and sex did not divide them. Yet they were dissatisfied. When they agreed, 'I want to go on living a bit,' or 'I don't believe in God,' the words were followed by a curious backwash, as though the universe had displaced itself to fill up a tiny void, or as though they had seen their own gestures from an immense height— dwarfs talking, shaking hands and assuring each other that they stood on the same footing of insight. (Ch. 29)

This I think has its this-worldly as well as cosmic connotations. Adela and Fielding, among the finest of the Britons we are shown and between them embodying much of Forster's own self, are nevertheless aware of a drastic limitation: they have somehow missed out on some central experience validating Life itself. As the work unfolds and we meet a considerable cross-section of Indian and British types alternately, we come more and more to feel the justice of the qualification with which Fielding endorses his Indian friend's appeal: 'Kindness, kindness, and more kindness—yes, that he might supply, but was that really all that the queer nation needed? Did it not also demand an occasional intoxication of the blood?' (Ch. 11). And we are liable to respond with ever greater seriousness to the remark Syed Ross Masood addressed to Forster as something only too sadly apt: 'As for your damned countrymen, I pity the poor fellows from the bottom of my heart, and give them all the help I can.'[4]

The gap in the English people's nature is what gives a sharp cutting edge to one of the questions which pulse through the book and stitch it as a tale together, so that the 'Temple' section at the end is not architecturally an adjunct but integral at the level of its revealed social let alone religious relations: 'whether or no it is possible [for an Indian] to be friends with an Englishman' (Ch. 2). Occidentals have so much need of the insights and attitudes that other races possess.

But this is not the most important aspect in which *A Passage to India* unfolds its thematic interests. As Forster himself put the matter (and his last long fiction is perhaps the only one of his writings about which he was usually and consistently an apt commentator)

> the book is not really about politics, though it is the political aspect of it that caught the general public and made it sell. It's about something wider than politics, about the search of the human race for a more lasting home, about the universe as embodied in the Indian earth and the Indian sky, about the horror lurking in the Marabar Caves and the release symbolized by the birth of Krishna. It is—or rather desires to be— philosophic and poetic. . . .[5]

The novelist uses India as a phenomenon with which to confront the varieties of the world's religious experience, especially three of its major systems. He shows himself more in sympathy with Islam than Christianity, or *en passant* Buddhism, and with Hinduism more than the others; but none of these philosophies comes through the book's treatment unscathed.

Islam's appeal is registered in Aziz's devotion to it, but, like Christianity's in Mrs. Moore's case, very much from without. Before visiting the subcontinent a second time and well before completing his story (indeed after it had been effectually abandoned in its early stages at what is now Chapter 8), Forster had already signalized a quizzical respect for Muslim attitudes and theism: see for example 'The Mosque', an essay of 1920 in 'Part IV—The East' of *Abinger Harvest*. But his renewed experience of the Indian environment has dealt with even this tolerance roughly.

For that religious tradition participates in the human tendency to exalt engulfing absolutes.

> If this world is not to our taste, well, at all events there is Heaven, Hell, Annihilation—one or other of those large things, that huge scenic background of stars, fires, blue or black air. All heroic endeavour, and all that is known as art, assumes that there is such a background, just all as practical endeavour, when the world is to our taste, assumes that the world is all. (Ch. 23)

But as scenery, animal and vegetable orders, India mocks too suggestively for Forster's comfort all ideas of a grandeur in things which will be anthropomorphically understood or welcome. Whether it be the sun in April ('herald of horrors')

'returning to his kingdom with power but without beauty'
(Ch. 10) or the way 'no Indian animal has any sense of an
interior' (Ch. 3), the text continually insinuates the presence
of a Nature here uncongenial, of its intrinsic character, to
belief in major goals or conclusive terminations.

We are shown this not only through the narrator's eyes but
as passing recurrently across Mrs. Moore's senses, so that her
experience in the Marabar Cave comes as the logical upshot of
her trip to Chandrapore altogether.

> The crush and the smells she could forget, but the echo began
> in some indescribable way to undermine her hold on life.
> Coming at a moment when she chanced to be fatigued, it had
> managed to murmur: 'Pathos, piety, courage—they exist, but
> are identical, and so is filth. Everything exists, nothing has
> value.' . . . Devils are of the North, and poems can be written
> about them, but no one could romanticize the Marabar, because
> it robbed infinity and eternity of their vastness, the only quality
> that accommodates them to mankind. (Ch. 15)

To this ontological debunk, this pricking of the bubble of all
mortal hope or consolation, Godbole's response after Adela
Quested's experience in *her* Cave returns the sole answer
which the novel affirmatively offers: 'good and evil . . . are not
what we think them, they are what they are, and each of us has
contributed to both' (Ch. 19). The mode of Adela's injury is
symptomatic. Has she really been assaulted by somebody in
that cave and if so, by whom? If not, is the episode an
hallucination (in which case did she break the binoculars'
strap herself)? Likewise is Evil a species of event, a quality
which all beings and forces in the cosmos recognize as *we* see
it—perverse willed privation of Good? Or is it a human
hallucination and part of a total experience Creation-wide (the
Creation unfolding itself, Nature naturing as it were) which
our limited sensoria fail to grasp *as a whole*? The Universe in
that case is the scene of a real drama, yes, but one which
mankind has not defined adequately, for all that we inescapably
take part.

Godbole's hint to this effect has further flesh put upon it by
the Mau ceremony near the end, where Forster recounts the
Gokul Ashtami festival he himself had assisted at in Dewas

Senior, 'and which was the strangest and strongest Indian experience ever granted me'.[6]

This of itself can be seen as suggesting active conscious participation, on the part of the humans present, in the cosmic ritual of which at other times of year they are merely unconscious agents and victims; and it leads, the author suggests in his turn, to a heightened mode of awareness in which kindness and unity do come to the fore in relations even between living and the dead: Professor Godbole's vision of the wasp at the end of Chapter 33 is a strange telepathic intuition of the scene much earlier at the end of Chapter 3.

So far, we may say, so good; and one is very grateful—or ought to be—for a novel which makes both these experiences available to attentive receptive pondering; the nullity in 'the twilight of the double vision' (Ch. 23) and the Hinduistic reconciliation of life's contrarieties which is enacted across the 'Temple' section at the end of the book.

Yet our problem with all this dimension of the work—the core of it if you like—seems to me the same as with imaginative fictions which are overtly partisan in other ways. *A Passage to India* mirror-images the practice of novels that require the reader to be, say, explicitly Christian or Marxist for the tale wholly to convince, but it has the same flaw. An act of faith is required in an inappropriate mode. Here we are to believe that while 'Visions are supposed to entail profundity. . . The abyss also may be petty, the serpent of eternity made of maggots . . .', but allowing this of itself entails credence on no mean scale. *Why* are we to be convinced by Mrs. Moore's sensation that other types of religious aspiring are irrelevant, and by Professor Godbole's that certain elements in Hinduism are more efficacious than anything Islam or Buddhism has to say? What makes the English lady's intuition in the cave definitive (of the nature of reality) or Professor Godbole's at Mau?

D. H. Lawrence was putting his finger on this central weakness I think with his remark 'I don't care about Bou-oum—Nor all the universe'[7]; a legitimate riposte that just by being uttered exposes the novel's failure to validate itself on this score; indeed the impossibility of such final and definitive justification as would vindicate the work's philosophical proceeding. If with Lawrence we turn on Forster's elderly heroine and say 'But *we* have not read into the "ou-boum" echo what *you* do', what could she, what can the book as a whole reply? Likewise when we get the 'telepathic appeal' at the end of the ceremony of Krishna's Birth, the effect in its place is, as Peter Burra has noted, 'Such beauty' as 'is not to be reckoned'[8]:

> It was his duty, as it was his desire, to place himself in the position of the God and to love her, and to place himself in her position and to say to the God, 'Come, come, come, come.' This was all he could do. How inadequate! But each according to his own capacities, and he knew that his own were small. 'One old Englishwoman and one little, little wasp,' he thought, as he stepped out of the temple into the gray of a pouring wet morning. 'It does not seem much, still, it is more than I am myself.'

Yet does Godbole's thinking of a wasp in connection with Mrs. Moore all unpromptedly at that hour mirror a true existential ligature in the nature of things or is it something contrived, *voulu* (however delicately) on the author's side and not necessarily to be found in the relations which the cosmos provides? A thorough-going materialist presumably makes the same objections (*inter multa alia*) to the novels of Charles Williams.

Our problem is partly one of degree, partly of kind. When Mrs. Moore and Adela Quested earlier at the Marabar picnic muse over the glories of Westmorland—' "Ah, dearest Grasmere!" Its little lakes and mountains were beloved by them all. Romantic yet manageable, it sprang from a kindlier planet' (Ch. 14)—we take the point. India's landscape suggests a dispensation of things far less anthropocentric than England's. Here visibly is a philosophical challenge. But how far the disorderliness of Nature in the subcontinent where they sit discredits monotheistic doctrines from (say) Palestine or southern Arabia is hard to define. The earliest of the Old Testament's authors knew they were up against a cosmos with some very queer physical features—and so does the Qu'ran. The issue is amongst the most interesting available to the notice and debate of men, but needs tougher working-over than Forster gives it here. All his treatment does, perhaps all it can do, is relentlessly to imply an alien Nature—alien to traditional theologies of coherence in things, as humanly understood—and to infer, in the case of (for instance) Mrs. Moore's received beliefs, a long-held misreading of the universal phenomena.

We are similarly grasping at a fog in trying to evaluate the authority of the experience associated with the Nawab Bahadur's motor-upset on the Marabar road (Ch. 8). On hearing of this from two of the participants, Ronny Heaslop and his fiancée, 'Mrs. Moore shivered, "A ghost!" ' and this episode has the following odd postlude:

> Down in Chandrapore the Nawab Bahadur waited for his car. He sat behind his town house (a small unfurnished building which he rarely entered) in the midst of the little court that always improvises itself round Indians of position. As if turbans were the natural product of darkness a fresh one would occasionally froth to the front, incline itself towards him, and retire. He was preoccupied, his diction was appropriate to a religious subject. Nine years previously, when first he had had a car, he had driven it over a drunken man and killed him, and the man had been waiting for him ever since. The Nawab Bahadur was innocent before God and the Law, he had paid double the compensation necessary; but it was no use, the man continued to wait in an unspeakable form, close to the scene of his death. None of the English people knew of this, nor did the chauffeur; it was a racial secret communicable more by blood than speech. He spoke now in horror of the particular circumstances: he had led others into danger, he had risked the lives of two innocent and honoured guests. He repeated: 'If I had been killed, what matter? It must happen sometime; but they who trusted me—' The company shuddered and invoked the mercy of God. Only Aziz held aloof, because a personal experience restrained him: was it not by despising ghosts that he had come to know Mrs. Moore? 'You know, Nureddin,' he whispered to the grandson—an effeminate youth whom he seldom met, always liked, and invariably forgot—'you know, my dear fellow, we Moslems simply must get rid of these superstitions, or India will never advance. How long must I hear of the savage pig upon the Marabar road?'

Yet Mrs. Moore's unpromptedness, distant from a scene she has not herself observed, suggests if not telepathy, something in addition, greater even than 'a racial secret communicable more by blood than speech' for it is a strong presumption that she has none of the Nawab Bahadur's ichor flowing in her veins. It implies that collective unconscious which Jung believed in; that mortals have each a part of one great Mind, unified across time and space. Whether the phenomenon encountered on the Marabar road has been a savage pig or a ghost after all remains another question again; yet, while we ought to pay full critical honour to the suggestiveness of the episode, the fineness of the author's handling of it so that his tale grows another dimension and indicates that aspect of living in which spiritual ligaments *are* apprehended though not to full interpretation by mankind, as an ingredient in the Hinduistic elements of the book it maintains a questionable status, like Professor Godbole's intuition of Mrs. Moore and the wasp at the end. Is it 'Zeus' or is it Forster who has arranged for the elderly Englishwoman to mutter 'A ghost!' at that stage?

A Passage actually enfeebles its case—its presented image of a world wherein order as traditionally conceived (especially by non-Hindus) does not inhere but another sort of coherence does—by slashing out so gratuitously at the religions its author finds uncongenial. For instance Buddhism—which gets no more consideration than a brief tilt that leaves a lot of questions begged:

> Some saddhus did once settle in a cave, but they were smoked out, and even Buddha, who must have passed this way down to the Bo Tree of Gaya, shunned a renunciation more complete than his own, and has left no legend of struggle or victory in the Marabar. (Ch. 12)

In this novel Forster's lifelong temperamental antipathy to Christianity—some of its laws at least, its Founder and its impact on his civilization—nags away on a scale positively heroic. The language of the Bible, especially the New Testament, is steadily parodied on practically every page, and the scolding becomes mere dismissiveness when we get to the caves themselves:

> But suddenly, at the edge of her mind, Religion appeared, poor little talkative Christianity, and she knew that all its divine words from 'Let there be light' to 'It is finished' only amounted to 'boum'.

The whole woodpeckering *parti pris* can strike one as rather remarkably silly in a work whose most essential theme of all is humanity's need of an epiphany, 'the difficulty of living in the universe'[9] without such an accession. If *A Passage to India* voices anything, it is first and last a desire for the revelation of Life's Meaning, *and* in a particular form: 'the Maker of al thing' visiting the world and befriending our species— explaining existence and justifying suffering *that* way.

Now of all the hieratic documents on record, interpretations of History and readings of mortal phenomena, the one which *par excellence* asserts that Krishna *has* arrived and—in the terms of Professor Godbole's song—coming to the milk-girl which is mankind (end of Chapter 7 and recurrently through the book) has by that act altered her fate, transfigured her happiness, is the corpus of orthodox Christian belief ('My soul doth magnify the Lord, And my spirit hath rejoiced in God my Saviour. For he hath regarded the low estate of his handmaiden . . .'). It seems odd to write a novel which enters so continually and feelingly that plea—'it voiced our loneliness nevertheless, our isolation, our need for the Friend who never comes yet is not entirely disproved'—and yet deals in so summary off-handed a way with precisely the religious tradition which responds to that appeal.

But artistically regarded *A Passage* is a more even success than *Howards End* in that its moralizing commentary, rather an overblown feature in the earlier volume, here is perfectly balanced with 'straight' narrative, description and dialogue; and we can certainly use Forster's last novel as a fine exemplum of his truly remarkable skills in writing.

As a storyteller he has only one flaw and very few peers. Take, for example, the opening of each of the three sections into which this novel is divided. They are deliberate pro-logomena and we apprehend them as standing back somewhat from events. Detached in mood thus, they answer the author's purpose to advertise the whole work's character as a piece of philosophizing, yet when once Chapter 1, which is only two pages long, is read, we are in possession of all the scenic background of the story, the topography of Chandrapore and those buildings in it which will have a significant rôle in the forthcoming action, much important plot-information; and the principal thematic notes of the tale have been sounded.

Hereafter scenes populated by Indians alternate with scenes where the British predominate: Hamidullah's small supper-gathering is followed by a visit (on our part) to the red-brick Chandrapore Club (sandwiched between these, meeting and speaking—significantly—alone and on equal terms, are Aziz and Mrs. Moore in their little episode at the mosque). The 'Bridge' Party follows—then we observe Aziz on the maidan outside the town practising polo—then Fielding and *his* tea-party. The canvas of a Forster novel is actually, in comparison with many other artists', crowded and busy, a multitude of different human figures are disposed and active upon it, but the early sequences unfold in a relaxed, apparently leisurely manner, even though substratographically the work's thematic life is all on the move and the story is developing from page to page.

An instance of this effect of relaxed narration—the absence of coerced, drilled events in a strained hectic fabliau—is the way the character of Fielding is introduced. A certain modest momentum has been gained by the preparations, complications and immediate aftermath of the Bridge Party but the concerns prompted in Adela Quested by this far from really delightful or civilized event are hung up in abeyance for a few pages (Chapter 7's first half). There is, as it were, a new intake of breath on the narrator's part, the beginning of a fresh subject.

> This Mr. Fielding had been caught by India late. He was over forty when he entered that oddest portal, the Victorian terminus at Bombay, and—having bribed a European ticket-inspector—took his luggage into the compartment of his first tropical train. . . .
> His career, though scholastic, was varied, [etc.]. . . .

But the work is not at a loose end, turning up out of an ill-assorted pack, desultorily, one card after another (however much in biographic fact it is the case that Forster himself felt bothered for inspiration in writing this novel early on and late). There is always something to draw us on and inward into the tale. First it has been the irritation mutually worked up by Major Callendar and his subordinate in the service of the District hospital (in Chapter 2): will this, we wonder, lead to a row? Worry on that score is followed by another uneasiness, at once more particular and more generalized; a clash is foreseeable between the new English girl coming out here and the City Magistrate, her possible fiancé *et pour cause*: the whole set of Anglo-Indian attitudes towards the local people (as expressed in Chapter 3) possesses an ugly fascination for us, makes almost every human encounter in this environment bristle with suppressed tension; and our path through the Collector's invitation and hospitality towards these latter on the Clubhouse lawn (Chs. 4 and 5) is an anxious one—to which Chapter 6 is an appropriate appendix. By this time— fifty-two pages into the saga by the Abinger edition's account— we have got interested enough in the various characters already introduced to bide our patience a moment while the novelist disposes new materials from a different, although nearby, angle of the tapestried loom. Yet the enfranchisement from urgent historiographic exigencies implicit in his choosing to do so not only serves his basic need *quâ* narrator at this juncture: to bring in, more fully introduced, another major character and topic (Fielding and his friendship with Aziz) before things progress any further on the main lines of the tale. It incarnates Life's own quality of moving at an uneven pace, not a forward rush of events, all equally significant and numbered in sequence in an intense order of fates. Having said which, it ought in justice to be noted that *Howards End* is a still superior achievement in just this regard. If the later book is a large full canvas, tall and broad, with perfect balance of groups and lines upon it, the earlier is a wide mural, an image that covers the whole wall of a long corridor (the corridor of humanity's progress through our Industrialized Age) and still more manages to combine the twin virtues of being really significant in practically every part as an organized fictional ado, with giving the impression of existence's own a-rhythmic apparent looseness of plot-weaving.

All the while however developments have been gathering, we have sensed this—for instance, in the tensions of outlooks opposed between Mrs. Moore and Miss Quested on the one side and Ronny Heaslop on the other—and in the next phase of the tale they do so more visibly, with (Ch. 8) the ghost?-

bumped car-drive, (Chs. 9–11) Aziz's reception of callers at his bedside of sickness in his bungalow, and (Chs. 12–14) the journey to the Marabar. *A Passage to India* is constructed upon a series of social amenities—offered motor-rides, invitations to dinner, to parties, group trips to see this or that—which all go wrong (even at Mau near the very end the tourists' boats overturn and they tumble into the water).

This fine management of activity in the interests of a story's rhythm can be traced through the railway journey to the caves, during which the two English ladies' grim experiences to come are, in thematic terms, very quietly but relentlessly prepared for; or in the way events thin out once the climax of the action has been passed with the trial scene's conclusion, yet the book does not lose *moral* momentum or interest as a narrative.

Forster's only flaw indeed in this aspect of his art is that first and last in his career he is fuddled in the matter of the distance between an author and his characters' fictional time. He believes on principle in the novelist's right to 'shift his viewpoint'; considers 'this power to expand and contract perception . . . one of the great advantages of the novel-form'[10]—and for the matter of that, I agree entirely with him—but this credo has led him at some aboriginal date in his imagination's career to infer that it denotes competence on the fictionist's part if he speaks about events, occasionally, as from some huge distance of years, of generations, after his characters have encountered them, or as if they have happened in the actual historical world.

These are heresies, mistakes which destroy, rather than enhancing, the illusion of life. As early as Chapter 4 of *Howards End* we are told of Helen Schlegel concerning her brief encounter with Paul Wilcox,

> A man in the darkness, he had whispered 'I love you' when she was desiring love. In time his slender personality faded, the scene that he had evoked endured. In all the variable years that followed she never saw the like of it again.

The pretence, sustained through the novel, that its author has seen his heroines across the whole of their lives from cradle to grave already and can comment on their careers as viewed wholes cannot in the given case win anything, as it happens, for this particular endeavour, can only blur its perspective. In *A Passage* still more glaringly, but uniquely, not a frequent fault, we have the following:

> Aziz yielded suddenly. He felt it was Mrs. Moore's wish that he should spare the woman who was about to marry her son, that it was the only honour he could pay her, and he renounced with a passionate and beautiful outburst the whole of the compensation money, claiming only costs. It was fine of him, and, as he foresaw, it won him no credit with the English. They still believed he was guilty, they believed it to the end of their careers, and retired Anglo-Indians in Tunbridge Wells or Cheltenham still murmur to each other: 'That Marabar case which broke down because the poor girl couldn't face giving her evidence—that was another bad case.' (Ch. 29)

The trouble with this sort of thing is that it suddenly projects the author into a seat of Olympian detachment way above the action without gaining anything thereby, and raises implausibility in unexpected forms. If the narrator can talk about his personages as though writing about 100 years after they have lived their lives, in what sense are they contemporary figures (at the time of publication)—not inhabitants of the eighteenth century—and what sort of date is *he* writing at: A.D. 2020? Further, if they are literally a part of our visible diurnal world, the one in which we are holding the book in our hands and reading it, why does none of us ever—in Cheltenham and Tunbridge Wells—come across a retired Anglo-Indian who puts his point of view *sotto voce* to us about that Marabar Case?

Questions are raised in short which would never lift up their heads at all if Forster did not suppose it incumbent on a fictionist to offer proofs of his divinity. Somebody has sold him that idea at the age of thirteen or whatever, and he has never found it out. The fact is that a good storyteller is divine, by nature, by definition, for the moments he speaks *urbi et orbi* in that rôle. He demonstrates the fact by creating a world and peopling it, like Boethius's God, at once foreseeing their ends and yet permitting them freedom of choices and personal self-development. But Time in the world so created is an 'alongside' chronology. It relates by analogy, not directly, to the calendar on the novelist's own personal mantelpiece—as I believe time in our world has an anagogic relation to the phenomenon of Succession as Boethius's God (the actual Deity in whom I believe) 'experiences'—one would rather say issues—it. There is a past and a future in both dimensions but one is a metaphor of the other, they do not connect as lengths of twine upon the same rope.

We must be cautious in our measurements here. The ending of *Maurice* is flawless in this regard, the beautiful paragraph where we are told one of the main characters' after-history:

> They were his last words, because Maurice had disappeared thereabouts, leaving no trace of his presence except a little pile of the petals of the evening primrose, which mourned from the ground like an expiring fire. To the end of his life Clive was not sure of the exact moment of departure, and with the approach of old age he grew uncertain whether the moment had yet occurred. The Blue Room would glimmer, ferns undulate. Out of some eternal Cambridge his friend began beckoning to him, clothed in the sun, and shaking out the scents and sounds of the May Term. (Ch. 46)

Such utterance is legitimate as it is fine because the novelist exactly does not try to link up the story's 'action-date' (according to the 'Terminal Note' 'about 1912') with the real-world chronometer to the accompaniment of which he is actually penning those words (in 1914). Absurd the attempt would be since Clive's old age must then be assumed to approach *circa* the yet far distant 1960s.

This blemish, infrequent enough to be trivial, is the only thing which from aesthetic causes actually makes one wince in Forster; unless objection be made to the 'downbeat' tenor of most of his longer stories. Four of the six novels cannot be said to end happily, after all, and few of his shorter tales.

In this matter he was, I think, on the horns of a dilemma which impales any modern fictive mind. Comoedic devising as a mode of creation is more than ever in our age simultaneously exigent, artistically the decent thing to do, yet lacking plausibility. Here from his *Commonplace Book* are some

Notes on a talk with Bob

> Life, so far as we know, is a freak in the universe, and even in the solar system. It does not even persist through this globe, but

is confined to its surface. Of living forms, only a small proportion utilise sex to continue themselves, and of that fraction only
a fraction is monogamous. Yet we are invited to regard
marriage as natural! If anything is 'natural' it is the entire
universe. What an aberration are we all in relation to it!

Consciousness the unique experiment. I consider that you
are romantic about the Life Force, whereas I with better reason
am romantic about what can be made out of it. Love and art
have been made out of it. They are the aberrations of an
aberration.

Goldie and the Platonists, going further than I can and much
further than you, regard them as premonitions of reality.
(p. 193, entry of 1948)

In a culture where such as the above are the background
fundamental assumptions about Man's environment and fate
in most people's minds and where the views of a Goldsworthy
Lowes Dickinson or a Platonist are not the norm, tragic
wailing art is otiose. What is there to beat the breast about if
we are all water-insects, creatures of an hour in a cosmos itself
impermanent as to its forms, where there is nothing more to
the whole of Reality than that, and where traditional human-
moral significances have been voided by the 'discoveries of
Science'? Still more, where are the good manners in mourning
like a bereaved Hecuba over the grave of things? If one must
enlist one's fellow-victims' attention at all for 'creative' pro-
ductions of one's improvising they should be cheerful; otherwise one is guilty of the same gross unkindness as rushing up
and down the gangway of a stricken airliner screaming (so
uselessly and cruelly) 'We're going to be killed! we're going to
be killed!' Such effusions of panic and misery may offer a
species of personal relief at the time but what help are they to
the others sitting beside you, no less white-faced but at least
properly behaved because restrained, on this Death Row? In
the same degree there is little virtue in moaning about those
woes and cruelties in mortal affairs not signalized by extinc-
tions of consciousness. In an intrinsically 'unfair' universe
where everything—again, on the human view—ultimately
goes wrong anyway, the sole really appropriate function for
the poets of our *homo sapiens* tribe, the *minnesinger* in whatever
literary form, is to be cheering, to take for their themes such

possibilities on the bright sides of existence, its happy elements, as they can glean, polish and make shine in their imitations of life—so that we are temporarily encouraged and comforted even though so haplessly doomed in every essential hope. The truly decent preoccupation for the skald in a culture with the cosmogonic assumptions which characterize our Occidental one now is exclusively, as one may say, 'what there is in all of this to buck us up'. Tragedy, which was always a little *bit* of a pose in any case (let alone sub-tragedy, merely gloomy stories and the like), has, in the wake of 'the New Philosophy' that got under sail in John Donne's time, become more and more and is now entirely an outrageous posture, a cheap self-indulgence on the artist's part, a narcissistic exploitation of society. The most deeply, genuinely intelligent nineteenth- and twentieth-century *poesis*, though for the same reasons exactly this is much harder to do than heretofore, is positively jocund and unhysterically blithe.

Art in our era, then, ought to be comic—'eucatastrophic' in J. R. R. Tolkien's term—or silent. But how much can a novelist, committed to producing happy plots (in the form of, say, fulfilled love-aspirations, achieved good purposes, contented merry societies, banished ills) mirror the facts—if not of a troubled earth (it always has been troubled within the ken of Clio), rather, of Man's apportionment at large, the principal determinants in the observed, the nowadays-believed-in Universe?

This is just as much a problem for someone who is (for instance) a Christian living and writing in the Occident, as a thoroughly modern agnostic. Your own personal vision, assumptions, about Man's 'long home', his destiny and his environment's meaningfulness, will colour your products, maybe; but they can only be strong artefacts to bear the weight and pressure of others' thought if they address themselves to the Areopagus of your own contemporary world—wherein (in our culture again—not, I agree, in Islam or possibly Thibet) the groundwork suppositions are so opposed to eucatastrophic theories of *The* Creation.

Because I do not personally share his vision of Life I find, for my personal taste, Forster's *oeuvre* a little too replete with sadness and hurt. But I think he has been as fair and balanced in treating of the human fate as his means and outlook in the circumstances allowed—the circumstances I have adverted to above—and not least in avoiding the begetting of 'Boo-hoo' art (as he would have called it: that is a favourite term of derision in his private critical record). Too many people may die or be frustrated, for our comfort, in his pages; but that reflects life as he sees it and the balance is redressed as far as conscientiously he can, by his all-enlivening humour. For it is time to emphasize afresh and more thoroughly than heretofore one of the principal features of his achievement; how Forster is one of the great *funny* writers, the provokers of laughter and producers of means to mirth.

We are assailed by one accession after another of jocose delight when we turn his pages from the way, which is the case in Jane Austen, so slily compassionate, so compassionatingly sly an intelligence reproduces with deadly accuracy the various manifestations of motive in human doings and the gaps between the cause of a given action or utterance, as it really is in itself at root, the image presented by its perpetrator for his own inward easement, and the vizard in which it is guyed up for public acceptation. Again, as with Jane Austen, Forster is an expert at showing the illogic of unworthy discourse or aims, the absurdities in which small-mindedness must necessarily obtrude itself on self-righteous occasions. The moment in *Mansfield Park* when, in a throwaway clause super-added to an already lengthy hypertactic sentence Jane Austen adjoins of Mrs. Norris's busy winter when she had so much to do during Sir Thomas Bertram's absence, 'and Mrs. Grant's wasteful doings to overlook' (Ch. 4, para. 3), has a fine successor in this ludicrous interlude during the courtroom proceedings of *A Passage to India*:

> And the party, including Miss Quested, descended from its rash eminence. The news of their humiliation spread quickly, and people jeered outside. Their special chairs followed them. Mahmoud Ali (who was quite silly and useless with hatred) objected even to these; by whose authority had special chairs been introduced, why had the Nawab Bahadur not been given one? etc. People began to talk all over the room, about chairs ordinary and special, strips of carpet, platforms one foot high. (Ch. 24)

181

Just as the kind of 'sprack wit'[11] which produced in *Pride and Prejudice* 'Lady Lucas was a very good kind of woman, not too clever to be a valuable neighbour to Mrs. Bennet' (Ch. 5) runs across all the earlier novelist's pages so the management of a tonic art of bathos travels an exhilarating thread through every chapter of Forster: tonic because it is not malicious merely, vindictive or an essay in reduction. He is, in the main (with his perennial nag at Christianity, his obsession against that, excepted) a writer singularly open, reverently available to experience's possibilities and unattended meanings. But regularly we have a phrase like the following—'A community that bows the knee to a Viceroy and believes that the divinity that hedges a king can be transplanted . . .' (Ch. 3). In each case, his and Jane Austen's, the power, the value of this stylistic posture resides in its balance. It is neither feral contempt nor wide-eyed credulity, but an attitude to life is constituted which is no more easily befooled than it is easily sceptical. It invites us thoroughly to deploy that piece of human equipment called intelligence, in short; it presents a mode of looking out upon the world which we want to appropriate and make our own. And of course the comic charge which throbs under so much of this novelist's writing and gives it in certain essentials therefore—exactly because it is a balanced kind of life-*affirming* humour—a very joyous tone, redresses the impact of his stories in their plot-aspects as tragedies and sub-tragedies.[12]

All this is possible to Forster because he is quite simply a master of language. *A Passage to India*, like all other great works of prose or verse, like most of his other writing, is a long succession of *mots justes*

> (where every word is at home,
> Taking its place to support the others,
> The word neither diffident nor ostentatious,
> An easy commerce of the old and the new,
> The common word exact without vulgarity,
> The formal word precise but not pedantic,
> The complete consort dancing together)[13]

—he can handle the English lexicon as a great pianist knows how to touch the ivories on his keyboard. One instance, by

way of proof, is the episode in Ronny's private room just before
the trial where, on a cue from Major Callendar—' "I say
there's not such a thing as cruelty after a thing like this" '—
Mrs. Turton is berating her male British compatriots for not
being sufficiently brutal towards the Indian community's
manhood within their rule:

> 'Exactly, and remember it afterwards, you men. You're
> weak, weak, weak. Why, they ought to crawl from here to the
> caves on their hands and knees whenever an Englishwoman's in
> sight, they oughtn't to be spoken to, they ought to be spat at,
> they ought to be ground into the dust, we've been far too kind
> with our Bridge Parties and the rest.'
> She paused. Profiting by her wrath, the heat had invaded
> her. She subsided into a lemon squash, and continued between
> the sips to murmur, 'Weak, weak.' (Ch. 24)

Her pronouncement is a very terrible thing and in a century
where this sort of effusion has been acted upon all over the
map—though rarely by the British: the Amritsar Massacre
(1919) was a terrific shock and scandal exactly for being an
exceptional atrocity in the latter-day conduct of the Raj, not
the rule, unlike Hitler's dealings with Europe and Russia or
quotidian administration in many Communist slave-states—
we are not inclined to dismiss it as having no serious side. One
of the book's many quieter ironies is that its chief expatriate
medical officer is a vicious bad-tempered sadist who keeps
venting aloud his longing to mutilate and murder people, and
has a certain sphere of 'operations' (in the case of the hapless
Nureddin, for example) at the Minto Hospital. But the author
manages to make Mrs. Turton's savagery contemptibly absurd
as well as frightening (as so often does Jane Austen with her
villains) and by stylistic as well as pictographic means. Her
repeated 'Weak, weak', becomes ludicrous, the feeble cheep-
ings of a stupid fowl when she has so far hurled herself against
the edicts of Nature as to defy the enormous heat all around
and quickly exhaust her physical powers. For the huge
temperature's implacability is further embodied to our senses
by the homophony of the long vowels in 'Profiting by her
wrath'.
  Similar skill in characterization informs the moment where,

in *A Room with a View*, rounded on at last, Charlotte Bartlett's head is described as '[driving] backwards and forwards, as though demolishing some invisible obstacle' (Ch. 16) which beautifully images the way Lucy Honeychurch's cousin is emphatic in a life which has no true purpose; she is a sort of besotted machine which drills away without any real goal to attain. The same command of expression informs the crucial account of what has happened, philosophically, to Mrs. Moore in the Cave. The narrator tells us of her echo,

> Coming at a moment when she chanced to be fatigued, it had managed to murmur, 'Pathos, piety, courage—they exist, but are identical, and so is filth. . . .' (Ch. 14)

It is the late entry of 'filth' into that sentence which graphically conveys how identical all experience suddenly does seem to this elderly lady. The initial power of the alliterative 'pathos' and 'piety' is sapped by the brittle 'i' of 'exist' (the author doesn't use here a large long-vowelled word, such as 'are', nor labour the idea as with 'coexist') and by the blotting-paper effect, the cotton-wool-like sound of the 'f' and 'lth' in 'filth'.

Accomplishment in these kinds, sustained over the course of whole volumes at a time, are what one means by poetic grasp of language and true novelistic power. Though his every work has its failures, they enable Forster to realize richly many of his mystical as well as prosaic purposes.

NOTES

1. Op. cit. (see note 6 to previous chapter), pp. 204–6.
2. Reprinted in Abinger edition of *A Passage to India* (London, 1978), p. 328.
3. *Life*, Vol. I, p. 262.
4. Recorded in Forster's obituary tribute 'Syed Ross Masood' in *Two Cheers for Democracy*.
5. See Abinger edition of *A Passage to India*, p. xxv.
6. Author's note to Chapter 33 in Everyman edition (of *Passage*) 1942, p. xxi; reproduced in Abinger edition, p. 364.
7. See *Life*, Vol. II, p. 124.
8. Op. cit. (in Abinger edition of *A Passage to India*), p. 320.
9. *Life*, Vol. II, p. 308; Forster's own phrase about the work's essential theme, uttered in 1960.

10. *Aspects of the Novel*, Ch. 4.

11. Mrs. George Austen (the novelist's mother)'s term for an element common to all her children's conversation. *The Shorter Oxford English Dictionary* usefully condenses its parent volume's entry as follows: '**Sprack**, *a.* Chiefly *dial.* 1747. [var. of SPRAG *a.*] Brisk, active; alert, smart; in good health and spirits.'

12. Nevertheless it is interesting that he could jib against the bit in just this regard and that *Arctic Summer* was abandoned because he could not see his way to giving its two heroes a happy ending. That at root was *why* he could not conceive a central event like 'a mountain round or over or through which . . . the story must somehow go' (see pp. 137ff. *supra* and Abinger Edition, Vol. 9, p. 162, where he insists that it remained a torso because the possibility of an unhappy conclusion did not interest him).

13. *Four Quartets*, 'Little Gidding', lines 217–23 (from Section V).

6

Biography and Memoirs by Forster; his *Commonplace Book*. Personal Reminiscences

Next in interest, to date, after his novels and tales have come Forster's biographic (with which I include autobiographic) writings. These take various forms. There are whole volume-length studies of a contemporary's life: *Goldsworthy Lowes Dickinson* (1934) and *Marianne Thornton* (1956, the account of his paternal grandmother's family, of Clapham Sect fame, through the eyes and doings of this great-aunt who played so significant a part in his own destiny). Of the two books I think the former is the more valuable for giving us insight into some of Forster's own inspirations. Dickinson as a teacher evidently fed his attraction to Ancient Greek civilization. He provided the younger man with the positive element in his philosophy:

> . . . he feels that until human nature has expanded fully, we cannot be either saved or safe, and views civilization as a pilgrimage towards a harmony which may never be realized, but it is our only proper goal.[1]

(Is not this the theme of *Howards End*?—a mysticism far more exhilarating because it is unwilled.) This 'goal' emerges again explicitly in the essay 'What I Believe':

> Not by becoming better, but by ordering and distributing his native goodness, will Man shut up Force into its box, and so

186

gain time to explore the universe and to set his mark upon it worthily.

And Dickinson himself constituted, as Forster's beautiful account of his later life attributes to him, a model of the human sanity which this disciple desired to emulate in is turn.

> Few men can so have combined the powers of the head and the heart, and by the use of reason have so fortified the affections to withstand the inevitable shocks which await them. (Ch. 9)

It is sadly amusing to remark the terms in which Beatrice Webb acknowledged grateful receipt of this fine biography.

> Why don't you write another great novel (analogous to the *Passage to India*) giving the essence of the current conflict all over the world between those who aim at exquisite relationships within the closed circle of the 'elect' and those who aim at hygienic and scientific improvement of the whole of the race?[2]

In effect Forster had been trying to do this, with *Arctic Summer*, and lost his way. But 'No more of that; I have noted it well.' In the way of thinking on that loss, madness lies.

On a similar principle it helps to have in his other Indian writings (now superbly edited by Dr. Elizabeth Heine[3]) additions to his novelistic account of India. That country was recurrently for Forster a matrix of profound experience, and one which drew out of the increasingly materialistic vision towards which his personality developed throughout our century susurrations of other kinds of feeling. As late as 1952–53 when he was recollecting his *ad hominem* studies of religious attitudes in Native States four decades previously, the ruler of Dewas Senior could evoke this from him:

> From start to finish, from the days when he behaved well and was officially petted down to the days when he misbehaved and was punished, he was never simple, never ordinary, never deaf to the promptings which most of us scarcely hear. His religion was the deepest thing in him. It ought to be studied—neither by the psychologist nor by the mythologist but by the individual who has experienced similar promptings. He penetrated into rare regions and he was always hoping that others would follow him there. He was never exclusive, despite his endless pujahs [prayer sessions]. To recall the conversation that we had

forty years ago in an upper room at Delhi, he was hopeful that we should all be recalled to the attention of God.

That, in the 'Pondicherry' section of *The Hill of Devi*, offers but one flavour and instance of fresh thinking from a book which is all round a very valuable supplement to *A Passage to India*. Indeed the region inspired him to new modes of consciousness as an artist early and late. On 2 February 1913, just after his first encounter with this great extraordinary region, we find him writing to Forrest Reid on the subject of his advancing sterility as a fictionist, 'I want something beyond the field of action and behaviour: the waters of the river that rises from the middle of the earth to join the Ganges and the Jumna where they join.'[4] In a much later piece begotten by travel there, the Journal he wrote on his visit in 1945 (an extract from which has been expertly edited by Dr. Michael Halls), recurs the theme of a new way of 'expounding the lovely world':

> Young writer wanted—space not as I knew it, or time . . . I should have a cinema mind—I detected it neglecting its opportunities. [From entry of 6 October]

> O lovely world, teach others to expound you as I have not been able to do: O untroubled spaces, seldom looked upon by men's eyes, and unmarked by their activities: These clouds over the Mediterranean which will keep moving when I have passed, those deserts in Arabia which I flew over coming out, and again the other night in the dark, You remain pure and unconquered, and the imagination of others shall conquer you. [From entry of 30 December][5]

Surely the reason why Forster took to India and its people as G. L. Dickinson did not was in part at least that thought and attitudes of the kind he found in (for instance) the Hindu rulers he especially knew expressed a response to living that his novels had already, and emphatically, embodied.

> Salvation, then [according to the Maharajah of Dewas State Senior], is the thrill *we* feel when God again becomes conscious of us, and all our life we must train our perceptions so that we may be capable of feeling when the time comes. (From a letter of 6 March 1913 to Mrs. Aylward[6].) About a month earlier, I had had a Krishna conversation with another Ruling Prince: the fantastic and poetical Maharajah of Chhatarpur. It took

place not in a dull Delhi room, but amidst the magnificent scenery of Bundelkhand. . . . 'I try to meditate on Krishna. I do not know that he is a God, but I love Love and Beauty and Wisdom, and I find them in his history. I worship and adore him as a man. If he is divine he will notice me for it and reward me; if he is not, I shall become grass and dust like the others.'[7]

This harmonizes with much in Forster's fiction, for instance the conclusion of Chapter 28 of *Maurice*:

> No reward awaited him. This work, like much that had gone before, was to fall ruining. But he did not fall with it, and the muscles it had developed remained for another use.

Again, for more explicit affirmation of the novelist's ideals, yet delicate, lacking the rhetorical crudities which jostle the reader through so much of *Maurice*, there is the brilliant, the wonderful 'Letter to Madan Blanchard' (in the 'Places' section of *Two Cheers for Democracy*). Here, going round the world to the almost antipodean Pelew Islands and backwards in time, Forster celebrates someone who seems to have been 'a solid fellow who suddenly jibbed'. And I think it was the element that jibbed in Forster himself which took him up in a glider above Cambridge one day, at 88, given the offer of the ride. 'There was nothing much to it really', he told me. 'We just went up and then'—small smiling uh-hm of a conspiratorial chuckle—'came down.' Or likewise the element which kept him utterly unflustered and unflustering the time in his mid-eighties he was left overnight locked in that city's Guildhall at the end of a concert during which he had dropped off to sleep, so that he spent the dark hours entirely unillumined and alone in that big building—surely a frightening ordeal for another kind of very old person—calm and quiet till the cleaners arriving in the morning discovered him and let him out.

But of the more extended works of this author I believe the most significant after his novels is his *Commonplace Book*, the tome he found in 1925 which had been bought in 1804 by Bishop Jebb of Limerick, had been elaborately indexed and but slightly written in by him (considering it is six quires of paper long) and which, left to the Forster family, the grandson of his chaplain appropriated upon discovery for continuing with entries of his own.

The *Commonplace Book* collects other people's sayings and writings as well as excogitations of Forster's and as yet exists only in a facsimile issue of 1978.[8] The letterpress edition, when it comes, ought to popularize it (like Gide's *Journals*) and awaken a larger awareness of its importance. It is a major work because it shows us one of the most finely articulate minds of the age pursuing its inheritance, the materialist outlook on life, with as much sensitivity and rigour as it can manage wherever that outlook may lead and attempting to come to terms with the facts of human consciousness through the same, eschewing anti- or non-materialistic 'consolations' and their (to his sense unproved) premises.

The volume does other things too. As the record of a mind assaying to cope with war, love, frustration, literature and other phenomena across a trajectory of more than forty years, given that the talent in question is as precisely expressive as Forster's, it would anyway be an important read even if it had not the larger theme running through it and constantly being worked and reworked at, that I have named above.

One proof of its distinction is that we don't weary of the author's self-analysis. This is either so clever, so generalized in its application or so (genuinely) modest, that the book is an epitome of a man's experience as such approached in a particular way, not the inexhaustible nose-pickings, as it were in front of a mirror, of an anxious infatuated egoist. The general tendency of the whole is downbeat and its vision ultimately and in sum is of the human fate as a yawning vacuum; yet it makes good reading, in doses, as does the Book of Ecclesiastes or certain other—in the last resort—nihilistic affirmations, and for similar reasons. It is so very well written; 'if way to the better there be, it exacts a full look at the worst'; and the whole is enlivened by Forster's deadly-impish sense of humour. An instance exemplifying at least two of these features is the entry in which he ends a quotation from letters by Thomas Gray.

> I reckognize [*sic*] an affinity. Laziness and loyalty have a connection. And sexuality? E. Fitzgerald. How this academic gentle gentlemanly type has survived! 3 Trumpington Street, where I write, is in a straight line with Gray's rooms in Pembroke and Fitzgerald's in King's Parade. We have our place in history—the small enclosure reserved for old dears—and if

noticed will awake some affection. Coleridge and Goldie have left
us to follow larger visions.

I think though, to be honest, that I am a more important
writer than either Fitzgerald or Gray. I have taken more trouble
to connect my inner life with the world's, even though I have not
been strong enough to stick. (p. 192 of the original autograph
and therefore of the facsimile edition; entry of 1948)

The *Commonplace Book* embodies in entry after entry his
sterling ability, unique, well beyond that of other British
writers in our age, to walk right round a human being or social
phenomenon and articulate precisely, without the prim
nannyish governessiness of which he was sometimes justly
accused, the virtues and flaws which are its most determinant
characteristics. It is like reading extracts from the dossiers of
the Recording Angel. Here is *the* definitive account, very
amusing, not deliberately so, not unkind, ruthlessly just,
unconsciously stern, appreciatively generous, grateful, fair, of

> *Bloomsbury*, hopes W. J. Turner, will not enjoy Schnabel, a
> pianist whom he enjoys himself. Why drag the place in, I
> wonder. I suppose ∴ [= because] it is the only genuine
> movement in English civilisation, though that civilisation con-
> tains far better and more genuine individuals. The other
> cheap, envious ⎫
> movements are anti-Bloomsbury and self-conscious ⎬ —wh. Bl.
> as a movement is not, being composed of people who hold similar
> opinions and dont quarrel violently with one another.—But
> unkind, despite irritable protests to the contrary; Orlando regards
> the centuries of flesh and spirit as fresh fuel for her bonfire, and
> death can only be laughed at (I remember their laughter at
> Massingham's) or adorned with a tasteful garland like Lady
> Strachey's.—Its contempt of the outsider plays a very small part
> of its activity, and rests on inattention rather than arrogance.
> Once convinced that he is not a figure of fun, it welcomes and
> studies him, but the rest of humanity remains in a background of
> screaming farce as before. Meanwhile the intellect—thinking
> and talking things out—goes steadily ahead, 'things' looking
> rather like small Xmas trees when they come into the room, and
> trees minus their leaves and decorations when they are carried
> out. The final bareness isn't tragic, the horrors of the universe
> being surveyed in physical comfort, and suffering apprehended
> only intellectually. Essentially *gentlefolks*. Would open other
> people's letters, but wouldn't steal bully, slander, or blackmail

like many of their critics, and have acquired a culture in harmony with their social position. Hence their stability. Contrast them with (a) gamindom—Joyce, D. H. Lawrence, Wyndham Lewes [*sic*] (b) aristocracy who regard culture as an adventure and may at any moment burn their tapering fingers and drop it. Academic background, independent income. Continental enthusiasms sex-talk, and all, they are in the English tradition.

I dont belong automatically—from 1916 on the gulf was bound to widen. And I couldnt go there for any sort of comfort or sympathy (p. 59)

Will the Court of Heaven in plenary session on Judgement Day be able to pronounce more discriminatively, more comprehensively than that?

Nor do we meet in this volume merely with humane judiciousness at its most expert and given supreme tongue. Forster can speak as one whose lips have been touched with celestial flame out of the heart, the mystery of passion. Surely this next entry signalizing the apparition and impermanence of a perfect erotic mutuality is the finest our modern literature has to show on the glory and problem of mortal amorous relationship:

> *I have to read* a book at a certain rate and cannot look backwards or on. One of the pages turns out to be gold. I come to it with surprise joy and terror, and know it must be turned over like the others. How lovely if the next page could be The End.[9]

The 'Commonplaces' as a whole are not written to that standard of perception. They can be trite as Forster is always capable of being; for example in an entry of 27 October 1943:

> Wisdom, when acquired, proves incommunicable and useless and goes with our learning into the grave. The edges of it occasionally impinge on people, though and strike a little awe into them.[10]

That is too glibly bleak, facilely pessimistic, and will not bear thorough searching. Its author is deliberately seeking exhilaration in the turning of a gloomy aphorism. But then this sort of lapse is as well in its way too; one wants the tome to be fallible at times, for as W. H. Auden has said of the writer's craft

> We're not musicians: to stink of Poetry
> is unbecoming, and never
> to be dull shows a lack of taste.[11]

If every phrase in the *Commonplace Book* were pure irrefutable Wisdom freshly fetched off Olympus, we should feel choked by encounter with the asphyxiating airs breathed by a god, not a fellow-human whose record of his progress through the world may assist our own. But very many of Forster's sentences (in both senses of the word) here *will* take a heavy weight of pondering: •

> *Love of Danger:* enviable but disgusting; coprophagist. (p. 177, entry of 1944)

> *The difficulty of growing old* is that one doesn't know what to do, through want of experience, helplessly watches the waves breaking and civilisation growing older at the same rate as oneself. In youth experience is unnecessary: in age we count on it and, generally speaking, only act successfully when it is to hand. Inverted adolescence. The decay of our powers more puzzling than their birth, because our consciousness was born with them, but here it lags behind, looking at the symptoms and unable to decide which is to be taken seriously. Apart from its discomfort, its so baffling. (p. 67)

and under an entry on Shakespeare's management of language:

> Death.—what a grand easy proprietor! Romeo & Juliet & Hamlet were his banqueting halls, Macbeth his dormitory, and nobody either ignored or belittled him. Thus they strutted around grandly themselves, and attained *Poetry through Rhetoric* in a way we can't. If I died like Romeo I should do so in irritability. (p. 99: [dated] 18.11.32)

which in inimitable Forsterian voice manages to amuse while making entirely seriously some interesting points.

This long vade-mecum also testifies to Forster's intense commitment to reproducing Life's actual flavour in his pages; that this is one of his central concerns as a fictionist. In a note made in 1927 he says on a new

> *Novel, beginning one*: . . . How to get down the first hand experiences of my life—today I heard F.V. was not going to prison, helped to lift garden seats, planted tulips, ate Scotch bun inside bread and butter, read Thomas Mann, fear the elm will be blown down—I might have spent such a day 20 years back, here it is, and what can I do with it? Digested by my literary mind, it will tend to reappear as a young man's day, and all the

incidents will be haloed with a spurious novelty and wonder, they will be falsified by 'oh this was the first time he . . .' which insensibly perverts and pervades modern literature, and turns the numerous and fascinating noises of life into a mechanical morning song. Abjure freshness, underemphasise surprise. Each incident should fall on to a thick bed of previous impressions ['previous' replaces 'its own', crossed out], like the tree on to mould that has been formed by its own dead leaves. . . . (pp. 42–3)

Stitched in and out of the multitude of heterogeneous reflections and *trouvailles* which make up the work runs Forster's principal proceeding. He takes by slow but progressive advances to its logical conclusion as full an imaginative response as he knows how to the materialist vision of the Universe prevailing since the eighteenth century. In this regard *A Passage to India*, with such apophthegms as e.g. 'Geology, looking further than religion . . .' (para. 1 of Ch. 12) is transitional, in theme and mood. He tries to come to terms with this in two aspects: (1) abandonment of hope about the future of the human race; (2) facing the prospect of his own personal extinction.

Early and late, at least as far as he is conscious of the business, the latter is much the easier of these difficulties. Celebrating in 1940 his find, the folio itself—'And what paper! paper manly yet seductive, paper which persuades the lagging and corrects the errant pen, sustains the heavy ink, retains the light, tempts even the twentieth century into calligraphy'[12]— he remarks of his death in comparison with the previous user's, it 'interests me less than his interested the Bishop'.[13] It is not that a stiff upper lip comes more easily to him than the next man, though he is very keen on its possession.

> *We cease to grieve*, cease to be fortune's slaves
> Nay cease to die by dying.
>
> —Webster, *The White Devil*

> All very well and courage is the goods, but my snag is that I try to be plucky in order to gain peace of mind and have no use for bravery for its own sake.[14]

But from early on Forster has digested pretty thoroughly the logic that if Death means annihilation it will not be an

experience, therefore no sweat is the least bit due on the score
of one's own destruction: an entirely apt response to that
bother, it seems to me; our problems all start and multiply like
the Hydra if, as I believe, Death is *not* the end. (One reason
why I think so is that by temperament and experience I am
too little easily comforted to suspect the Law of Things as
kindly-simple enough. After all of Life's strenuosities, with the
whole show such an uphill struggle 99% of the time, sheer
plod and constant worry, complication and complexity so
major a part of its intrinsic character, its very 'trick' and
signature, you have to be indefatiguably sanguine entirely to
be convinced—an optimist practically raving utterly to
believe—Death will prove so straightforward and accommo-
dating. Oh no, brothers, we are tied to a wheel. It is all a much
toughter show than that.) More difficult for him is the
adjustment to Science's latest concept of the cosmos as itself a
thing impermanent, fluxive, with aeons of matter imploded, so
that Forster cannot even hope after his day to extend in space
if not in time (see note called 'Book' at the end of the volume,
written as late as 1956).

Most troublesome of all, and this seems to have required all
his ninety-one years to learn to live with, is the degeneration of
the countryside in his own land and the degradation of Nature
world-wide.

> And like a man in wrath the heart
> Stood up and answered 'I have felt'

From Tennyson's duel between reason and emotion across a
grave. The lines had some magic and power yesterday which
now that I copy them out have faded. I should never think of
applying them to Rob's death [his beloved godson, deceased in
early life 1962], though I might forty years ago to Mohammed
el Adl's. Such love as I can feel no longer asserts or fights. It is
bound up with my own impermanence, with the consent I have
given to disappear, with the disappearance of the fragile
Tennysonian Lincolnshire which I hope to see next week. The
death of our countriside [*sic*] (which will *never* be renewed)
upsets me more than the death of a man or of a generation of
men which be [*sic*] replaced in much the same form. 15.4.63
I can't read any one of the lovely nature-references in In
Memoriam or Maud without pain.[15]

Well if the gods award prizes for selfless beautiful kinds of love, the species of attachment which ought to gain Forster his accolade will surely be his passionate devotion to man's natural environment. First and last in his career he adored it and longed for its remaining untrammelled, unsullied. This worship is discriminative and careful, like the best of loves in any kind.

> Next day 8.4.28 I take a longer walk to Honeysuckle Bottom. The path is blocked by trees that had fallen in the snow. Wild, wild, wilder than the genuine forests that survive in the south of Sweden. I excite myself by learning the names of the woods on the Ordnance Map, by hearing a wryneck and by seeing a swallow and a bat—all three pleasures early. Think I will learn the names of all the fields in the parish, although the lease of the house expires in a few years' time. Wish I had talked to old men. (pp. 48–9)

It extends, such searching and feeling responsiveness, even quite far into physics and metaphysics.

> Now, the other day, from dining room, underneath little oak trees' boughs on lawn, there appeared on the down: yellow green strip below, purple grey one above. They were in such perfect relationship to each other and to the level boughs of the tree ruled above them, that I feared my mother would speak. For two or three seconds I had that rare pleasure an aesthetic emotion. It vanished or became utilitarian as soon as I realised it had brought me peace, but for several seconds I was content that the strips shouldn't recall something else or even be fields. Is this the pleasure trained artists can command? Their lives ought to be happy. Here, as with the bacteria, I am at the frontier of a kingdom but cannot get in. (Conclusion of note on 'Evening Walk 8.8.28', pp. 51–2)

He reads through many documents of scientific research and its collations with the aim of apprehending phenomena as they 'really' are (e.g. 'Eddington', 'Guinea Worms', entries on pp. 57 and 59 respectively) and 'in the hope that through this scrutiny "my new Ethic will emerge" '.[16] And in a sense it does. He comes to accept as inevitable, though tragic, the human species' collapse no less than his own demise. He travels from aching over the nations' imperfectibility and their endless possibilities of strife and mayhem (p. 95 under 'Ah No Ah No')

to a certain quietude of spirit before their apparently likely
self-extinction. He was explicit indeed, if asked, about this
likelihood. One evening I was sitting briefly with him at the
pre-Dinner hour and said 'Mr. Forster, do you think the human
race will survive?'

> FORSTER: No. Do you?
> SELF: Yes.
> FORSTER: Why?
> SELF: I don't know (*shuffling a bit, embarrassed at the method not the
> content of my argument*). I just feel it will.
> FORSTER: I can't see it myself.

But man's latter-day raids upon the encompassing scene
distressed him with little solace the length of his whole career.
Yet through or in spite of what is set down in that quotation
under the heading from Tennyson ('And like a man in wrath')
there is, as he abandons one position and then another, a
smaller loss of humanity than might be expected. Surprising
(it could be said) the affirmation of values in even the gathering lurid sunset, the general void, the Abysm ahead of all his
hopes' defeat.

It is happy that he came across this empty tome in the year
immediately following *A Passage to India*'s publication and
wrote in it from then on. It is a more solid, because serious,
piece of work than the mechanically sceptical twitterings of
Pharos and Pharillon (1923)[17] and more substantial than the
short stories he wrote after this time.

A major testament from so intelligent and articulate a
personality, albeit with blindspots and intermittencies in its
perceptions, the *Commonplace Book* is one of the big accessions of
twentieth-century letters: as well worth having as a new novel
from its writer; indeed it presents that condition and development of his mind wherein a new novel was not forthcoming.

The subject of *E. M. Forster: A Life* however does not come
across as so great a boon or blessing through most of his years.
This is a little bit the responsibility of his biographer who (with
the best intentions) has represented the central figure as much
as possible by his own diary, etc. entries and autoverdicts

(which therefore makes not a balanced account of the career, though a very valuable); but more largely it is Forster's own fault. Through all but the last pages of the two volumes he afflicts the reader's nerves as everything but truly amiable and, though such an impression may be little looked for by any devotee of his work who knows that only, it is not hard to say why.

Forster was, in intention from early on and increasingly over the years in practice, a thorough-going committed hedonist. That type of individual can, when intelligent and witty, be fun as a companion, a conversationist, a social item, but it is impossible to respect. His own note on the subject is really a tombstone: 'Without a moral effort (which I cannot ever make) I am steering through disappointments and betrayals.'[18] Hedonists are generic to those people who roam around begging to be loved ('I'm lonely! *Love me!*'): exactly the kind of person nobody *can* fall for, however earnest an attempt be made. Human beings are as personalities ultimately interesting and attractive only when they are thinking about something else: the duties of the day, their neighbours' preoccupations, the job in hand and *not whether they themselves are happy*. To be in presence of someone who has, however implicitly, secretly, that as the essential concern on his mind, is always embarrassing and off-putting. Forster was continually asking 'Am I having a good time?' and comes over as wonderfully unappealing. He was generous on many occasions, sensitive, thoughtful, he was anything you like; but when on earth did he ever choose to *pay*—I mean really pay in some way it hurt—for a moral commitment? When did he ever put himself out deeply?

There is a big divorce here between the man and the work. His novels are the very accents themselves of Love in Love's aspects of Brotherly Feeling (Philadelphia) and Kindness (Caritas): those are their central notes and one of the reasons why they are more important than D. H. Lawrence's, whose sex-pother is a much more facile achievement. But these things, which Forster was a rare expert about on paper and could practise in the flesh, do not get the final attestation in his own life, the one that counts, that of self-sacrifice in a really significant degree—not at least as his biographer or he himself ever presents the business. A much lesser author does seem to have touched this matter with, alas, only too much point.

His most formidable detractor was Graham Greene. Greene caricatured him in *The Third Man* as the old-maidish writer Benjamin Dexter, who 'took a passionate interest in embroidery' and calmed 'a not very tumultuous mind with tatting'. He also attacked him in *Why Do I Write?* as an irresponsible liberal, a typical member of the PEN Club, always signing appeals in *The Times*. 'So long as he [i.e. such a writer] had eased his conscience publicly in print, and in good company, he was not concerned with the consequences of his letter.'[19]

This is travesty of the life as a whole but not very answerable as a *compte rendu* for much of and in it—again, as revealed by the biography, the known facts and the character of Forster's own memoranda. So that in the light of these considerations the paradox is not as surprising as at first blush it would seem; that 'people fell in love with him through his books' (*Life*, Vol. II, p. 278)—this is certainly why I took upon myself to call on him when I went up to Cambridge in the October of 1968—but not when they met him in the flesh.

Yet the man who was E.M.F. during his very last years. . . . Lately it has occurred to me, and for the first time, during the writing of this book, to wonder if I knew him not just at the tail-end of his earthly existence—as who should presumptuously say its mere fag-stub—but, my acquaintance being of the last twenty months, over part of its very best segment of all. For the human being I met was significantly unlike the figure only too accurately reflected (I make no doubt) in his own private writings and in most of P. N. Furbank's narrative. In extreme old age[20] Forster was deeply impressive, a higher form of life altogether.

The first thing to say, or to repeat here for some insistence, is that at this time of life he was not the least bit senile. Very old in physical terms, burdened with age, yes. But gaga? Quite the opposite. In fact he is the only great writer of our literature's history I have met and the only one I have hoped since then I ever shall have encountered by the time my days are done: precisely because, unpretentiously enough, he talked exactly as his books read—with the same pith, insight, economy, the same voice entirely. This begets a happy illusion: if not that, could we have once called upon Shakespeare or Milton, it would have meant, at the feeblest, hearing them discuss their laundry-bills in immortal verse; rather, that in the case of the really big authors, the personality in the texts and the actual man are identical spirits. It is not just, now, that it can never seriously occur to me that Jeremy Taylor might conceivably have fumbled cack-handedly through the language when he wanted an euphonious synonym in the course of diurnal chat, but that the light of day ever beheld him in the rôle of an extortioner.

One time Forster recollected a fine performance of *Götter-dämmerung* at Dresden 1905 where the Germans enthusiastically staged Brünnhilde's Immolation as realistically as possible and all went well until the horse started eating the scenery. When the first Moon-'probe' took place in 1969, I had excited mixed feelings and said 'But it is a new frontier'. 'Yes', replied he, 'and my generation had not expected that there would *be* another.'[21]

'What was D. H. Lawrence like, Mr. Forster?'

'He was frightening.'

'To you or to other people?'

'*I* found him frightening. He was very fierce. He would challenge you to justify everything you said.'

His face lit up, and speech, when I told him one day about the variegated assortment of bantam poultry I kept at home. Like myself he had an insatiable appetite for the small homely details of life and could be wondrously regaled with the arrangements of a chicken-run. Most of the other people I have ever known cannot (alas); and I suppose it may be regarded as an old-maidish trait. But I never knew he was homosexual until on some of the radio tributes immediately after his death this element in his nature was very relishingly discussed.

Once or twice he chuckled over the sheer fact of his age: 'You see, I am so *very old!*' as if entirely in the light of a joke. But the jest, all undeliberately, may really have been upon me. Of the two of us in that saloon (on 'A' staircase at King's), he was so much the younger in that he had somehow got outside Time.

Let me try to explain.

To Mr. Furbank's expert description of Forster in his last years (*Life*, Vol. II, Chs. 13 and 14) I can add little. But what greatly struck me then, what has become more articulate in my consciousness lately, is the serenity and aliveness of the spirit inside that very aged, worn, ungainly body. It was hugely glad in a quiet and wholly un-'valedictory' way. He makes Yeats's great poem 'Lapis Lazuli' real as no other experience has done.

Normally when I read W. B. Yeats's verses I rejoice in the virile beauty of the poetry in them and am coldly unconvinced by their (so much more wishful, it seems to me, than proven) 'thought'—if I may expose myself as daring crudely to bifurcate these elements out of their alleged and offered unity. I always used to think in just this way that the vision, and near the end of *his* career, of the two old Chinamen across the world's sadness and their own mortality was another lovely hoax on the part of the Irish bard.

> Every discoloration of the stone,
> Every accidental crack or dent,
> Seems a water-course or an avalanche,
> Or lofty slope where it still snows
> Though doubtless plum or cherry-branch
> Sweetens the little half-way house
> Those Chinamen climb towards, and I
> Delight to imagine them seated there;
> There, on the mountain and the sky,
> On all the tragic scene they stare.
> One asks for mournful melodies;
> Accomplished fingers begin to play.
> Their eyes mid many wrinkles, their eyes,
> Their ancient, glittering eyes, are gay.

Yet I now realize this is not mere whistling in the dark. Forster's eyes were gay, his whole personality was so just in the manner of the Yeats figures, on the very eve of his own extinction; an event which, since he travelled through old age with all his intelligence intact, he was consciantly anticipating in the very near future through the seasons I knew him.

In fact he knew pretty exactly when he was sentenced. In the late afternoon of 25 May 1970 I called on him flourishing my Tripos Shakespeare Paper of that morning all ready for a mutual laugh upon the fact that one of its questions was simply a half-statement rather than interrogative or really a challenge at all.

But on arrival I found matters altered.

Mr. Furbank was there—my first and so far only meeting with that gentleman—and Forster was seated in his chair beside the fireplace with his legs beshawled. He seemed all his cheerful self, however, and introduced me to his friend, as indeed his appointed biographer, and both were very kind. Drinks were discussed and I was ensconced opposite (on the other side of the fireplace) with a glass of sherry, Mr. Furbank doing the honours, and Forster was provided with a very large Martini Bianco: which in the light of later confirmed knowledge seems to me exquisitely right. What a perfect occasion to start, for the first time in your life, some really solid drinking: when you realize that you have just had your final stroke. (I like it, I like it.)

It became apparent to me—for that matter they neither of them much baulked the matter as far as delicately glancing off the surface of hints could go—that notice had been served, that Dame Kind had knocked upon the door for her debt. Our host confessedly had lost the use of his legs, Mr. Furbank declared he had been taken rather poorly—and from behind its owner's chair occularly signalled to me that a graver term would better apply; yet they pressed me to stay for that glass of sherry (though I did not, of course, linger long) and we talked over different subjects. Forster recurrently chuckled at my exam paper, both men averred their commitment to a biography which would not contain literary criticism of his writings— 'There has been so much of that already'—we giggled at some things and were serious upon others.

Yet roll-called and (I more clearly perceived looking back) clearly aware he had now a matter of hours left, not possible months, Forster was as he wrote once of his beloved Bapu Sahib 'gay, gay'—and, I hurry to add, *before* quaffing, in slow modest sips, the big Martini libation. His was, as in all my acquaintance it had been, a blitheness that was in no smallest degree one of bravado or indifference in the face of things. His concern with this world remained as keen, as grave, as committed as could be desired. But his cheer was—well, if *of* this world, something one rarely sees in it.

A month earlier as the General Election of that year loomed I had come out with the usual hackneyed wisdom on British political contests: 'Well Mr. Forster, we've simply got to go for the lesser of two evils.'—'Yes,' bleakly, 'if you think there's a choice.'[22]

A later morning's call discovered to me Bob Buckingham—in these days a tall robust elderly man who had shed the stoutness which shows in more distant photographs; it was, likewise, the only time I met *him*. He and Forster had been toiling over arrears of correspondence. 'We've just been saying, how on earth did the Victorians accomplish so much with their time? Here it is now 11.30 and we've managed in all this morning to answer five letters!' Said Forster: 'And not even long ones.'

Both had a hurt to confess which our host by no means just waved or laughed off. Someone had crept into the unlocked apartment and stolen a plate—a treasured family heirloom—from the mantelpiece sometime during the previous morning when its ancient tenant had briefly been out of his sitting-room. At this nasty meanness they were pained. Upon Ian Smith's government in what is now Zimbabwe they were vituperative: 'Those White Rhodesians are shits.'

Yet alongside everything else there ran a deep cheer in Forster, a happiness in his eyes which, one strongly suspected, was there most hours of the day, which did not come in stray gleams or fitful snatches but inhabited like a bird brooding eggs upon its nest.

On reconsideration the tone of 'Lapis Lazuli' does not quite convey what I want to testify to—not with perfect exactness. All of that was there in the man when I visited him once a week or a fortnight, but we are also talking about someone who had reached

> A condition of complete simplicity
> (Costing not less than everything)

where the promise

> And all shall be well and
> All manner of thing shall be well[23]

had been, was from minute to minute being, fulfilled.

One day Forster pointed out to me his inscription 'from Pindar's Eighth Pythian Ode which had become a charm or maxim for him':

E. M. Forster: Our Permanent Contemporary

Man's life is a day. What is he, what is he not?
Man is the dream of a shadow. But when the god-given
   brightness comes
A bright light is among men, and an age that is gentle comes
   to birth.[24]

It put me then, it puts me now, in mind of that part of Greek
mythology which tells of the gods Castor and Pollux visiting a
town and passing amidst its human population unrecognized.

The word contentment has little meaning left to my senses
but when used to express what was in E. M. Forster's mien
during the months I saw him. Though his body *was* burdened
with age, his hearing and memory defective, it was as if it was
near the end given him to *be* at last what he had always
wanted, an Ancient Hellene and, like Oedipus Colonneus,
amongst the most privileged of the same. Acquaintance with
him was, yes, searching and strenuous—Mr. Furbank's
account of his conversation[25] is unmatchable. His was a
presence still which in some sort put you on trial. But legiti-
mately now—not with that slight questionableness of aloof-
ness, superiority, call it what you will, which Frank Swinner-
ton's memoir of 1935 signalizes as having

> consciously affected [me]; by which I mean that something in
> him moves me to slightly affected boisterousness of behaviour.
> But the fault is not in him: one has the sense of perfect integrity,
> calm, sympathy; however, a little remoteness, too.[26]

These things were there yet; but transmuted; just as the
fretting which can distinguish even the latest pages of the
Commonplace Book had been outsoared.

Wholly of this world in so far as being anxious about it,
interested in and caring for it, the opposite of dismissive or
bored—it isn't even enough to say he struck me as having
gained on a full-time basis the sense of life's magicality so that,
no longer the least bit afraid of living—rather, finding it all an
amazing adventure—he had lost any approach to death that
wasn't—well, *gay*, again. That was true, too, as far as it went;
but there is still more behind.

It was as if the gods *he* had worshipped all his days appeared
to him at the last, as if the Divine Twins swayed his spirit out
of all real woe into unassailable happiness, so that like them he

remained entirely human yet was translated also. His blitheness at this season (not that of a spirit anticipating release and looking forward to mere rest), his utter gladness of essential being I can only explain by this simile. It was as if he beheld, seated or standing beside so many other ordinary comers like myself in those days and in that sitting-room, visitors not mortal.

NOTES

1. From Forster's review of G. L. Dickinson's *Points of View* in *Nation and Athenaeum*, 10 May 1930.
2. Letter to Forster of 24 April 1934.
3. Abinger Edition of *The Hill of Devi and Other Indian Writings* (London, 1983).
4. *Life*, Vol. I, p. 249.
5. *India Again: Extracts from an Unpublished Journal*, ed. M. A. Halls (Cambridge, 1982).
6. A lady 'who was profoundly Christian and was furthermore interested in all manifestations of religion'; in *Letters of 1912–13* section of *The Hill of Devi*.
7. Loc. ibid.
8. Scolar Press, London, 300 pp., with a fine introduction by Mr. Furbank, to whom once again be it said, as I thus take my leave of him here, Forster study and scholarship owes in gratitude so much.
9. Ibid., p. 98.
10. Ibid., p. 171.
11. *Collected Poems* (London, 1976), p. 523 (from 'The Cave of Making' in 'Thanksgiving for a Habitat').
12. 'Bishop Jebb's Book', para. 1, in Part 2 of *Two Cheers for Democracy*.
13. Ibid., id. loc.
14. *Commonplace Book*, p. 108, entry of 1936.
15. Ibid., p. 271.
16. From 'Growing Old Watchfully', a publicity sheet advertising the *Commonplace Book* facsimile and published in London 1978 by Scolar Press.
17. Though that is capable of rare beauty, a severe disciplined pathos, too, on just this subject of our species *versus* 'the quiet persistence of the earth'—in the essay 'The Solitary Place' ('Pharillon' section).
18. *Commonplace Book*, p. 58.
19. *Life*, Vol. II, p. 309, n. 2.
20. As we term it, although I don't entirely see by what warrant. Everything is relative in this dimension; nine decades are the briefest tick of a carbon clock; sea-turtles live two centuries; and the legends of our race

speak of a time when better-adjusted, more integrated Man dwelt hundreds of years upon the earth before entropy had much to say to him and made him expire. Then, also, youth and age are very much states of mind as well as body. I earnestly beseech the heavens I may never again be so old as I was at 16.

21. I suppose after the 1911–12 South Polar Expeditions.

22. A Cambridge don was informed by him one day that in sixty years of voting conscientiously in British elections he had never had the gratification of seeing his suffrage once help actually to choose the winning candidate!

23. *Four Quartets*, 'Little Gidding', lines 253–56 (Section V).

24. *Life*, Vol. I, p. 101.

25. Ibid., Vol. II, pp. 293–94.

26. *The Georgian Literary Scene*, Chapter XIV, Section II, para. 2; p. 286 of Everyman edition (London, 1938).

Conclusion

In his study *E. M. Forster: The Endless Journey* (Cambridge, 1976), John Sayre Martin writes:

> To what extent, it must finally be asked, does Forster's fiction reflect the literary conventions and social conditions of a bygone era, and to what extent does it transcend that era and speak to us?[1]

My own monograph has been written in the desire to answer 'Very Much' to both these questions. Forster's work reflects a society now departed, the world which was contemporary for his youth; and, like the other great novelists', goes on being relevant to our concerns today because his vision is permanently contemporary.

What gives it this importance; wherein is its human centrality? I think a clue to the answer can be found in his own 'Notes on the English Character', that essay of 1920 published at the beginning of *Abinger Harvest*. There Forster typifies one aspect of his countrymen's temperament with the following anecdote:

> For when [my Indian friend and I] met the next month our conversation threw a good deal of light on the English character. I began by scolding my friend. I told him that he had been wrong to feel and display so much emotion upon so slight an occasion; that it was inappropriate. The word 'inappropriate' roused him to fury. 'What?' he cried. 'Do you measure out your emotions as if they were potatoes?' I did not like the simile of the potatoes, but after a moment's reflection I said, 'Yes, I do; and what's more, I think I ought to. A small occasion demands a little emotion, just as a large occasion demands a great one. I would like my emotions to be appropriate. This may be measuring them like potatoes, but it is better than slopping them about like water from a pail, which is what you did.' He did not like the simile of the pail. 'If those are your opinions, they part us forever,' he

207

cried, and left the room. Returning immediately, he added: 'No—but your whole attitude toward emotion is wrong. Emotion has nothing to do with appropriateness. It matters only that it shall be sincere. I happened to feel deeply. I showed it. It doesn't matter whether I ought to have felt deeply or not.'

Forster concludes his account of the episode with the suggestion that the Englishman in himself may be in error, that perhaps 'the wealth of the spirit is endless; that we may express it copiously, passionately, and always; and that we can never feel sorrow or joy too acutely.'

He allows for this possibility, as do his novels (cf. Fielding's self-communion at the end of Chapter 20 in *A Passage to India*). But their strength resides, for me, in *being* spiritually precise; this commitment is what centrally sets him above most other writers and among the brightest stars of our literary pantheon.

His sack-of-potatoes approach to the world of feeling runs through narrative and characterization both, when these are strongest—and they are so most of the time—and makes a major extension of the humanly thinkable because it is under-taken not for the sake of coldness, of cynically dominating the life of the emotions, but rather with regard to getting the emotional life *right*: i.e. honest, fair, healthy and fulfilled.

There are many features of his *oeuvre* I have passed by—virtues and vices, excellencies and faults—because space is limited and they have already been well hymned or trounced in turn. There is the way, for example, artfully preparing for events which he then springs on the reader as a shock (e.g. Mrs. Moore's death in *A Passage to India*), Forster is a past master at getting most out of them as artistic elements: milking his plot for utmost generally irradiative effect. There is his self-discipline as a writer. He can manage one of the easier literary tricks, a 'dying fall' in narrative and rhythmic cadence together, with the best of them; Fielding's tea-party and Professor Godbole's (thematically crucial) song are wound up thus—

> 'I say to Him, Come, come, come, come, come, come. He neglects to come.'
>
> Ronny's steps had died away, and there was a moment of absolute silence. No ripple disturbed the water, no leaf stirred. (Ibid., Ch. 7)

but this sort of thing is much the more effective in that Forster does not go in for it the least bit too often.

There is his brilliant ability as a fictional letter-writer. He is an absolute master in the mode as development of his story, revelation of character and expression (in a new avatar) of the work's intrinsic theme. The perfect instances here are to be found in *Maurice*—Alec Scudder's letters to the eponymous hero in Chapters 40 and 42—which novel will also furnish us with good examples of the stylish waspishness Forster can turn on from time to time by way of another colour in his mosaic: 'Church was the only place Mrs. Hall had to go to—the shops delivered' (Ch. 2); or the slyness with which he can exploit even the tiniest details. 'Hill and Hall' is the title of the solicitorial firm his hero is apprenticed to inherit; as if in suburbia everyone is so mass-produced, it is only the differ-ence of a letter, one sole vowel, which distinguishes one identity from another.

But Forster is hopeless at treating of Love in its forms of Agape or of Eros, sexual and religious affinity, which I think my study, like most others, has sufficiently made clear. His great cards are Kindness,[2] Charity, brotherly mutuality between people who do not expect to go to bed together— which accounts after all for at least 99% of our human dealings.

This is the basis of his social wit. It starts with the human heart. Authoritative yet tentative is his tone; and the moder-ation of so many of his judgements makes the fierce ones far more telling when they arrive. He is witty, supremely. But discrimination is not his *raison d'être* as a writer for its own sake. The incising power of his moral calibrations is all recruited in the service of objects and goals beyond the simply evaluative. *The Longest Journey* alone testifies to that. All its references to man—this man, that one, men and women generally—feeling their relation to their environment; the detailed description, unidealizing, unexaggerated, individualized, of rural scenes and country persons: from all this comes the book's strength as incarnation of the Spirit of landscape in England.

Its author's repute, however, is still in a state of flux— unnecessarily. He is the most important British-Isles-born writer of imaginative English prose to have published in this

century so far, and even were a new Dickens or Emily Brontë
with us now, about to arise, what would that displace? The
publishers and editor of the Abinger series ought to take heart
by recognizing once for all they are performing a most valuable
function in accurately establishing his scripts in their fullness
before time has dispersed or destroyed texts and memories.
For Forster is with the really very best in our creative annals.
Others still abide our question indeed; but he is free.

NOTES

1. Op. cit., p. 164.
2. The supremacy and loveliness of this instinct in his imagination is
   exemplified not only by each of his novels (bating *Maurice*'s stridencies
   and injustices) but also in a noble *Commonplace Book* entry of 1943. His
   attempt to attain almost Buddhistic detachment with no loss of
   humanity—that is the measure of his *oeuvre*'s greatness.

   > *I simply dont mind* is the last word in human wisdom, but I recoil
   > from saying it. It would deliver me from fear, wastage of strength,
   > entanglement with the unworthy or the perishable. It offers an
   > inviolable sanctuary. My reluctance to enter implies some form of
   > faith. It *is* my goal, but I would rather be dragged to it protesting.
   > When I seek it and shed things or people, guilt mixes with my relief,
   > and when I see anyone going further than myself, like Joe, I feel
   > horror. *Not to mind* is to present a retreating back. 'Which is bad
   > form?'—An insufficient answer, because it reduces the problem to
   > personal pride; it's greater.

   > To *forget* people or things because more interested in something else
   > would be excellent. Up with Art therefore. Up even with work. The
   > negative is all right while it is accepted as a negative. But when 'I
   > simply don't mind' presents itself as something positive, I get scared.
   > (p. 167)

Index